AMERICAN UNIVERSITY PROGRAMS

IN

COMPUTER SCIENCE

Their Resources, Facilities, and Course Offering

William W. Lau, Ph.D., Editor
California State University, Fullerton

GGL Educational Press, Fullerton, California

IMPORTANT NOTICE

While extensive effort has been made to collect the most up-to-date data during the preparation of this book, neither the editor, nor GGL Educational Press, makes any warranty, expressed or implied, regarding the accuracy of information contained herein. In no event shall they be held liable for errors, omissions, or any consequential, incidental, or collateral damage in connection with the use of this book.

Interested readers must contact the respective department or the university for the latest and the most accurate information on their program.

First Edition

Library of Congress Cataloging in Publication Number: 84-80037

ISBN-Hardbound: 0-915751-25-9

Printed in the United States of America

To My Sister, Grace

PREFACE

This book is the outgrowth of some of my recurring observations.

First, to maintain a comprehensive collection of college catalog, and keep it current, is getting extremely expensive even for university libraries. Many institutions have stopped sending free catalogs. As such, most public and school libraries carry catalogs of local colleges only.

Some universities do subscribe to microfilm service to supplement their catalog collection. However, to look up detailed description of several computer science programs on such media is certainly a difficult task. It takes the hand-eye coordination of a tennis pro to maneuver these films on the viewing screen, not to mention the subsequent eye and neck-strains, or the agony at the sight and smell of those unreadable photocopies made from the attached machines.

Second, even college catalogs do not generally provide coverage on such information as size of the programs, department computing facilities, hardware acquisition plans, areas within computer science to be expanded or strengthened through faculty recruitment ...etc. These could be significant factors for consideration before students make their choices. For doctoral applicants and computer scientists seeking an academic career, additional information on department's resources, faculty research activities and their specialty is particularly vital.

Considering the rapid growth of computer science programs throughout the nation, the publication of this compendium of information is timely and perhaps inevitable. Therefore, I decided to undertake such a task in March of 1983, striving to develop a publication that would serve as a comprehensive guide for:

- college-bound and graduate students who contemplate a university education in computer science, or in a specialized area within the discipline;
- industrial and other employers of computer science graduates who wish to know more about the various program offerings to help formulate their recruitment plans;
- public and private organizations who are interested in contracting universities for research, special training or other consulting assignments;
- computer scientists who seek a teaching or research career with a university.

The book starts with an introduction chapter written primarily for laymen or beginning students. Examples of computer systems allow them to develop some familiarity with models mentioned in the computing facilities section of the university program. The glossary provides the simplest explanation of some acronyms, or fields of study within the computer science discipline, that often appear in the description of university programs throughout the book. They are by no means formal definitions of these terms.

The universities are grouped by states. Within each state, they are arranged alphabetically with the provision that institutions offering doctoral programs are listed first. Readers should know that university resources, program offerings, and curriculum continue to evolve rapidly. One must contact the individual department for the most accurate information about the program.

The data collection phase of this project turned out to be a far more arduous task than I had anticipated, spanning a five-month period from June through November of 1983. However, I shall feel remiss not to thank many department chairs and program directors, who had responded to our questionaires, and generously provided us with additional materials that further describe their programs. Without their cooperation, this book could never come into existence. We hope they will notify us any error or changes of their program, so that future printings of this publication will always contain the latest information available to us.

Finally, my gratitude goes to my wife Geegym for the layout and design work of this book; regrets to myself for having missed many of my little Loraine's piano practices, bedtime chats, and goodnight kisses. Gregory must have benefited from the periodic absence of tennis matches with his daddy, for these boring matches have actually dulled his reflex and impeded his progress considerably. Now, if only I would undertake a new project shortly, he might make the freshmen team of his high school next year.

June, 1984   W.W.L.

vii

CONTENTS

KANSAS
  Kansas State University
  University of Kansas

KENTUCKY
  University of Kentucky
  University of Louisville

LOUISIANA
  Louisiana State University
  University of Southeast Louisiana
  University of New Orleans

MAINE
  University of Southern Maine

MASSACHUSETTS
  Boston University
  Harvard University
  Massachusettes Institute of Technology
  University of Massachusettes
  Boston College
  Brandeis University
  Framingham State College
  Wellesley College

MARYLAND
  John's Hopkins University
  University of Maryland
  Towson State University

MICHIGAN
  Michigan State University
  Wayne State University
  Northern Michigan University
  The University of Michigan
  University of Michigan, Flint
  Western Michigan University

MINNESOTA
  University of Minnesota, Minneapolis
  Moorehead State University
  University of Minnesota, Duluth

MISSOURI
  University of Missouri, Rolla
  Northwest Missouri University
  University of Missouri, St Louis

MONTANA
  University of Montana

NEBRASKA
  University of Nebraska
  Creighton University

NEVADA
  University of Nevada, Reno

NEW HEMPSHIRE
  Dartmouth College

NEW JERSEY
  Princeton University

NEW MEXICO
  New Mexico Institute of Mining
      & Technology
  New Mexico State University
  University of New Mexico

NEW YORK
  Columbia University
  Cornell University
  New York University
  Polytechnic Institute of New York
  State University of New York, Buffalo
  State University of New York, Stony Brook
  Syracuse University
  University of Rochester
  Adelphi University
  City University of New York
      The City College
      Hunter College
  Long Island University
  Rochester Institute of Technology
  St John's University
  State University of New York Colleges
      Brockport
      Fredonia
      Oswego
      Plattsburgh

NORTH DAKOTA
  North Dakota State University

OHIO
  Case Western Reserve University
  Ohio State University
  Bowling Green State University
  Miami University
  Ohio University

OREGON
University of Oregon

PENNSYLVANIA
Pennsylvania State University
Temple University
University of Pennsylvania
University of Pittsburgh
Edinboro University of Pennsylvania
Indiana University of Pennsylvania
La Salle College
Mansfield State College
Slippery Rock State College
Spring Garden College
Villanova University

RHODE ISLAND
University of Rhode Island
Bryant College

SOUTH CAROLINA
University of South Carolina
Clemson University
Furnam University
Lander College

SOUTH DAKOTA
South Dakota Schools of
Mines & Technology

TENNESSEE
Vanderbilt University
Memphis State University
University of Tennessee

TEXAS
North Texas State University
Texas A & M University
University of Texas at Arlington
The University of Texas, Austin
Baylor University
Southwest Texas State University
Stephen F Austin State University
University of Texas at El Paso
West Texas State University

UTAH
University of Utah
Utah State University
Weber State University

VIRGINIA
University of Virginia
Bethany College
Hollins College
James Madison University
Virginia Wesleyan College

WASHINGTON
Western Washington University

WISCONSIN
University of Wisconsin
Madison
Eau Claire
Milwaukee
Parkside
Superior

WYOMING
University of Wyoming

APPENDIX

Industrial Employers of Computer Science Graduates

INTRODUCTION

EXAMPLES OF COMPUTER SYSTEMS

The list below covers sample current models of hardware manufactures whose computer systems are used in the universities described in this publication. Because of the overlapping capabilities, the classification of computers into four broad categories is at times quite debatable.

bw-bit words; K-kilobytes of primary storage
MB-megabytes of primary storage
MIPS-million instructions per second
s/t-storage and transfer word sizes respectively in bits

SUPERCOMPUTERS

Control Data
    Cyber 200 Model 203: 1-2MB; 64bw.
    Cyber 200 Model 205: 1-4MB; 64bw.
    Cyber 205 Series 600: 8-16MB; 32-64bw.
Cray Research
    Cray X-MP: 2-4MB; 64bw; 200MIPS.
    Cray-1: 4-32MB; 64bw.
    Cray-1S: 4-32MB; 64bw.

MAINFRAMES

Amdahl
    Models 470 V/5,6,7,8: 4-32MB; 32bw; 2.7-6.8MIPS.
    Models 5840,50,60,70,80: 16-32MB; 32bw; 7.6-22MIPS.
Burroughs
    B 1905,55,85: 0.256-2MB; 24bw; 0.25-0.43MIPS.
    B 6930: 6.2MB; 48bw; 0.84MIPS.
    B 7850: 1.5-3.1MB; 48bw; 7.7MIPS.
    B 7900: 12-96MB; 48bw; 4.4-13.7MIPS.

MAINFRAME COMPUTERS

Control Data
    Cyber 170/815-875: (12-bit) 1-16MB; 60bw.
Digital Equipment
    Models 2020,40,60: 0.256-6MB; 36bw.
Four-Phase
    System 3122: 1-4MB; 32bw; 0.5MIPS.
Honeywell
    DPS 7,8: 1-64MB; 36bw.
    DPS 88: 16-128MB; 64bw.
    Level 66 DPS/B: 12-64MB; 36bw.
    Level 66 DPS/C: .016-.064MB; 36bw.
    Level 66/05-80: .384MB; 36bw.
IBM
    3031,3032: 2-8MB; 64bw; 1.1-2.5MIPS.
    3033N,3033S: 4-16MB; 64bw; 2.4-4.2MIPS.
    3033U,A,M: 4-32MB; 64bw; 4.7-8.0MIPS.
    3081: 16-48MB; 64bw; 10-15MIPS.
    3083: 8-32MB; 64bw; 3.7-7.9MIPS.
    4331,4341: 1-16MB; 32bw; 0.2-1.2MIPS.
    370/115,125: .064-.512MB; 32bw.
    370/138 (3138), 148(4148): .512-2MB; 32bw.
    370/158,168: .512-16MB; 32bw.
Magnuson
    M80/20-43: .512-16MB; 32bw; 0.22-1.1MIPS.
National Advanced Systems
    AS/6620,30,50: 2-16MB; 64bw.
    AS/7000: 2-16MB; 32bw; 2.2-5.5MIPS.
    AS/8040,50,60: 8-24MB; 31bw.

MINICOMPUTERS

Appolo Computer
    DN400/420: 0.5-3.5MB; 32bw.
    Domain: 3.5MB; 32bw.
Charles River
    MH-11: 128-256K; 16bw.
Control Data
    Cyber 18 Series: 16-256K; 16bw.
Data General
    Eclipse MV/10000: 1-16MB; 32bw.
    Eclipse MV/4000,6000,8000: 1-12MB; 32bw.
    Eclipse S/120,130,140: 32K-2MB; 16bw.
    Eclipse S/250,280: 64K-2MB; 16bw.
Digital Equipment
    Datasystem 700: 0.512-8MB; 32bw.
    VAX 11/730,750: 0.512-8MB; 32bw.
    VAX 11/780,782: 0.512-32MB; 32bw.
    PDP 11/23,24: 0.128-4MB; 16bw.
    PDP 11/34: 32-256K; 16bw.
    PDP 11/44 Series: 0.256-1MB; 16bw.
    PDP 11/70: 0.512-4MB.

Four-Phase Systems
   IV/40,50,70: 24-96K; 24bw.
   IV/60,65,80: 240-864K; 24bw.
   IV/90M,S: 192-480K; 24bw.
   IV/95: 0.48-1.536MB; 24bw.
Harris
   Models 300,500: 0.196-3MB; 48bw.
   Series 700,800: 0.384-12MB; 48bw.
   MIND Series: 0.144-1MB; 16bw.
   Models 1650,1660,9240: 0.144-1MB; 16bw.
Hewlett-Packard
   HP1000 Models 16,17,18: 0.128-6MB; 16bw.
   HP3000 Series 39,40,40SX: 0.256-2MB; 16bw.
   HP3000 Series 48,64,68: 2-8MB; 16bw.
Honeywell
   DPS 6/92,94,96: 1-16MB; 32bw.
   DPS 6/30-76: 0.256-2MB; 16bw.
   DPS Level 6 Models 23-57: 16K-1MB; 16bw.
IBM
   System/38 5381 Models 3-8: 0.512-8MB; 32bw.
   Series/1 Models 4954-4956: 16K-1MB; 16bw.
   System/7 Model 5010: up to 128K; 16bw.
Microdata
   Sequel Series VMS 3210,3265: 1-2MB; 32bw.
Perkin-Elmer
   Model 3200MPS: 2-16MB; 32bw.
   Models 3205,3210: 0.512-4MB; 32bw.
   Models 3230,3250: 0.512-16MB; 32bw.
Prime
   Models 250,450,550: 0.512-4MB; 32bw.
   Models 750,850,9950: 1-16MB; 32bw.
Sperry Univac
   V77-400,500,600,700,800: 32K-2MB; 16bw.
Texas Instruments
   Business 600,800 Series: 0.256-2MB; 16bw.
   Models 990/10A,12LR Processors: 2MB; 16bw.
Wang Laboratories
   VS 50: 0.128-0.512MB; 32bw.
   VS 85,90: 1-4MB; 32bw.
   VS 100: 0.256-8MB; 32bw.
   VS 25,45,80: 0.256-1.2MB; 16bw.

MICROCOMPUTERS

Alpha Micro
   AM-1000: 128-256K; 32/16 bits storage/transfer words.
   AM-1062: 128K-4MB; 32/16 bits.
Appolo
   DN 300: 512K-1.5MB; 32/32 bits.

MICROCOMPUTERS

Apple
    Lisa, Macintosh: 128K-1MB; 32/16 bits.
    Apple IIc: 128K; IIe, III: 64-256K; 8/8 bits.
Atari
    800,1200,1400XL: 64K; 8/8 bits.
Charles River
    Universe 68/05: 256K-12MB; 32/32 bits.
    Universe 68/27,37,47: 256K-5MB; 32/8,16,32.
    Universe 68/80: 256K-12MB; 32/8,16,32 bits.
Columbia
    Models 1600-1,1,2: 128K; 16/8 bits.
Commodore
    Commodore 64: 64-128K; 8/8 bits.
    C128/80: 128K; 8/8 bits.
    VIC 20: 5-32K; 8/8 bits.
Compac Microelectronics
    CEC 8000S: 512K-8MB; 32/16 bits.
Control Data
    Model 110: 64K; 8/8 bits.
Corona Data Systems
    Corona PC: 128-512K; 16/16 bits.
Corvus Systems
    Concept, Concept+: 256-768K; 32/16 bits.
Data General
    Desktop Generation 10,20,30: 128K-1.5MB; 16/16 bits.
Digital Equipment
    DECmate II: 96K; 12/8 bits.
    Professional 325,350: 256K-1MB; 16/16 bits.
    Rainbow 100: 64-256K; 16/8 bits.
Eagle
    1600: 128-512K; 16/16 bits.
    Eagle IIe: 64K; 8/8 bits.
    Eagle PC: 128-512K; 16/8 bits.
Epson America
    Model QX-10: 64-256K; 8/8 bits.
Fortune
    Fortune 32,16: 128K-1MB; 16/16 bits.
    System Five, Ten, Twenty: 256K-1MB; 16/16 bits.
Harris
    Model 9240, 9200 Workstations: 64K; 8/8 bits.
Hewlett-Packard
    HP Series 200 Models/16,26: 64K-2MB; 32/16 bits.
    HP 9000 Series 500/20,30,50: 512K-1MB; 32/32 bits.
    HP Series 100: 64K; 8/8 bits.
    HP 150: 256-640K; 16 bits.
IBM
    PC XT,5160 Model 87: 128-640K; 16/16 bits.
    PC 5150 Models 104,114,164,174: 256-640K; 16/16 bits.
    PC: 64-256K; 16/8 bits.
    PCjr: 64-128K; 16/8 bits.
    System/23 Datamaster: 32-128K; 8/8 bits.

Intel
    System 80/300X: 384K-1MB; 16/16 bits.
    System 86/330,380,735: 320K-1MB; 16/16 bits.
Megadata
    Model 8174-1,2: 768K-16MB; 16/16 bits.
Motorola
    M-6809: 64K; 8/8 bits.
NCR
    Tower 1632: 256K-2MB; 32/16 bits.
    Decision Mate V: 64-512K; 16,8/16,8 bits.
North Star
    Advantage: 64K; 8/8 bits.
    Advantage 8/16: 64-256K; 16,8/16,8 bits.
Pacific Microcomputers
    PM 100,200,300,400: 256K-1.5MB; 16/16 bits.
Radio Shack
    TRS-80 Model 16: 128-512K; 32/16 bits.
    TRS-80 Model II: 64K; 8/8 bits.
    TRS-80 Model 12: 80-512K; 8/8 bits.
Texas Instruments
    Professional Computer: 64-256K; 16/16 bits
    200 Series: 64K; 16/16 bits.
    300 Series: 128-512K; 16/16 bits.
Wicat Systems
    Systems 155: 512K-4.5MB; 32/16 bits.
    System 200: 512K-5MB; 16/16 bits.
    System 220: 512K-14MB; 32/16 bits.
Zilog
    System 8000 Model 11: 256K-1MB; 32,16,8/32,16,8 bits.
    System 8000 Model 21: 1-8MB; 32,16,8/32,16,8 bits.
    System 8000 Model 31: 8MB; 32,16,8/32,16,8.

GLOSSARY

Many technical terms and abbreviations will appear in the description of university programs throughout the book. The glossary below helps explain some of these terms in the simplest way.

ADA-- a high-level language developed in the late 70s and early 80s at the initiative of the Department of Defense. Aiming to improve software reliability, portability and maintainability, the language has been implemented for large complex systmes and embedded real-time applications.

Algebraic Language-- a programming language whose data are algebraic expressions and whose operations include such algebraic manipulation as factorization, simplifications, multiplying out brackets, differentiations ...etc.

ALGOL-- a programming language developed for arithmetic and logical processes. It is taken from ALGOrithmic Language.

Algorithm-- a set of rules or procedures developed for the solution of a problem in a finite number of steps. Compare it with heuristic.

ANSI-- American National Standards Insititute, an US organization that establishes industrial standards for such items as linked-level protocols, pin positions and meaning in chips, and some software standards e.g. FORTRAN, COBOL.

Architecture-- a specific design, layout and interconnections of various components of a computer systems, e.g., the number and functions of registers, instruction set and formats, memory organization and addressing, I/O operations and control.

ARPANET-- Advanced Research Projects Agenency (ARPA) Network, a packet-switching computer network linking over 100 host computers of major universities, private and public research organizations throughout half of the world. Originally sponsored by ARPA, the network is now under the control of the Defense Communication Agency.

Array Processor-- a processor designed specifically for processing arrays (tables, matrices). A single operation can apply to all elements of the array simultaneously, thereby providing extremely fast processing of iterative computations. Extensive application is found in image processing, signal processing, scientific computing ...etc.

Artificial Intelligence (AI)-- investigates the way human thinks. Such studies would lead to the development of machines' capability to perform some human-like functions as reasoning, learning, self-improving ...etc.

Assembly Language-- a low level language which uses symbols (mnemonics) instead of ordinary words to give instruction to the computer. It can be translated directly into binary machine codes or data formats.

Automata-- the study of the principles of operations and applications of automatic machines.

Baud Rate-- a measure of signal flow which is expressed in bits per second.

C Language-- a machine independent programming language developed by Bell Lab as the systems programming language of UNIX.

CAD-- an abbreviation for Computer-Aided Design, which is concerned with automated designs of industrial applications through the use of computers, visual display devices, and graphic symbols.

CAM-- an abbreviation for Computer-Aided Manufacturing.

CAD/CAM System-- an automated design and drafting system that provides a connection between numerical control and CAM functions which include: design of machine parts, diagramming of complex arrangements, generation of printed-circuit boards ...etc.

Chip-- a tiny device containing many transistors and other microscopic components photoetched on the surface of a piece of silicon.

Combinatorics-- a branch of mathematics that deals mainly with counting, enumeration, and other computational problems of discrte structures.

Complexity-- is concerned with various ways to measure how "difficulty" it is to compute some problems. The degree of difficulty is often described in terms of resource consumed during the computation.

Computability-- is concerned with the existence of effective algorithms that would yield computational solutions of some mathematical functions.

Concurrent System-- a system that allow several operations (e.g., writing, reading, seeking, addressing) to proceed simultaneously in various parts of the system.

Correctness Proof-- a mathematical proof to demonstrate that the semantics of a program is consistent with the formal specification of that program.

Cybernetics-- the science that studies the control and communication in information handling machines, and in the nervous systems of human or animals.

Data Base Management System (DBMS)-- a collection of utility programs designed to create, maintain, and retrieve the databases of an organization.

Distributed System-- refers to the various arrangements of separate computing facilities that work cooperateively to serve the needs of an organization.

Expert System-- a software system that solves problems by making use of knowledge acquired previously from human experts. Application of this artificial intelligence technique can be found in medical diagnosis, fault-finding system, mineral prospecting ...etc.

GLOSSARY

Fault-Tolerant System-- a system capable of functioning fully (fail-safe) or partially (fail-soft) despite failure in parts of the system.

Formal Language Theory-- studies the structures and representation of languages which are considered merely as sets of strings, apart from any semanics of such languages.

Heuristic Programming-- a programming method that patterns after human's exploratory approach to solve problems, (e.g., trial and error, or learning while doing). Contrast with an algorithmic approach which is based on some prior knowledge of solution methods.

Integrated Circuits (IC)-- involves the use of transistors for computer circuitry. Circuits are often fabricated with a unipolar field effect transistor, known as the Metal Oxide Semiconductor (MOS) transistor, which is widely used in microprocessor and memory chips. The level of integration is measured in numbers of transistors to be put on a single chip. Medium Scale Integration (MSI): 100 to 10,000 transistors; Large Scale Integration (LSI): 10,000 to 100,000 transistors; Very Large Scale Integration (VLSI) over 100,000 transistors per chip.

Image Processing-- analyzes information contained in images, and perform such activities as tranformation, enhancement, restoration, and feature extracion of images through the use of computers and optical devices.

Local Area Network-- a communication system that connects workstations and/or other facilities in the same building or in areas nearby.

LISP-- a computer programming language designed for the manipulation of non-numeric data. It is often used in artificial intelligence research.

LSI-- Large Scale Integration, see Integrated Circuit.

MOS-- Medal Oxide Semiconductor. It refers to the three layers used in forming the gate structure of a field-effect transistor (FET). See Integrated Circuit.

MSI-- Medium Scale Integration, see Integrated Circuit.

Natural Language-- a language whose rules are quite flexible and whose intepretation is often ambiguous. The rules describe current instead of prescribed usages. While such a language makes verbal arts and poetry expressive of human feeling, it is difficult for computer use. On the contrary, an artificial language, created for machine processing, is precise and logical.

Operating System-- a collection of programs that controls the operation of resources and components of a computer system.

Packet-Switching Network-- a communication network where messages are broken into packets, each of which is transmitted as a single unit. A packet is a group of binary bits that consists of data and control signals arranged in a prescribed format.

Parallel Processing-- simultaneous execution of several sequences of instruction by a machine having multiple arithmetic and logic units.

Parallel Programming-- programming that allows several arithmetic or logic operations to be executed simultaneously even though there is only one processing unit. This can be accomplished by using different parts of a word for holding the operands.

Parsing-- the process of deciding whether a string of input characters forms a sentence of a given language.

Pattern Recognition-- the identification of patterns through a machine, capable of scanning and converting input into digital signal patterns, to be compared with patterns in storage.

Performance Evaluation-- evaluate a system to see if its computing resources are being utilized effectively by analyzing the data of its dynamic behavior. Tools for evaluation include benchmark programs and simulation methods.

Privacy and Security-- is concerned with the protection against unauthorized retrieval or alteration of stored data.

Program Specification-- a precise statement of the requirements that a program is designed to meet, without any commitment as to how such program could be written.

Robotics-- involves the study and development of a general-purpose programmable machine that can perform certain human tasks. Robotic systems have been developed and utilized in the automobile, steel, and aerospace industries.

Systems Programming-- involves the development of operating systems, language processors, utilities, file and data base management systems.

Software Engineering-- studies the process of creating software systems, which include the following stages of develoments: requirement analysis, design specification, implementation, testing and validation, operation and maintenance.

Semantics-- a set of rules that gives clear and precise meaning to each symbol or strings of symbols of a programming language.

SNOBOL-- a programming language for processing strings of characters.

Text Processing-- the interactive use of software tools to create, revise, and maintain text materials.

Theorem Proving-- refers to programming a computer to prove theorms, a subject of considerable interest to artificial intelligence researchers. There are two general approaches. A proof-finding program is first given a theorem and then proceeds to find a proof; whereas a consequence-finding approach is first given some axioms, and then proceed to deduce consequences from those axioms.

UNIX-- a trademark of Bell Laboratory, is a general-purpose multiple-user multi-tasking time-shared system that is widely used on a variety of computers. It offers a hierarchical file system, programmable command language interpreters, portability, and a wide collection of application programs, especially useful for program development and document preparation.

Virtual Memory-- addressable space that appears to the user as real storage. It is made possible by a combination of hardware and software techniques to effect expanded capacity of the main memory.

ALABAMA

UNIVERSITY OF ALABAMA
Birmingham, AL 35294
(205) 934-4011

The University of Alabama is a public university, whose 240-acre campus at Birmingham supports a population of 15,000 students with a faculty student ratio of 1 to 10, and a library containing over 650,000 volumes.

The Department of Computer Science offers bachelor's, master's, and PhD programs in which 821, 50, and 12 students are enrolled currently. Prospective students should apply through the Department at 901 S 15th St. No deadline is specified. Computer systems in use include: IBM 4341, Data General Eclipse S/130, DEC VAX 11/750, PDP 11/23, and the Zenith Z90 and Terak microcomputers. CSNet is available. A second VAX will be acquired in the near future.

There are 8 full-time faculty members in the department. Positions are open at the assistant and associate ranks. Background in any area of computer science will be considered.

Course Offerings:

105	Intro to Inform Processing	530	Computer Design I
115	Elem Comp Instr for Chemitry	531	VLSI Systems Design I
210	Intro to Programming	532	Computer Design II
215	Business Data Processing	533	VLSI Systems Design II
250	Theoreical Foundations of CS	535	Computer Comunications Networks
310	Algorithms & Data Stuctures	536	Microproccessor Laboratory
320	Intro to File Processing	542	Compiler Design
325	Machine Oriented Programming	544	Computer Operating System Design I
330	Comp Org & Microprocessor	546	Computer Operating System Design II
405	General Purpose Prog Languages	552	Design & Analysis of Algorithms I
425	Systems Analysis	553	Design & Analysis of Algorithms II
426	Database Management Systems	555	Theory of Automata & Computability
430	Systems Programs	556	Formal Linguistics
437	Intro to Telecomunications	560	Artificial Intelligence Programming
440	Computer Operating Systems	562	Artificial Intelligence
455	Design & Analysis of Algorithms	563	Computational Logic
477	Intro to Comp Graphics	564	Pattern Recognition
480	Modeling & Simulation	567	Algebraic Manipulation Systems
491	Special Topics in Biomed Computing	568	Biomedical Information Systems
508	Micrprocessor Design	570	Num Analysis I
524	Software Design Methology	572	Num Analysis II
526	Database Systems I	574	On Line Data Acquisition & Display
528	Database Systems II	577	Num Optimization Techniques

578 Num Soln of Partial Diff Equations	730 Rsrch Topics in Architecture & Organization
580 Modelling & Simulation I	739 Seminar on Systems Organization
581 Modelling & Simulation II	740 Rsrch Topics in Systems Software
586 Computer Performance Evaluation	749 Seminar on Software Systems
591 Special Topics in Biomed Computing	750 Rsrch Topics in Theorical Foundations
594 Computer Graphics	759 Seminar on Theory
700 Rsrch Topics in programming Language	760 Rsrch Topics in Intelligent Systems
710 Rsrch Topics in Data Stucturec	769 Seminar on Intelligent Systems
720 Rsrch Topics in Information Systems	770 Rsrch Topics in Num Analysis & Computing

JACKSONVILLE STATE UNIVERSITY
Jacksonville, AL 36265
(205) 435-9820

Jacksonville State University's 175-acre campus supports 6,500 students with a faculty student ratio of 1 to 24 and a library that contains over 350,000 volumes.

The Department of Computer Science and Information Systems offers undergraduate and master's programs: Computer Science for those interested in the theory and application of computers in a scientific environment, and Computer Information Systems for computer applications in a business environment. Prospective students should apply through the Admissions Office; deadline Aug 20.

The Department has 8 full-time faculty members. Three openings exist at the assistant professor level. Background in any areas of computer science will be considered.

Computing facilities at Jacksonville State include an IBM 4341 Model II with VM/DOS, IBM PCs and the Apple IIe's. Future acquisition plan calls for more microcomputes.

Course Offerings: (generally 3 units)

201 Intro to Data Processing	366 Information Storage and Retrieval
220 RPG II Programming	410 Microcomputing
231 Intro to Computing	411 Management Information Systems
233 Computer Elements and Digital Logic	412 Computer-Oriented Numerical Methods
240 BASIC Programming	417 Systems Modeling and Simulations
250 Intro to COBOL	432 Computer Graphics
254 Intro to FORTRAN	441 Computer Systems Programming
305 Adv FORTRAN	442 Compiler Contruction
310 Fundamental of Systems Analysis	448 Data Base Systems
320 Data Processing Systems Management	450 Communications and Security
330 Adv COBOL Programming	495 Management Business Decision Making
331 Data Stuctures	496 Laboratory Practicum (1)
334 Discrete Conputational Stuctures	497 Business Computer Science Practicum
350 Fundamentals of Computer Operating Systems	498 Indep Adv Programming Problems
353 Intro to Programming Languges	499 Indep Adv Programming Problems
354 Assembly Language Programming	Courses for Individualized Intruction
358 PL/I Programming	407 Computer Mapping
361 Digital Computer Organization	432 Computer Science

11

ARKANSAS

UNIVERSITY OF ARKANSAS
Fayetteville, AR 72701
(501) 575-5346

The University of Arkansas is a public university whose 330-acre campus at Fayetteville supports a total of 16,000 students with a faculty student ratio of 1 to 18, and a library with over a million volumes.

The Department of Industrial Engineering & Computer Science consists of five full-time faculty members. It offers bachelor's and master's programs in computer science. Currently, 300 and 15 students are enrolled in the two programs respectively.

Computing facilities at the university include: an Amdahl V-6 (8 meg VM/370), TI 990/12 with 15 CRT's, 15 TI 99/4A's, 3 TRS 80s. Future acquisition calls for 4 minicomputers to serve nodal function of a computer network.

Course Offerings:

1013 Introduction to Computer Science	4653 Computer Organization & File Structure
2813 Information Structures	4803 Introduction to Formal Languages
2823 Computer & Programming Systems	4813 Computer System Design & Implementation
2943 Theory of Digital Machines	4933 Computer Systems Analysis
3743 Computer Graphics	
3823 Digital Computer Org & Assembly Language I	Graduate
3843 Data Structures & File Management	4833 Software Design & Development
3943 Control Structure of Computers	4933 Computer Systems Analysis
4633 System Configuration & Evaluation	4653 Computer Organization & File Structure

ARIZONA

ARIZONA STATE UNIVERSITY
Tempe, AZ 85287
(602) 965-7788

Arizona State's 566-acre campus, located just east of Phoenix, provides easy access to the substantial number of high technolgy industries in computer and elecreonics. Serving a student population of 38,000 students, the university has a faculty student ratio of 1 to 25, and a library system containing 1.7 million volumes.

The Department of Computer Science offers a bachelor's, a master's and beginning in the fall of 1983, a PhD program in computer science. Currently, there are 1100, 75, and 10 students enrolled in these three programs respectively. 16 full-time faculty belong to the department. Faculty openings exist at all ranks. Computer scientists with specialty in software engineering, expert systems, compilers, data base, computer science theory, operating systems and architecture are particularly desired.

Computing facilities at the university include an IBM 3081, two IBM 4341, Honeywell 68/80, two VAX 11/780, two Harris 800, many Motorola and Intel based microcomputer systems. Computer networks CSNET and UUCP are accessible. Operating systems in use include VMS, CMS, UNIX, Multics. Future acquisition plan calls for additional VAXs. New research facilities have just been completed and the development of a nearby research park is well underway, providing ample employment and consulting opportunities.

Faculty positions exist at all ranks. All areas in computer science will be considered. Background in programming language design and implementation, operating systems, theory of computation, data structures, algorithms, database systems, and artificial intelligence is particularly desired.

Course Offerings: (generally 3 semester units)

100	Intro to Computer Science I	383	Applied FORTRAN Programming
101	Intro to Computer Science II	400	Advanced Assembly Language Programming
180	Computers & Society	410	Intro to File & Database Structures
181	Programming in BASIC	412	Database Systems
182	Elementary FORTRAN Programing (2)	420	Computer Architecture I
183	Programming in FORTRAN	421	Microcomputer Fundamentals (4)
200	Assembly Language Programming	422	Microcomputer Systems Design I (4)
210	Data Structures	423	Microcomputer Systems Design II
304	Intro to COBOL	430	Elementary Concepts of Operating Systems
305	Intro to PL/1	438	Systems Programming
309	High Level Languages	440	Compiler Construction I
320	Computer Organization	450	Analysis of Algrthm
340	Structure of Programming Languages	457	Theory of Formal Languages
355	Intro to Automata Theory	460	Software Project Management & Development

13

ARIZONA STATE

470 Computer Graphics
473 Functional Language Applications
474 Modeling For Computer Simulation
475 Simulation Theory & Languages
483 FORTRAN Programming for Graduate Research
512 Database Systems Design
515 Information Storage & Retrieval
520 Computer Architecture II
521 Microprocessor Applications (4)
522 Microprogramming
523 Microcomputer Systems Software
525 Digital Testing & Reliability
530 Operating Systems Theory

532 Security in Computing Systems
535 Performance Evaluation
540 Compiler Constructrion II
542 Translator Writing Systems
545 Programming Language Design
550 Combinatorial Algrthm & Intractability
552 Sorting Algrthm
554 Advanced Switching Theory
555 Automata Theory
560 Software Project Mngmnt & Development II
565 Software Reliability
571 Artificial Intelligence
572 Pattern Recognition

CALIFORNIA

CALIFORNIA INSTITUTE OF TECHNOLOGY
Pasadena, CA 91125
(818) 356-6811

The California Institute of Technology is an independent, privately supported institution with an 82-acre main campus in Pasadena, which is 25 miles from the Pacific Ocean. The Institute maintains a small, select student population, (about 875 undergraduate and 930 graduate), and 780 faculty members who are unusually active in research. Its nine-story main library and other library collections together subscribe to 5,664 journals and series, and contain 400,000 volumes. One of the world's major research centers, Caltech's small size fosters an environment of scholarly intimacy among the students, faculty members and staff scientists.

PhD and MS in Computer Science are offered here. A computer engineering specialization within the Electrical Engineering Option, and a computer science specialization within the Engineering & Applied Science Option, are available to the undergraduates. Admission is extremely competitive, granted only to a limited number of students with superior ability. Interested students should apply as early as possible (before Jan 15 for September admission) through the Dean of Graduate Studies, or through the Office of Admissions.

Caltech has unusual strength in the design of very-large-scale integrated circuits. State-of-the-art IC designs, prepared by students and faculty, as classroom or research projects, are sent to industrial suppliers for fabrication. The resulting circuits are assembled into computing systems. Areas of research at Caltech include:

1) Computer design where memory and logical processing are commingled in common circuits. Such designs may provide tremendous increase in computing power. They include many thousands of processing elements, located very close to the data on which they operate, thereby avoiding the speed limitations inherent in conventional memory bus.

2) Development of software tools for integrated ciucuit design, that would make extensive use of interactive terminals and real-time computing to greatly simplify the disign of complex ciucuits.

3) The study of interaction between hardware and advanced software systems, that would allow systems programming tasks to influence hardware designs.

4) High-level computer languages appropriate to specialized tasks. Natural languages, graphical languages, algebraic languages, and languages for associative processing are beign studied here.

5) Information retrieval from very large data bases, including the development of natural-language inquiry systems and efficient searching of large data bases.

The department's computing facilities consist of: a DEC 2060 with TOPS 20AN, 1024K words of primary storage, six RPO6 disks and ARPAnet connection; a VAX 11/780 with Berkeley UNIX and 4 megabytes of primary storage, 900 MB of mass storage and ARPAnet connection; a VAX 11/750 running Berkeley UNIX; a PDP 11/34, Applicon plotter, Trilog printers, Evans & Sutherland graphics system, GIGI terminals, HP9845s, HP9826/36s, HP7580 color plotter, Versatec printer, Data General NOVA, an XGP, an HP 2635A. The department's digital electronics lab is equipped with facilities for packaging chips.

Faculty of the department and their interests: R Ayres, (formal & informal systems, languages, compilation), J F Blinn (animation, modeling, three dimensional data), R E Bryant (VLSI dsgn, parallel cmptrs, distributed systems), S L Johnsson (modeling large systems, control thry, num analysis, architecture & algrthms concurrent computation, VLSI), J T Kajiya (prgmng languages, signal prcssng, sensory system), A J Martin (correctness, concurrent & distributed computation, highly parallel computers), C A Mead (VLSI design, ultraconcurrent systems, physics of computation), C B Ray (logic dsgn, architecture, microprocessors), M Rem (prgmng, correctness proofs, concurrent computation), C L Seitz (architecture & dsgn, VLSI systems, swtchng thry, self-timed systems, concurrency, graphics & image systems), F B Thompson (computational linguistics, user interface, philosophy & dynamics of information).

Course Offering:

4	Intro to Digital Electronics	144abc	Artificial Intelligence
6abc	Intro to Discrete Mathematics	146ab	Concurrent Algorithms
10	Intro to Computing	171ab	Computer Architecture
11	Digital Electronics Lab	180	Masters Thesis Research
80abc	Undergraduate Research in Cmptr Science	181abc	VLSI Design Lab
112	Prncpl of Micropression-Based Info Systems	183ab	Integrated Digital Communication
114	Microprocessor Systems	237abc	Design & Implmntn of Prgmng Languages
117abc	Computability Theory	247	Formal Models of Digital Systems
119abc	Prncpl of Waveform Processing	250ab	The Physics of Computation
121	Microprocessor Lab	251abc	Potentialities & Limitatns Cmptng Mchnes
137a	Systematic Programming	270abc	Computer Aided Design
138ab	Computer Algorithms	274abc	Computer Graphics
139ab	Concurrency in Computation	280	Research in Computer Science
140abc	Programming Lab	282abc	Readings in Computer Science
141abc	Formal Semantics of Prgrmng Languages	284abc	Special Topics in Computer Science
142abc	Computer Mdeling & Data Analysis	286abc	Seminar in Computer Science

STANFORD UNIVERSITY
Stanford, CA 94305
(415) 497-2091

Stanford is a private university with 13,000 students, a faculty student ratio of 1 to 10, and a library system with 4.7 million volumes. Among Stanford's faculty are 10 Nobel laureates, 11 winners of the National Medal of Sciences, 75 members of the National Academy of Sciences, and 37 members of the National Academy of Engineering.

The Computer Science department offers a PhD program in Computer Science and two MS programs: MS in Computer Science, and MS in Computer Science: Artificial Intelligence. Currently, there are 124 students in the PhD program, and 150 in the MS programs. Because the department is extremely selective, candidated should apply through either the Office of Graduate Admissions or the Department Chair as early as possible (before January).

MS in CS: Artificial Intelligence is intended as a terminal professional degree. Students in this program usually spend two years beginning in the Autumn Quarter. They will register 9 units and serve as a teaching or research assistant 20 hours per week each quarter. The first year of study emphasizes course work, while the second the implementation and documentation of a substantial application in AI. Students in this program will have no advantage over other PhD applicants. In fact, admission to MS/CS: AI may negatively affect a subsequent PhD application. Therefore, students intending for the doctorate should apply directly for admission to the PhD program.

The department actively pursues the following research areas: analysis of algorithms, complexity theory, databases, data structures, design of computer networks, design of program systems, graph theory, heuristic programming, measurement and performance evaluation, natural language understanding, numerical linear algebra, operating systems, optimization, partial differential equations, program verification, programming languages, reliability of computer systems, robotics, spline functions, vision and perception. The department conducts a weekly colloquium, presented by the staff and visiting scientists, covering a wide range of current topics in computer science.

Computing facilities available to computer science students include three large systems: SCORE, SAIL, SUMEX. Each is a host on the ARPANET, and each is a host on the experimental ethernet (SUNet) operated by the department. SCORE, a DECSYSTEM 2060 running TOPS-20 with 2 million words of memory and 2.2 billion bytes of online storage, is used primarily for departmental research. SAIL, a DECSYSTEM 1080 with two central processors, 2.3 million words of memory and 1.6 billion bytes of disk storage, runs the WAITS timesharing operating systems and supports 64 display consoles, plus other local and remote terminals. The SAIL system controls specialized peripherals such as TV cameras, artificial hands and vehicles for robotics research. SUMEX, a large DECSYSTEM 2060 owned by the National Institute of Health, is used for applications of artificial intelligence to problems in medicine and biology.

In addition, the department operates several Xerox Alto computers connected by the Ethernet networks, a VAX 11/780 for research in large-scale numerical problems, several VAX computers for other specific research projects, a variety of Hewlett Packard systems, and several kinds of personal work stations.

Members of the department and their interests: C Bigelow (digital & typographic dsgns); T O Binford (cmptr vision, robotics, geometric modeling, cmptr graphics, AI); R Brooks (robot planning, vision, spatial reasoning, lisp compilers & language systems); B G Buchanan (heuristics, medical reasoning, chemical reasoning, scientific discovery, reprsntatn of knwodg, mthds of inference); D R Cheriton (operating system dsgn, distrbtd systems, cmptr communications, office automation, high performance graphics & parallel computation); G Dahlquist (numerical analysis, ordinary differential equations, generation of random numbers).

G B Dantzig (modeling & optmztns of large-scale energy systems, combinatorial math, math prgrmng); E A Feigenbaum (AI, heuristic prgrmng, languages for symbolic prcssng, symbolic prcssng cmptr archtctrs, highly parallel cmptr strctrs, national & international policies for cmptr industry develpmnt); R W Floyd (math thry of computation, prgrmng languages, appl computational complexity thry); M R Genesereth (AI, knwldg reprsntatn, prblm solving & learning, with applns to hrdwr diagnosis & testing, man-machine interaction, and robot prblm solving); G H Golub (numerical analysis, math prgrmng, statistical computing).

J H Herriot (numerical analysis); D E Knuth (analysis of algrthms, prgrmng languages, math typography, combntrl math, history of computer science); D B Lenat (AI, prcsses of discovery, knwldg acquisition, expert systems); Z Manna (math thry of computation, logical analysis & synthesis of prgrms, semantics of prgrms); E Mayr (descrptn & math analysis of behavior of parallel prgms, systems, decidability & complexity prblms, efficient scheduling algrthms for parallel prgms, IC layout algrthms & sftwr tools); J McCarthy (AI, math thry of computation, computing with symbolic expressions, time-sharing).

expressions, time-sharing).

E J McCluskey (faulty-tolerant computing, cmptr reliability, diagnosis & testing, orgnztn of computer systems, switching thry & logic dsgn); W F Miller (cmptr system dsgn, sftwr systems, strategic planning & mangmnt, automatn & control); J Oliger (numerical anaylsis, numerical mthds for part diff equatns, applns in meteorology, oceanography & geophysics); C H Papadimitriou (computatnl complexity, thry of algrthms, database thry, concurrency control, math prgrmng, combinatories, graph thry); V Pratt (computatnl complexity, computatnl logic, comptr architctr, sftwr engnrng). A L Samuel (AI).

R Schreiber (numerical analysis, numerical soln of ord & part diff equatns, high speed scientific cmptng, parallel cmptng, supercomputers, numerical linear algebra, digital signal prcssng); J D Ullman (massively parallel computatn, database systems, silicon compilatn, analysis of algrthms); G Wiederhold (databases, prgrmng systems, distrbtd & parallel prblm solving, applns in medicine & planning); J H Wilkinson (numerical linear algebra); T Winograd (thry of natural & cmptatnl languages, specific langauges, system specificatn & devlpmnt); A C Yao (computatnl complexity, analysis of algrthms, data structures, combntrcs, VLSI computatn, commnctn protocols).

Course Offerings: (generally 3 quarter units)

75 Computers & Language (5)	Graduate
101 Computers: Their Nature, Use, & Impact	200 Departmental Lecture Series (1)
102 Intro to LISP Programming	204 Problem Seminar
103 Programming in Fortran (2)	206 Recursive Programming & Proving
104 Programming in PASCAL (2)	209 Topics in Computer Science
105 Intro to Computing	211 Logic Design
106 Intro to Structured Programming	212A Processor Design
107 Systematic Programming	212B Prcssr Dsgn-Mmry Hierarch & Cntrl Unit Dsgn
108 Fundamentals of Computer Science (4)	222 A I Programming
109A Assembly Language Programming	223 Fundamentals of A I
109B DECSYSTEM-20 Assem Language Prgrmng	224 Survey of Research Topics in A I (2)
111 Intro Cmptr Org, Machine & Assem Lang	226 Epistemological Problems of A I
112 Digital Computer Organization	227A Intro to Robotics & Computer Vision
120 Medical Computer Science	227B Intro to Robotics & Computer Vision
121A Computer-Based Medical Decision Aids	227C Advanced Robotics
121B Computer-Based Medical Decision Aids	228 Applying Cognitive Psychology to CS
135 Numerical Methods	229 Topics in A I
137 Numerical Analysis A,B,C	234 Numerical Methods of Optimization
143 Compilers	235 Statistical Computing
145 File Database Systems	237 Advanced Numerical Analysis A,B,C
146 Intro to Operating Systems	238 Adv Topics Numerical Analysis A,B,C
147 Basic Tools in Cmptr System Modeling	242 Programming Language Design
150 Intro to Combinatorial Theory	243 Advanced Compilers
154 Formal Languages	244 Networks: Architecture & Implmntatn
155 Concrete Mathematics	245 Database System Theory
156 Intro to Math Theory of Computation	246 Advanced Operating Systems
157A Logical Basis for Cmptr Prgrmng	249 Topics in Prgrmng Systems
157B Deductive Systems	250 Graph Theory
161 Intro to Data Structures & Algrthms	254 Logical Algorithms
162 Sorting & Searching	256 Advanced Theory of Computation
163 Arithmetic & Combinatorial Algrthms	257 Adv Computability & Complexity
192 Programming Service Project	258 Mathematical Theory of Computation
193 Digital Logic Laboratory	259 Topics in Theory of Computation
194 Microcomputer Laboratory	262 Analysis of Algorithms
198 Teaching of Computer Science	263A Combinatorial Algorithms
199 Independent Work	263B Combinatorial Algorithms

264 Combinatorial Optimization	318 Testing Aspects of Computer Systems
265 Probabilistic Algorithms	319 Fault Tolerant Computing Systems
266 Lower Bounds	320 Artificial Intelligence Seminar 1-3
267 VLSI Theory	321 Seminar on Computers in Biomedical Research
268 Computational Geometry	327 Robotics Seminar
269 Topics in Analysis of Algorithms	330 Numerical analysis Seminar
271 Writing Seminar	343 Topics in Concurrent Programming
272 Digital Grammatography	344 Distributed Systems
273 Text and Image	345 Database Research Seminar
275 Cmptatnl Models Syntax of Natrl Language	347 Computer Networks: Modeling & Analysis
276 Cmptatnl Models Syntax of Natrl Language	350 Theory of Computation Seminar 1-3
277 Topics in Cmptatnl Linguistics	355 Combinatorics Seminar 1-3
293 Computer Laboratory	370 A I & Language Seminar 1-3
300 Computer Science Colloquium 1	390 Adv Reading & Research
312 Advanced Computer Organization	400A Reprsntatn, Meaning & Inference
315 Digital Reliability Seminar 1-4	400B Thry of Robot Cognition & Action
316 Advanced Computer Architecture	400C Cell Discretization Algrthms & Applns
317 Digital Signal Prcssng: Archtctr & Circuits	

UNIVERSITY OF CALIFORNIA, BERKELEY
Berkeley, CA 94720
(415) 642-0200

UC Berkeley has a 1,200-acre campus serving a population of 30,000 students with a faculty student ratio of 1 to 14, and a library with over 6 million volumes. The Engineering Library contains 98,000 volumes and 2200 periodicals. The San Francisco Bay area and the nearby Silicon Valley offer unparalleled opportunity for computer scientists. IBM, Xerox, Amdahl, Hewlett-Packard, Tandem, Fairchild, Intel, Zilog, Apple, Atari are all within a short driving distance, thereby providing ample employment and consulting possibilities for students and faculty in computer science.

The Department of Electrical Engineering & Computer Science offers bachelor's, master's, and PhD programs in which 460, 100, and 60 students are currently enrolled. Prospective students should apply through the Office of Admissions & Records; deadline Nov 30.

The Department offers an exciting environment for research and teaching. There are numerous weekly seminars and Computer Science Division Colloquium where scientists from universities and industrial research laboratories participate and interact with Berkelely's own faculty, research scientists and students. Research areas actively pursued here include: analysis of algorithms, code generation and optimization, computational complexity, computer architecture, computer aided design, computer graphics, computer networks, data base systems, formal language theory, natural language processing, numerical analysis, operating systems, performance evaluation, programming language design ...etc. Examples of some areas of specialization here:

1) Theoretical Computer Science investigates: timing and storage requirements of algorithms, development of new algorithms, application of network flow theory to combinatorial optimization, efficent algorithms for the matching problems in graphs. Faculty in this area include Professors: Blum, Gill, Harrison, Karp, Lawler, and Thompson.

2) Programming Language & Methodology develops automating compiler constru-

ction, language retargetable programming tools, error diagnostics and error recovery, table-driven method for code generation based on efficient pattern matching, database application development tools and language (RIGEL), experimental langauge with abstract data types (Model), a portable P-code-based compiler, efficent implementation of parameterized types and tasking mechanisms in ADA, Efficent compilation of typing in Smalltalk. Faculty in this group include Professors: Graham, Rowe, Powell, Hilfinger and Fateman.

3) Architecture is concerned with advanced parallel or pipelined machines, influence of Very Large Scale Ingegration of future computer systems, development of integrated software system (Smalltalk '80), implementation of Smalltalk under UNIX on a SUN station, design of a VLSI chip for Smalltalk. Faculty in this area include Professors: Despain, Ramamoorthy, Patterson, Sequin.

4) Operating Systems and Performance Evaluation is concerned with: the development of reliable, efficient and secure computing systems, multiprocessor and distributed operating systems (OSMOSIS), the development of the Berkeley UNIX project (UNIX 4.2BSD), distributed file systems, naming sevices, automatic load balancing, distributed system instrumentation, and distributed program debugging. Faculty here include Professors: Powell, Fabry, Ferrari, Ousterhout and Smith.

5) Symbolic Manipulation and Numerical Analysis is interested in the development of: scientific software support, arithmetic hardware, compilers and lanauges, numerical algorithms, large virtual memory algebraic manipulation systems, the MACSYMA algebraic system, interfaces to numerical and natural languages, diagnostic procedures, IEEE standard for floating-point arithmetic, matrix computation. Faculty in this area include Professors: Fateman, Kahan, Parlett.

6) Graphics and Computer-Aided Design investigates: the synthisis of images and their communication, computer aided geometric design and modeling, free-form curves and surfaces, mathematical techniques for curve and surface representation, image generation, algorithms for clipping and ray-tracing, hidden surface removal, antialiasing, color graphics tools for designing integrated circuits and creating text illustrations, interactive graphical systems (VAXIMA, UNIGRAFIX). Faculty in this group include Professors: Barsky, Fateman, Ousterhout, and Sequin.

7) Data Base Systems is involved with the development of distributed data base and data base programming languages (RIGEL, FADS, INGRES). Professors here include Rowe, Stonebraker and Wong.

8) Artificial Intelligence consists of two major groups. Professor Wilensky directs the Berkeley Artificial Intelligence Research project that includes the development and application of UC (UNIX Consultant), Pearl, PHRAN, PHRED, PANDER. FAUSTUS. Professor Zadeh directs the development of knowledge representation and approximate reasoning which include PRUF, a natural language that can be used to represent the meaning of complex propositions, inference, analysis of evidence and the design of expert systems. In addition, there are 15 faculty from various departments participating in the the Berkeley Cognitive Science program that concentrates on the understanding of cognitive processes.

Computing facilities available at Berkeley include: 7 VAX 11/780, 13 VAX 11/750, 20 SUN workstations with a few dozen more expected. These workstations offer high resolution bit-mapped graphics and run UNIX. Most computing systems are linked locally via Ethernet and tied to the ARPAnet and CSnet national networks. Languages available on Berkeley's UNIX include C, Pascal, SNOBOL, and INGRES which was developed here. A collection of color graphics stations support the research in computer aided design. Teaching facilities include 6 PDP 11/70, 7 VAX's, and an IBM 4341. In addition, some external resources are also available: The Lawrence Berkeley Lab and the Lawrence Livermore Lab maintain major computational facilities such as the CDC 7600, the STAR Processors, and the CRAY-1. The university's Computer Center will operate an IBM 3081, a significant portion of which will be made available to Berkeley's computer scientists.

The Berkeley Computer Graphics Laboratory is equipped with an Evans & Sutherland PS300 system, and an Ikonas RDS-3000 raster display system hosted by a VAX 11/750, running the Berkeley UNIX 4.2BSD with a floating-point accelerator and Ampex Capricorn Model 330 disk.

There are 30 full-time faculty in the department. Openings exist at the assistant professor rank. The department seeks outstanding individuals in all fields of computer science, particularly those with background in artificial intelligence, graphics, networking and distributed systems. Faculty and their interests:

B A Barsky (computer aided geometric dsgn & modeling, interactive 3-dimnsnl graphics); M Blum (applns of recursive functn thry to computatnl complexity & inductive inference, automata in 2- or 3-dimnsnl space, protocols for protecting electronic transactions, cryptography); A M Despain (archtctr, micros, specialized computers); R S Fabry (sftwr, operating systems, archtctr, protection, performance evaluation of UNIX); R J Fateman (scientific sftwr, algebraic manipulation systems, LISP, analysis of algrthms, analysis of large prgrmng systems).

D Ferrari (computer system performance evaluation & meawsurement, operating systems, distrbtd systems); A Gill (automata thry, prgrmng, data structures, complexity of algrthms); S L Graham (prgrmng languages dsng & implmntatn, code generation & optimiztn, sftwr development environments); M A Harrison (protection & security in operating systems, fast parsing tchnqs, text prcssng systems); P N Hilfinger (prgrmng languages, compilers, sftwr engnrng, prgrmng environments).

W M Kahan (numerical & scientific computatn, algebraic symbol manipulation, exception handling & execution time diagnostics, error analysis, arithmetic units); R M Karp (computational complexity, combinatorial algrthms); R H Katz (VLSI dsgn data mangmnt, VLSI on archtctr, rapid hardware prototyping); E I Lawler (combinatorial optmztn, computatnl complexity thry); J K Ousterhout (interactive graphics, computer-aided dsgn tools, VLSI circuits, operating systems).

B N Parlett (numerical analysis & sparse matrices); D A Patterson (VLSI archtctr, sftwr directed hardwr); M I Powell (multiprcssr, distrbtd & adaptive operating systems, operating system dsgn & implmntatn, prgrmng languages dsgn & implmntatn, prgrm development systems, large sftwr systems); C V Ramamoorthy (systems archtctr, sftwr engnrng, hardwr & sftwr reliability); L A Rowe (prgrmng languages dsgn & implmntatn, data base systems, computer ntwrks).

C H Sequin (archtctr & computer aided dsgn tools, computer graphics, influence of very large scale integratn on future computing systems, implmntatn of special purpose function in silicon, tightly coupled multiprcssr ntwrks); A J Smith (system modeling & analysis, performance evaluation, operating systems, computer archtctr, data compression); M R Stonebraker (database systems, database machines, distrbtd data bases, engnrng data bases); C D Thompson (thry of VLSI systems, parallel algrthms, computatinal complexity, computer archtctr); R Wilensky (AI, natural language prcssng); L A Zadel (AI, natural language prcssng, expert systems, fuzzy sets).

Course Offerings: (generally 3 semester units)

3	Intro to Programming 4	55	Machine Structures 4
7	Intro to Programming	95	Topics in Computer Science 1
7P	Intro Fortran Scientific Computation 1	99	Individual Rsrch for Undergraduates 1-2
7S	Self-Paced Intro to Programming 1-3	103S	Self-Paced Intro to Programming 1-4
8	Intro to Programming	106	Programming with Applications 4
8P	Programming in Pascal 1	150	Components & Dsgn Tchnq: Digital Systems
8S	Self-Paced Intro to Programming 1-3	150L	Digital Design lab 2
10	Principles of Computing	151	Input-Output Devices & Microprocessors 4
38	Self-Paced Intro to Programming 1-4	152	Computer Architecture & Engineering 4
50	The Science & Practice of Computing 5	154	Hardware/Software Microprocessor Lab
50P	Intro to CS for Programmers 2	160	Data Structures & Adv Programming 4

U C BERKELEY

162 System Programming & Operating Systems 4
164 Programming Languages & Compilers 4
170 Efficient Algrthm & Intractable Prblms 4
172 Formal Language & Automata Theory
174 Combinatorics & Graph Theory
184 Foundations of Computer Graphics 4
186 Intro to Database Systems
188 Intro to A I & Natural Lang Processing 4
189 Intro to Lang Prcssng & Query Languages
190 Programming Applications
195 Social & Econ Implctns of Cmptr Tchnlgy 2
196 Honors Seminar for Computer Science Majors
199 Supervised Independent Study 1-5
Graduate
250 VLSI Systems Design 4
252 Graduate Computer Architecture
253 Microprocessor-Based System Design 4
254 Implementation & Testing of LSI Chips 2
255 Microarchitecture & Microprogramming 2
256 Software Driven Computer Architecture 2
257 Adv Computer Architecture 2
258 Parallel Processors 2
259 Fault Tolerant Systems 2
261 Security in Computer Systems
262 Adv Topics in Operating Systems
263 Design of Programming Languages
264 Implmntatn of Programming Languages 4
265 Adv Prgrmng Language Implementation 2
266 Intro to System Performance Analysis 2
267 Computer System Analysis 2
268 Analytic Models of Computer Systems 2
269 Sftwr Engineering & Large System Design

270 Combinatorial Algrthms & Data Structures
272 Languages & Abstract Machines 2
273 Recognition & Parsing of Languages 2
274 VSLI Theory 2
276 Number Theory & Cryptography 2
277 Concrete Complexity 2
278 Machine-Based Complexity Theory 2
281 System Support f Scientific Computation 2
282 Algebraic Algorithms 2
283 Prgrmng Tchnlgy: A I & Symbol Manipulation
284 Computer-Aided Geometric Design & Modeling
286 Implementation of Data Base Systems
287 User-Interfaces to Computer Systems 2
288 A I Approach to Natural Lang Processing
289 A I, Knowledge Rprsntn & Expert Systems 2
292 New Topics in CS 2
292A Probabilistic Algorithms
292D Concurrent Programming 2
292N Video Graphics Languages & Techniques
292Q Computer-Aided Geometric Design
292V Distributed Systems & Computer Networks
292X VLSI Systems Implementation 4
298 Group Studies, Seminars or Resrch 1-8
299 Individual Research 1-12

Professional Courses
300 Teaching Practice 1-6
301 Teaching Tchnques for Computer Science 1-3

Interdepartmental Studies (IDS)
270 Error Correcting Codes 2
286 Neurobiology of Vision

UNIVERSITY OF CALIFORNIA, DAVIS
Davis, CA 95616
(916) 752-2971

UC Davis's 3700-acre campus is located 13 miles west of Sacramento. Operating on a trimester system with 2 6-week summer sessions, the university has 20,000 students of which 14,000 are undergraduates, a faculty student ratio of 1 to 19, and a library with 1.8 million volumes. Currently, there are 200 enrolled in the Bachelor's program in computer science, 70 in the master's and 15 in the PhD program. Interested students should apply through the Graduate Admissions Office before April 1 for the fall.

University computing facilities at the Davis Campus include: a Burroughs B7800, two VAX, PDP 11/70, HP3000, PDP 11/34, and a number of 8080, 8086/88, and 68000 microcomputers. Local network, ARPAnet and UCnet are all accessible. Operating systems include: MPL, UNIX, VMS, CPM, MSDOS.

There are 10 full-time faculty members in the computer science program. The

department seeks several faculty at various ranks. Computer scientists with specialty in programming languages and architecture are specially desired.

Course Offerings: (3 units unless noted otherwise)

Offered by the Mathematics Department

29A	Intro to Computer Science
29B	Adv Computer Programming Techniques
29C	Adv Computer Programming Techniques
123	Intro to Computer Organization
124	Intro to Minicomputers
128A	Numerical Analysis 4
129A	Computer Data Structures
129B	Algorithm Design & Analysis
129C	Programming Language & Compilers
168	Mathematical Programming
170	Data Processing
171	Automata Theory & Formal Languages
173	Computer Graphics
174	Topics in Artificial Intelligence
175	Techniques in Pattern Recognition
176	Software Design

Offered by Engrng: Elctrl & Cmptr Depts

8	Intro Computer Prgrmmng (PASCAL)
80	Intro to Software Development
88	Computer Programming (PASCAL)
89A-O	Sp Topics in Elctrl & Cmptr Engrng (1-5)
170	Computer Structure & Assem Language 4
171	Intro to Computer Architecture 4
172	Microcomputer-Based Systems Design 4
175	Computer Devices & Systems
176	Digital Systems I 4
177	Digital Systems II 4
180	Data Structures & Prgrmmng Tchnques 4
181	Programming Languages & Compilers 4
182A	Operating System Design 4
182B	Operating System Design
185	Database Systems 4
186	Discrete Event Simulation
189	Sp Topics in Elctrl & Cmptr Engrng 1

Graduate

201	Optimization Tchnques w Applications
202	Optimization of Dynamic Systems
204	Digital Processing of Signals 4
206	Digital Image Processing
207	Pattern Recognition & Classification
214	Computer-Aided Circuit Analysis & Dsng

273	Bit-Slice Microprocessor Systems
274	Adv Computer Architecture
276A	Intro to Fault-Tolerant Computing
276B	Intro to Digital Fault Diagnosis
277	Adv Programming & Data Structures
278A	Formal Language & Related Automata
278B	Translation of Programming Languages
279	Artificial Intelligence
280	Database Systems
282	Operating Systems Models

Offered by the Engrng: Applied Science Dept.
Davis

115	Intro Numerical Methods for Computers

Graduate

210A	Adv Methods of Computational Physics
210B	Adv Methods of Computational Physics

Livermore

101	Data Structures
103	Intro to Computer Architecture
106	Language Structures
108	Concurrent Programming
111	Intro to Foundations of Computing
115	Intro Numerical Methods for Computers

Graduate

201	Software Engineering
202	Data Base Management
203A	Computer Architecture
203B	Computer Architecture
206	Programming Languages
207	Compiler Construction
208A	Operating Systems
208B	Operating Systems
210A	Adv Methods of Computational Physics
210B	Adv Methods of Computational Physics
211	Automata Theory & Formal Languages
212	Analysis of Algorithms
214	Computing with Symbolic Expressions
215A	Computational Mathematics
215B	Computational Mathematics
216A-G	Sp Topics in Computer Science (1-5)
224	Micro Prgrmmng & Prgrmmable Archtctr

UNIVERSITY OF CALIFORNIA, IRVINE
Irvine, CA 92717
(714) 856-5011

UCI's 1510-acre suburban campus is located 5 miles from the Pacific and 40 miles south of Los Angeles, supporting 12,000 students with a faculty student ratio of 1 to 17, and a library containing over a million volumns.

The department of Computer Science at UCI offers graduate and undergraduate degrees in computer science. Currently, there are 600 students in the bachelor's program and 70 in the doctoral program. Prospective students should apply through the Office of Admissions or the Office of Graduate Studies and Research in November for the Fall Semester. With 16 full-time faculty members, the department continues to seek individuals at all ranks.

Computing facilities at UCI include: a Sigma 7, several DEC 10, DEC VAX 11/750, PDP 11/45, DEC 2020's, 18 TERAK's and 18 Western Digital Microengines. CSNET is accessible. Operating systems in use include TOPS-10, TOPS-20, UNIX, and UCILISP.

Research areas of the faculty include: multimachine and distributed machine architecture, data flows and reduction language machines, data flow representations of data base, programming languages, program development and maintenance environments, data structures, analysis of algorithms and concrete complexity, natural language processing, knowledge representation, computer models of music theory, software engineering tools and methods especially for analysis and design, social impacts of computing, and management of computing resourses.

Course Offering: (generally 4 quarter units)

1A	Programming & Problem Solving I	222	Adv Topics in Archtctr & Operating Systems
1B	Programming & Problem Solving I	231	Formal Analytic Techniques
2	Programming & Problem Solving II	232	Models of Computation
2L	Lab for Programming & Prblm Solving	233	Analysis of Algorithms
3	Programming & Problem Solving III	241	Computer Models of Human Behavior
10	Computers and Society	242	Knowledge Reprsntatn in AI
80	Spec Topics in Info & Computer Science	245	Intro to Software Engineering
90	Survey of Programming Languages	246	Economics & Administration of Computing
141	Programming Languages	250	Seminar in Prgrmng Languages, & Translators
142	Compilers and Interpreters	251	Seminar in Artificial Intelligence
145	Language Processor Construction	252	Seminar in Automata Theory
151A	Intro to Computer Systems Architecture	253	Seminar in Formal Languages
151B	Intermediate Cmptr Systems Architecture	254	Seminar in Pattern Recognition I, II, III
152	Process & Resource Mngmnt in Cmptr Systems	255	Seminar in Self-Organizing Systems I, II, III
154	Logic Design Laboratory	256	Seminar in Computer Architecture
155	Project in Computer System Organization	257	Seminar in the Economics of Computation
161	Design & Analysis of Algorithms	258	Seminar in Social Implcatn of Cmptrs & Automatn
162	Formal Languages & Automata	259	Seminar in Optimztn Tchnques
171	Intro to Heuristic Prblm Solvng in AI	260	Seminar in Natural Language Prcssng
172	Prgrmmng Tchnques in AI	261	Seminar in Numerical Analysis
175	Project in Artificial Intelligence	262	Seminar in Models of the Brain
180	Special Topics in Info & Computer Science	270	Workshop in Prgrmng Languages & Translators
181	Organizational Info Systems	271	Workshop in Artificial Intelligence
182	Tutoring in ICS	272	Workshop in Automata Theory
183	Data Processing & Tchnques	273	Workshop in Formal Languages
184	File & Data Base Management	274	Workshop in Pattern Recognition
186	Computer Graphics	275	Workshop in Self-Organizing Systems
191	System Measurement & Evaluation	276	Workshop in Computer Architecture
193	Individual & Orgnztnl Factors in Computing	280	Special Topics in Info & Computer Science
195	Project in System Design	290	Research Seminar
Graduate		291	Directed Research
211	Data Structures	295	Colloquia-Orientation
212	Programming Language Processors	298	Thesis Supervision
221	Computer Systems Architecture	299	Individual Study

UCLA's 411-acre campus is located in Westwood, Los Angeles. Among its 33,000 student body, two thirds are undergraduates. The university operates on a trimester (quarter) system with a 6-week summer session. Faculty student ratio is about 1 to 17. The library contains 4.4 million volumes.

The Computer Science Department offers four graduate degrees: MS in CS, MS in Engineering, PhD in CS and Phd in Engineering. Currently, there are 100 enrolled in the PhD program, 171 in the MS program. At the undergraduate level, a major in Mathematics / Computer Science is offered by the two departments. In addition to the appropriate studies in mathematics, the program permits study in the principal disciplines of computer science, including theoretical foundations of computer science, methodology of computing, computer system design, programming languages and systems, and computer applications. Students who intend to enter this major, but have not completed the courses required for entrance into the program, must enroll in the Pre-Math/CS program. Currently, 692 are enrolled in the Pre Math/CS, 272 in Math/CS, and 146 in Computer Engineering. In addition, a major in Linguistics and Computer Science is also available. Interested undergraduate students should apply through the Admissions Office, graduates through the Computer Science Department in Boelter Hall, UCLA; deadlines: Oct 1 for the winter quarter, Nov 30 for the spring and Feb 15 for the fall. Due to budget constraint, fewer students will be admitted than previous years. Therefore, students should apply as promptly as possible. After Fall 1984, there will be only annual Fall admissions for graduate studies.

The graduate program offers five academic fields of study: computer science theory, network modeling and analysis, system architecture, computer methodology, programming languages and systems.

I. Computer science theory encompasses: grammar & machines, computability and complexity, algorithms, automata, formal languages, program structure & correctness, discrete state system theory, analysis of heuristic methods, special topics. Faculty directing research in theoretical study includes: S Greibach (chair), D Cantor, J Carlyle, E Fiedman, D Martin, D S Parker, J Pearl.

II. Areas under computer network modeling and analysis are: computer networks, multiprogramming systems, parallel processing systems, distributed processing systems, computer communication, time shared systems, satellite and ground radio packet switching systems, packet communications, local network architecture, communication processors, communication protocols. Faculty directing research here includes: L Kleinrock (chair), J Carlyle, W Chu, G Estrin, E Gafni, M Gerla, S Greibach, B Miller, R Muntz, D S Parker, G Popek.

III. The computer system architecture field is reponsible for: arithmetic procesor systems and algorithms, fault-tolerant system and fault-tolerant computing, memory systems, distributed processing and distributed data bases, interactive graphics, methodology of synthesis of concurrent systems, comparative architecture, VLSI system design and implementation, high-speed computing. Professors directing research in these issues: A Avizienis, B Bussell, W Chu, G Estrin, M Ercegovac, T Lang, L McNamee, S Parker, D Rennels, V Tyree.

IV. Three options are grouped under the field of computer methodology: physical systems option, biological systems option, and machine intelligence option. In addition to fundamentals on such topics as data organization, random data analyis and measurement procedures...etc, the physical systems option studies advanced numerical methods, continuous systems simulation, distributed parameter system, digital processing, pattern recognition. Faculty in this option include: A Cardenas, J Carlyle, M Ercegovac, W Karplus (chair), A Klinger, L Levine, L McNamee. The biological systems option studies information processing in nerve unified systems, digital processing, biocybernetics, simulation of biological systems and statistical pattern recognition. Faculty here consists of J DiStefano, T Estrin, A Klinger, J Vidal (chair). The machine intelligence option studies pattern recognition, heuristic programming, artificial intelligence, data

25

structure, data representation, programming languages for A I, natural language processing, Knowledge-based system, problem solving and decision making models. Faculty here includes J Carlyle, M Dyer, M Flowers, A Klinger, L Miller, J Pearl (chair), Ruzgalis, J Vidal.

V. The programming languages and systems field, also known as the software systems, include three major areas: operating systems, programming languages, and data management systems. Fundamental to this field is computer programming. Graduate students in this field should be expert programmers in at least two high level languages such as FORTRAN, COBOL, Algol, PL/I...etc. The operating systems area studies operating systems concepts, probabilistic models of system behavior and related issues in language, data management and security. The programming languages area concentrates on specification, design validation, evaluation of programming languages and systems, and formal models of syntax and semantics. The data management area studies file management, database management systems, query languages and processing, data dependencies and normalization, database integrity and security, database design and development, and database operating systems.

The Computer Science teaching laboratories at UCLA include: 1) Introductory Digital Circuits Lab which provides students an opportunity to design, assembly, build, and test small digital subsystems to better understand the basics of computer operation. 2) Digital Systems Lab that allows students to attach small digital devices to microcomputers and write programs to operate the devices. 3) Computation Lab which is equipped with a large VAX 11/780, that has four megabytes of main storage, over 450 megabytes secondary storage, 90 terminal ports, capable of supporting more than 35 concurrent users under a paging UNIX operating systems. Fully dedicated to the needs of the Computer Science Department, it provides convenient interactive computing to faculty and students. In addition, a VAX 11/750 is networked to the larger VAX, permitting distributed system experiments and general reliability enhancement. This machine is extensively utilized for undergraduate instruction.

Facilities dedicated to system research include 18 VAX 11/750's. Most of the machines are connected together by a high bandwidth local area network, as well as being directly connected to the worldwide ARPANet. The Computer Aided Design Lab contains 6 IBM 3250's, one IBM 3277 GA and an IBM 2250 graphics work station. They are interconnected and the operating systems include Lockheed's CADAM and IBM's NGS systems. CADAM is a versatile layout design system with the ability to perform some analysis on completed designs and NGS is a three dimensional surface design and display systems. The VLSI Design Lab is equipped with advanced interactive color graphics terminals, multi-pen plotters and test equipments in support of VSLI mask design and VLSI chip testing.

Additionally, the department has won an NSF-DARPA award for experimental computer science. 15 VAX 11/750's have been ordered. Planned acquisition in the near future includes a network of Apollo Domain Workstations.

There are 28 full-time faculty in the department. Areas of primary recruitment interest are: theoretical foundations of computer science; computer network systems modeling, analysis and design; computer systems archtecture; methodology of application of computers; programming languages and programming systems. Contact the Department Chair for faculty openings, adjunct or research staff positions, visiting professorships, post doctoral scholars and research engineers.

Department faculty members: A Avizienis, D Berry, B Bussell, D Cantor, A F Cardenas, J Carlyle, W Chu, J DiStefano, M Ercegovac, G Estrin, T Estrin, E Gafni, M Gerla, S Greibach, W Karplus, D Kay, L Kleinrock, A Klinger, T Lang, L Levine, D F Martin, L P McNamee, M A Melkanoff, L Miller, R R Muntz, D S Parker, J Pearl, G J Popek, D Rennels, V Tyree, R Uzgalis, J J Vidal, C R Viswanathan.

Course Offerings:

5 Computer Literacy & Appreciation	252A Computer System Dsgn Arithmetic Prcssors
10C Intro to Programming	253A Computer System Dsgn Fault Tolerance
10F Intro to Programming	253B Adv Topics in Fault-Tolerant Computing
10S Intro Prgmmng for Life & Social Sciences	254A Computer Memories & Memory Systems
20 Programming & Problem Solving	255B Distr Prcssng & Distr Data Base Systems
30 Intro to Computer Operating Systems	256A Interactive Computer Graphics
99 Individual Programming Projects	257A Comparaive Archtctr & Synthesis Mthods
111 Systems Programming	258A LSI in Computer System Design
112 Computer System Modeling Fundamentals	258B Same as above
130 Software Engineering	258C Same as above
131 Programming Languages	259 Seminar: System Design (Architecture)
132 Compiler Construction	259A Computer Architectures VLSI Implmntatn
141 Basic Structure for Data Organization	259B Spec Topics in High Speed Computing
151 Computer System Architecture I	259C Computational Switching Structures
151B Computer System architecture II	259D VLSI CAD Techniques
152A Intro Digital Circuits Lab	270A Computer Methodology: Adv Numerical Mthods
152B Digital Systems Lab	271A Cmptr Mthdlogy: Continuous Systm Simulation
171 On-Line Computer Systems	271B Cmptr Mthdlogy: Distributed Parameter Systm
171L Real-Time Systems Lab	271C Sem: Advanced Simulation Methods
172 Simulation & Models	273A Digital Prcssng of Engnrng & Statstcl Data
173 Random Data Anlyss & Measrmnt Prcdures	274A Problem Solving & Decision Making
174 Elements of Computer Graphics	274B Knowledge-Based Systems
181 Theoretical Models in Computer Science	274C Cmptr Mthds Data Analysis & Model Formation
183 Discrete Systems & Automata	274Z Analysis of Heuristic Methods
198I Microprocessors & Microcomputers	275A Information Processes in Nervous Systems
199 Special Studies	276A Pattern Recognition
201 Computer Science Seminar	276B Structural Pattern Recognition
202 Advanced Computer Science Seminar	276C Machine Pattern Analysis
212A Queueing System Theory	277A Heuristic Prgmng & Artificial Intelligence
212B Queueing Applns: Schdlng Algrthms & Ntwrks	279 Seminar: Cmptr Applns in Health Sciences
215 Computer Communication & Networks	280A Algorithms: Principles of Dsgn & Analysis
2216 Distributed Multi-Access Control in Ntwrks	280G Algorithms: Graph & Networks
218A Network Protocols & Processor Design	281A Computability & Complexity
219 Current Topics: System Modeling Analysis	281D Discrete State Systems
221 Economics of Computers	284A Context-Free Languages
231A Advanced Topics in Prgmmng Languages	284P Parsing Algorithms
231B Sem: Currnt Topics Computer Language Dsgn	287A Theory of Program Structure
232A Opertnl Semantics of Prgmmng Languages	289A Current Topics in Computer Theory
234A Corrctness Proofs	375 Teaching Apprentice Practicum
234C High Level Language Computer Architecture	497 Field Projects in Computer Science
239 Sem: Curr Topics Pgmng Languages & Systems	596 Directed Study
241A Data Management Systems	597 Preparation for MS Comprehensive Exam
241B Data Base, Software, & Info Systems	597B Preparation for PhD Prelim Exam
242A Privacy & Security in Cmptr Info Systems	597C Preparation for PhD Oral Exam
243A Relational Data Bases	598 Research & Preparation for Master's Thesis
249 Current Topics in Data Structure	599 Research & Preparation for PhD Dissertation
251 Advanced Computer Architecture	

UNIVERSITY OF CALIFORNIA, RIVERSIDE
Riverside, CA 92521
(714) 787-1012

UC Riverside's 1200-acre campus is located 60 miles east of Los Angeles. Of the 4800 students, about 3100 are undergraduates. Operating on a quarter system with a 6-week summer session, the university has 1.1 million volumes in its library. Faculty student ratio is 1 to 14.

The Department of Mathematics and Computer Science has 21 full-time faculty, offering undergraduate and graduate programs in computer science. Presently, there are 240 enrolled in the bachelor's program, 28 in the master's and 19 in the PhD's. Interested students should apply through the Department. No application deadlines have been specified.

The university is equiped with an IBM 4341, a Prime 750, 3 VAX 11/750s, various TERAKs, Apple IIs, Apple IIIs, and the IBM PCs. The IBM, Prime, and VAX are all tied through a campus data switch. The IBM runs MVS, Prime runs PRIMOS, VAX runs UNIX and VMS.

Course Offerings:

11	Intro to Computer Science I	166	Data Base Management Systems
12	Intro to Computer Science II	170	Artificial Intelligence
13	Intro to Assem Lang & Real-time Prgmmng	175	Information Theory
18	Intro to Program	177	Modeling and Simulation
20	Intermediate Program	180A	Seminar in Computer System Design
Upper Division		180B	Seminar in Computer System Design
109	Intro to Data Processing	185	Progamming Languages
140A	Algorithms and Data Structures	190	Special Studies (1-4)
140B	Algorithms and Data Structures	191	Seminar in Computer Science (1-4)
150A	Theory of Computation	193	Projects in Computer Scince (1-4)
150B	Theory of Computation	194	Independent Reading (1-4)
160A	Org and Design of Computer Systems	Graduate	
160B	Org and Design of Computer Systems	201	Compiler Construction
160C	Org and Design of Computer Systems	202	Advanced Operating Systems

UNIVERSITY OF CALIFORNIA, SAN DIEGO
La Jolla, CA 92093
(619) 452-3160

U C San Diego's 1200-acre campus lies on the Pacific coast, 12 miles north of Downtown San Diego. Operating on a trimester system with summer sessions, the university has over 13,000 students, a faculty student ratio of 1 to 18, and a library with 1.4 million volumes.

The Electrical Engineering & Computer Science Department (EECS) offers BS in computer engineering, BA in computer science, BA in information science, MS, and PhD in computer science. Interested students are suggested to apply in November.

The BS in computer engineering places a strong emphasis on engineering mathematics and other basic engineering science, as well as a firm background in computer science. It prepares students for employment in the industry and for graduate work in the field. The BA degrees allow students more time for undergraduate studies outside their major subject. They prepare students for graduate study in computer & information science, as well as for certain types of employment.

The graduate program is concerned with fundamental properties of digital

28

information processing systems. Emphasis is placed on the design of computer systems, especially compilers, architecture, programming languages, operating systems, and the analysis of algorithms. The MS degree is designed to serve as a terminal master's degree for students who wish to seek immediate employment in the computer field. However, MS graduates are also in an excellent position to go on for the PhD program.

The UCSD computer center maintains a VAX 11/780 using VMS and UNIX. Graphic facilities include color hardcopy plotting and storage display video technology that use Disspla, Tektronix, and Zeta software packages. Advanced text processing facilities for thesis production journal, articles, and book manuscripts are provided through the Computer Assisted Typing & Typesetting (CATT) service that runs on the dedicated PDP 11/70 using UNIX.

The department is interested in computer scientists in all areas, especially those in graphics, database management systems, expert systems, VLSI, programming languages, operating systems, networking, architecture, and software engineering. The faculty of the EECS Department:

H Alfven, V C Anderson, H G Booker, W S Chang, W A Coles, M Fredman, C W Helstrom, T C Hu, S S Lau, S H Lee, R Lugannani, H L Luo, E Masry, B J Rickett, M Rotenberg, M L Rudee, V H Rumsey, W J Savitch, W A Burkhard, W E Howden, G J Lewak, L B Milstein, W F Appelbe, P Dymond, L G Meiners, R Reichman.

Course Offerings: (generally 4 quarter units)

Courses by EE-CS (a Partial Listing)

61 Intro to Computer Science	198 Directed Group Study
63 Non-Numeric Applns of Computers	199 Indep Study for Undergraduates
64 Scientific Applns of Computers	Graduate
65 Intro to Programming Theory	247 Intro VLSI Microfabrication Tchnlogy
69 Computers & Society	259A Info Theory & Digital Communication
70 Intro to Systems Programming	259B Same as above
136A Fundmntls Semiconductor Devices Fabrctns	259C Same as above
136B Microelectronics Lab	264A Software Engineering
159A Queueing Systems	264B Advanced Operating Systems
159B Queueing Systems	264C Advanced Compiler Design
159C Queueing Systems	264D Database Systems
160A Foundation of Computer Science	265A Automata, Formal Languages & Complexity
160B Same as above	265B Same as above
161A Data Structure I	265C Same as above
161B Data Structure II	268A Combinatorial & Searching Algorithms
163A Compiler Construction	268B Same as above
163B Compiler Construction	268C Same as above
165 Algrthms, Automata, & Formal Languages	269 Special Projects in Computer Science
166 Numerical algorithms	270A Concepts in Computer Architecture
170A Prncpls of Computer System Design	270B Same as above
170B Prncpls of Computer System Design	278 Topics in Artificial Intelligence
171A Prncpls of Computer Operating Systems	280 Special Topics in Computer Science
171B Prncpls of Computer Operating Systems	281 Special Topics in Computer Science
173 Comparative Study of Prgmng Languages	285 Sp Topics Natnl Security for Science Stdnts
175B Digital Hardware Lab	287A Special Studies in Information Science
175C Microprocessor System Design	287B Same as above
178 Artificial Intelligence	287C Same as above
179 Analysis of Algorithms	289 Special Topics in Information Science
195 Teaching	293 Graduate Seminar in Info & Cmptr Science
197 Field Study in EE & CS	298 Indep Study
	299 Research

U C Santa Barbara's 850-acre campus lies on the Pacific Coast, approximately 100 miles north of Los Angeles. The university maintains a faculty student ratio of 1 to 18, and a library with 1.35 million volumes.

The Department of Computer Science offers BA, BS in Computer Science. The BA is a College of Letters & Science major, while the BS is a College of Engineering major. Computer Science tracks leading to the MS and PhD in Electrical & Computer Engineering are available. Questions about computer science courses, requirements, application deadlines ...etc may be obtained by writing or calling Department of Computer Science, Enginering 2211, UCSB, (805) 961-4321; or Department of Electrical & Computer Engineering, Engineering 4121, (805) 961-3716.

The department has a DEC VAX 11/780 (UNIX) for instructional computing. The campus maintains an ITEL ASV6 (IBM 370 compatible) with OS/MVT & Wylbur, an IBM 4341 supporting VM & CMS, two PDP 11/70 with UNIX. Terminal rooms house Tektronix 4006 graphics terminals, a stand alone LSI/11 based Terak computer systems on which UCSD's Pascal system is available. The Computer Systems Laboratory runs three VAX. The UCSB Microcomputer Lab is a general-purpose instructional facility equipped with Apple II's.

Faculty of the department: J L Bruno (engnrng applns, scheduling, ntwrk, graph); P R Cappello (VLSI thry & applns, prgmng language & systems); D L Chaum (security, privacy, cryptography, archtctr); L M Chirica (prgmng, languages, methdlogy, info system dsgn); P R Eggert (prgmng languages, systems reliability); R A Kemmerer (spec & verfctn, security, reliablty, lang dsgn); A G Konheim (cmptr communications, modeling & analysis); M Marcus, (linear & multilinear algebra); M T Shing (dsgn & anlys algrthms, optimztn, dsgn automatn); R C Wood (system modeling, dsgn & analysis, archtctr).

Course Offerings:

Lower Division
5	Intro to Computer Prgmng & Organztn
11	Programming Language Lab
20	Programming Methods
26	Fundation of Computer Science
30	Intro to Computer Systems

Upper Division
110	Numerical Computation
130	Data Structure & Algorithms
130C	Algorithms for Graph & Network Prblms
140	Software Fabrication
154	Computer Architecture
160	Translation of Prgmng Languages
162	Programming Languages
170	Operating Systems
172	Software Engineering
174	Data Base Management Systems
176	Intro to Computer Communication Netwrk
178	Intro to Cryptography
180	Computer Graphis
185	Automata and Formal Languages
186	Theory of Computation
190	Special topics in Computer Science
192	Projects
194	Group Studies in Computer Science
199	Indep Studies in Computer Science

Graduate
220	Automation-Based complexity
221	Formal Languages
222	Computability
230	Topics in Algorithms & Complexity
260	Adv Topics in Translation
262	Adv Topics in Programming Languages
264	Automated Theorem Proving
266	Formal Specification & Verification
270	Adv Topics in Operating Systems
272	Software Engineering
274	Adv Topics in Data Base Mngmnt Systems
276	Distributed Computing & Computer Ntwrk
277	Security, Privacy and Computers
278	Simulation
290	Special Topics in Computer Science

UNIVERSITY OF CALIFORNIA, SANTA CRUZ
Santa Cruz, CA 95064
(408) 429-4008

CALIFORNIA

UC Santa Cruz is nestled in a 2000-acre redwood forest high above Monterey Bay along the Pacific Coast, offering spectacular views of the ocean & miles of forest paths to explore. It is located 75 miles north of San Francisco and 40 miles south of the Monterey Peninsula. Operating on a trimester system with two summer sessions, the university maintains a faculty student ratio of 1 to 18 and a library system with about 670,000 volumes.

UCSC offers a BA, MS and PhD in Computer & Information Sciences. Beginning in September 1984, a BS in computer engineering will be offered, while the corresponding MS & PhD programs are expected to open in 1985.

The priority filing of application is October for the spring quarter, and November for the following fall quarter.

There are four established subprograms within the BA program in Computer & Information Science: 1) computer science; 2) artificial intelligence & cognition; 3) information, coding & signals; 4) computer mathematics.

The Computer & Information Sciences board operates several computer systems: a VAX 11/750, a Wang VS-80, and microcomputers including Victor 9000s for instructional uses. In addition, the campus maintains: a Magnusion M80 (IBM compatible); timesharing systems through Wylbur and IBM's CMS; two DEC PDP 11/70s and two VAX 11/780s (UNIX). In addition, the Natural Science Division maintains a computer graphics laboratory in the Applied Science Building.

Faculty members of the department include: F DeRemer (programming languages, processors, automata theory, software engineering); A Goldberg (computational complexity, logic); L Hitchner (three-dimensional graphic displays); D Huffman (info thry & coding, graph, discrete systems); H Huskey (on-line computing, history of computing); D Perkins (VLSI, archtctr, organization, compiler); I Pohl (combinatorics, machine intelligence, heuristics); K Schimpf (parsing, compiler, AI, equational theories); R Tanner (info thry, error-correction, complexity, VLSI, fault tolerance).

Affiliated Faculty: R Abraham (graphics, visually-aided math); N Burgoyne (finite group, lie algebras & applns); A Kelly (numerical methods, symbolic computation); W Wipke (AI, computatnl chemistry, graphics).

Course Offerings:

1 Computers in Society	151 Signal Processing
10 Intro to Cybernetics	160 Intro to Computer Graphics
12A The Nature of Computation	192 Directed Student Teaching
12B Same as above	193 Field Study
15 Systems & Simulation	194 Group Tutorial
42 Student-Directed Seminar	195 Senior Thesis Research
100G Intro to Programming	198 Individual Study or Research
100N Intro to Programming	199 Tutorial
101 Data Structures	Graduate
103 The Math Foundation of System Science	200 Graduate Workshop
104A Programming Linguistics-Syntax	204 Topics in Programming Linguistics
104B Programming Linguistics-Semanics	207 Computational Logic
106 Graphs, Games & Structures	222 Intro to VLSI Design
110 Mechanical Translatn of Computer Languages	250 Information & Communication Theory
111A Assembly Language Programming	253 Analysis of Algorithms
111B Intro to Operating System	292A Seminar
120A Digital Logic & Computer Organization	292B Seminar
120B Computer Architecture	292C Seminar
120C Microprocessors	297 Indep Study or Research
130 Computational Models	299 Thesis Research
140 Artificial Intelligence	301 Supervised Teaching Experience
150 Information & Communication Theory	

31

UNIVERSITY OF SOUTHERN CALIFORNIA
Los Angeles, CA 90007
(213) 743-2311

The 150-acre urban campus of USC is situated in University Park, Los Angeles. There are approximately 29,000 students, among them 13,000 are undergraduates. The university operates on a semester system with summer sessions. Faculty Student ratio is about 1 to 14. The library system contains over 2.1 million volumns.

As part of the School of Engineering, the Computer Science Department offers BS, MS and PhD degrees. There are 456 students in the BS program, 214 in the MS, and 38 in the PhD program. Prospective students should apply through the Computer Science department; application date is open.

The Computer Science Lab is equipped with: Data General MV/8000, 2 DEC VAX/11-750, chromatics color graphic stations, 6 Sun workstations with 336 megabytes of disk storage and one megabyte internal memory each, 40 IBM PC's and an AED 512 color graphics display terminal. Planned acquisition in the near future includes a third VAX 11/750. The lab has been expanded to include equipment and facilities for research in software engineering, CAD/VLSI design, computer graphics, data management, text editing, and personal computing. The department has a Personal Computer Lab that allows students to write operating systems for personal computers.

The Engineering Computer Lab maintains 6 DEC KL10 and an IBM 4341. The KL10 systems, each offering a broad range of compilers and software packages, are used to support: funded research, word processing, electronic mail, ARPANET, Image Understanding research, instructional needs...etc. A DEC GT-42 mini supports graphics.

The Image Processing Institute is involved in basic and applied studies in the fields of digital, electronic, optical and hybrid methods of image processing, image analysis and machine perception. Maintaining close academic ties with the EE and CS departments, the Institute has access to the KL-10 system, ARPANET, TELENET. Several PDP-11 minis are used to control image digitizers, recorders and displays in the Institute's laboratory.

The Information Sciences Institute (ISI), located at Marina del Rey, 15 miles from the main campus, is involved in a broad spectrum of information processing research and the development of advanced computer and communication technology and systems. With 60 full-time researchers, about half at PhD level and 75 support staff personnels, ISI provides a number of special research assistantships. USC students are encouraged to become involed in research relevant to their graduate work. ISI in engaged in these research areas: specification formulation; testing and implementation; mapping designs; command graphics; internetwork concepts; machine composition of multiparagraph text; control of expert systems; cooperative interactive system; wideband communication; wafer and chip process; VLSI design technology; Interlisp etc. One of the largest nodes on the ARPANET, the Institute supports 6 PDP10's with TOP-20, two VAX 11/780 for Interlisp and ADA program development, four PDP11's, an FPS AP-120B array procesor, a QM-1 processor, several PERQ workstations, and 10 VAX-750.

The department has 17 full-time faculty and continues to seek outstanding individuals in a currently relevant field in computer science at all levels. Faculty of the department: F R Carlson Jr (human communication, AI, cmptr applns to education), L Adleman (complexity of number theoretic problems), P Brinch-Hansen (operating systems, concurrent Pascal), L Cooprider (multiversion systems, software construction), P F Dietz (efficient algrthms, constructive math & prgmng), L Flon (reliable system, verification, semantics), L Gasser (wrk spport, sftwr engnrng, AI, prsnl cmputng), S Ginsburg (automata, languages, grammar, database), L Horowitz (large-scale software design, workstations), R Hull (languages, theoretical models of database), D Jefferson (semantics, verification, thrm proving), D McLeod (database, distributed systems, prsnl IMS), A Motro (database models, semantics), W Scacchi (innovation in computing, AI, sftwr engnrng), P Vanderbilt (prgmng logic & semantics, spec lang, type thry).

Course Offerings: (generally 3 semester units)

501	Numerical Analysis & Computation	576	Logic Design & Switching Theory
502ab	Numerical Analysis	577	Dsgn & Constrctn of Large Scale Systems (4)
551	Computer Communications	578	Microprogramming
552	Logic Design & Switching Theory	579	Graph Theory & Applications
553	Computational Soln of Optmztn Prblms	585	Database Systems
554	Real Time Computer Systems	589	Algorithmic Aspects of Graph Theory
555	Operating Systems	590	Directed Research
556	Diagnosis & Reliable Dsgn of Dgtl System	599	Special Topics in Computer Science
557ab	Computing System Architecture	601	Adv Topics in Programming
558	Information Systems Processing	612	Program Correctness
559a	Mathematical Pattern Recognition	652ab	Seminar in Computer Theory
560	Adv Microcomputer-Based Design	653	Seminar in Programming Theory (1)
561	Survey of Artificial Intelligence	655	Automata & Formal Language Theory
565	Compiler Design (4)	656	AFL Theory
570	Design & Analysis of Algorithms	665	Programming System Design
571	Issues of Prgmng Language Design	691ab	Seminar in Automata & Formal Lang Thry
572	Adv Theory of Computation	692ab	Seminar in Pattrn Recgntn & A I
574	Machine Perception	693ab	Seminar in Database Theory
575ab	Man-Machine Interactive Systems	790	Research

CALIFORNIA STATE UNIVERSITY, CHICO
Chico, CA 95929
(916) 895-6116

Cal State Chico is located 90 miles north of Sacramento. The university operates on a semester system, with a faculty Student ratio of 1 to 18, and a library containing over 560,000 volumes.

The Department of Computer Science offers BS & MS in Computer Science. There are 1100 enrolled in the BS program and 105 in the MS program. Interested students should apply through Office of Admission in the month of November.

The university provides computing services with a CDC Cyber 170 and access to remote batch and timesharing facilities through the California State University computer network. The Department Lab also supports various minicomputers: HP2100A, HP1000E, HP1000F, HP3000, DG Eclipse 150, a CSPI MAP 300 array processor, as well as a number of Apples, Intels and Ataris.

Within the Computer Science major, the department created four options: Commercial Application, General Option, Math/Science Option, and the Systems Option that includes system analysis, machine architecture, programming languages and data structures.

Since its first offering in 1967, the department has grown to 22 full-time faculty. Recruitment is continuing. There are openings at all levels for all areas of computer science.

Course offerings: (generally 3 semester units)

CAL STATE CHICO

010	Computer Literacy		227	Discrete Simulation Systems
015	Introduction to Programming		231	Computer Graphics
040	Computer Assisted Art1		250	Complier Theory
050	FORTRAN language Programming		256	Theroy of Computing
050H	FORTRAN Language Programming		269	Mathematical Optimization Theroy
051A	Assembley Language Programming		270	Systems Design
051B	Assemblers	(1)	272	Multi-User Operating Systems
052	COBOL Language Programming		273	Structured Methods in Data Base
052H	COBOL Language Programming		278	Computer Networks
053	Programming Languages		280	Digital Logic Design Theory
054	Intro to Business Programming		283	Microprogramming Applications
055	BASIC Language Programming	(1)	285	Microprocessor Components & Syst
056	Intro to Computer Graphing	(1)	298A	Adv Topics in Computer Science (1)
058	Intro to Statistical Packages	(1)	298B	Adv Topics in Computer Science (2)
059	Programs & Files Utilities	(1)	298C	Advanced Topics in Computer Sci
110	Computer's Impact on Society		320A	Digital & Analog Transform Theory
125	Analog Simulation Dynamic Systems		320B	Digital & Analog Transform Theory
140	Computer Assisted Art2		322	Artificial Intelligence
151	Data & Program Structures		325	Hybird Computation
152	Operating Systems Programming		350A	Language Theory
160	Linear Programming Applications		350B	Language Theory
165	Numerical Methods Programming		360	Non Linear Math Optimization
171	Computer Architecture		370	System Design Theroy
172	Systems Architecture		371	System Design Techniques
175	Information Display Systems		372	Operating System Theory
189	Intern Program Analysis & Debugg	(1)	376	Theory of Information Retrieval
190A	Directed Programming Expierence	(1)	377	Automated Information Retrieval
190B	Directed Programming Expierence	(2)	380	Digital Systems Design
190C	Directed Programming Expierence		381A	Computer Morphology
199A	Special Problems	(1)	381B	Computer Morphology
199B	Special Problems	(2)	382A	Information Theory
199C	Special Problems		382B	Information Theory
225	Continuous Systems Simulation & Applns			

CALIFORNIA STATE UNIVERSITY, FRESNO
Fresno, CA 93740
(209) 294-4240

Cal State Fresno has a 220-acre main campus, a 1190-acre university farm, a population of 16,500 students, a faculty student ratio of 1 to 18, and a library containing over a half million volumes.

The university does not offer a formal bachelor major in computer science. However, the Department of Mathematics offers an undergraduate degree in mathematics with a computer science option. In addition, the business school offers an option in computer applications and systmes. Interested students should apply through the Office of Admissions in November for the Fall Semester.

Computing facilities to faculty and students include a dual processor CYBER 170/720, a PDP 11/45 for local timesharing, a CSU central network Cyber 174, and many Apple microcomputers.

Course Offering:

Courses by Math Dept (a Partial Listing):
10 Intensive BASIC Programming
20 Intro to Computer Programming
40 Computer Programming I
41 Computer Programming II
100 Programming Languages
110 Symbolic Logic
112 Assembly Language Programming
114 Discrete Structures
115 Data Structures
117 Structures of Programming Languages
118 Graph Theory
134 Compiler Design
144 Operating Systems & Computer Orgnztn
164 Artificial Intelligence Programming
184 Theory of Computation
186 Automata Theory & Formal Languages
190 Independent Study in Computer Science
191 Proseminar
Courses by Info Systems & Decision Science Dept
50 Computer Concepts

53 Programming Languages-FORTRAN
54 Programming Languages-COBOL
103 Prncpls of Office Management
104 Office Production
107 Management of Information
108 Inplementation of Information Systems
109 Data Communication
115 Office Automation
116 Word Processing Management
117 Records Management
151 Adv Applications Software-BASIC
152 Adv Applications Software-COBOL
159 Machine Language Programming
161 Information Systems Analysis
162 Information System Design
163 Business Models & Simulation
164 Computer Configurations
165 File Organization & Data Base Systems
168 Data Processing Management
189 Topics in Information Systems

CALIF STATE UNIVERSITY, FULLERTON
Fullerton, CA 92634
(714) 773-2011

Cal State Fullerton's 225-acre campus lies 30 miles south east of Los Angeles. Enrollment is about 22,000. Operating on a semester system with two 6-week summer sessions, the university maintains a faculty student ratio of 1 to 14, and a library that contains over half a million volumes with an increasing rate of 20,000 to 25,000 volumes per year.

The Department of Computer Science in the School of Mathematics, Science & Engineering offers programs leading to BS & MS in Computer Science. Currently, There are 1000, and 350 students enrolled in the two programs respectively. For further information, call the Department of Computer Science, (714) 773-3700. In addition, the School of Business Administration & Economics offers an undergraduate program in Management Information Systems, that provides students training in business computing, systems design, analysis, application programming...etc. Interested students may call (714) 773-2211 for more information. Both MIS & CS are impacted programs at the university. Students should apply through the Office of Admissions and Records early in November for the following Fall Semester.

CSUF offers a wide range of computing resourses. The host computer is a CDC Cyber 170/730 dual processors, 262,000 words of memory and two billion characters of on-line disk storage. In addition, users have access to a PDP 11/45 (UNIX), a PDP 11/70 (RSTS), and to a large Cyber 170/760 730 system located at CSU's Division of Information Systems in Los Angeles. IBM PCs and Apple IIs are available to students and faculty members. The university plans to acquire more IBM PC's in the immediate future.

There are 10 full-time faculty members in the department. The department continues to recruit specialists in: operating system, languages, compilers, data base system design, software engineering, microprocessors, automata, algorithms and complexity, data structure, artificial intelligence, pattern recognition, graphics, real-time systems.

Course Offerings: (generally 3 semester units)

112	Intro to Computer Programming	430	Software Engineering
130	Data Structure Concepts	440	Theory of Algorithms
210	Intro to Machine Languages & Logic	442	Firmware Techniques
212	Intro to Computational Languages	456	Data Communications
222	High-Level Language Workshops (1-3)	462	Interactive Systems Techniques
230	File Systems Concepts	463	Pattern Recognition
240	Low-Level Language Systems	465	Principles of Computer Graphics
242	Low Level Language Workshops (1)	470	Theory of Computation
252	Operating Systems Workshops (1)	471	Automata Theory
260	Structured Programming in FORTRAN	476	Information Theory & Cybernetics
261	Progrmming in PASCAL	487	Artificial Intelligence
270	File Concepts & COBOL Programming	510	Operating Systems Design
302	Information Structures	512	Compiler Design
310	Systems Programming	530	Advanced Software Engineering
371	Intro to Combinatorics	552	Microcomputer System Organization
402	Intro to Discrete Structures	566	Design of Administrative Info Systems
404	Intro to Microprcssrs & Microcmptrs	567	Design of Database Management Systems
410	Operating Systems Concepts	572	Formal Languages & Automata
414	Mini-Computer Software Systems	597	Project (1-3)
416	Computer Performance Evaluation	598	Thesis (1-3)
421	System Security & Encryption	599	Independent Graduate Research (1-3)

CALIF STATE UNIVERSITY, LONG BEACH
Long Beach, CA 90840
(213) 498-4111

The hilltop portion of Cal State Long Beach's 322 acre-campus overlooks the Pacific Ocean. 32,000 students are currently enrolled in the university, about 75% undergraduates, 56% full-time and 52% female. Operating on a semester system with summer sessions, the school maintains a 1 to 18 faculty student ratio, and a library with 780,000 volumes.

There are several ways students may acquire training in computer science: BS in Business with an option in Business Computer Methods; BS in Electrical Engineering with an option in Computer Science and Engineering; BA in Math with an option in Computer Science and Mathematics; and Certificate in Computer Applications. For detailed information of these options, contact respectively: Quantitative Systems, (213) 498-4993; Electrical Engineering, 498-4285; Mathematics Department, 498-4721; Certificate Computer Applications, 498-4986.

Interested students should file application during November for the following fall.

Course offerings:

Courses by Math Dept (partial listing):
170 Intro to Programming
171 Computer Calculus
270 Intro to Computing
272 Techniques of Programming
273 COBOL Programming
321 Files & Database Systems
325 Computer Systems & Programming
326 Operating Systems
330 Intro to Mathematical Logic
343 Discrete Structures & Combinatorics

421 Artificial Intelligence
422 Orgnztn of Programming Languages
424 Algorithmic Combinatorics
425 Data Structures & Files
427 Computer Graphics
430 Mathematical Logic
442 Intro to Algebraic Coding Theory
Graduate
521 Database Management Systems
524 Advanced Compiler Design
526 The Mathematics of Operating Systems

CALIF STATE UNIVERSITY, LOS ANGELES
Los Angeles, CA 90032
(213) 224-0111

Established in 1947, CSULA has grown to 23,000 students, of which 8500 are graduate students with a faculty student ratio of a 1 to 19, and a library containing over 800,000 volumes.

The Mathematics & Computer Science Department offers a BS in Mathematics & Computer Science. Currently, there are 450 students enrolled in the program. Interested students should apply through the Office of Admissions in November for the Fall.

The university has a CDC CYBER 730, a PDP 11/70, and a number of Apple II's. Future acquisition plan includes a PDP 11/24 with UNIX.

There are 8 full-time faculty in the department. The Department seeks several individuals at all ranks. Computer scientists with specialty in operating systems and programming languages are particularly desirable.

Course Offerings: (generally 4 quarter units)

CS 190 BASIC Programming (2)
BUS 283 Intro to COBOL Programming
CS 284 Data Structure for Business Applns
CS 290 Intro to FORTRAN Programming (2)
CS 333 Computer Structure & Machine Language
CS 380 PASCAL Programming
CS 390 Advanced FORTRAN Programming
CS 433 Assembly Language Programming

CS 454 Topics in Advanced Computer Science
CS 480 Systems Programming
CS 482 Programming Languages
CS 484 Data Structure
CS 486 Grammar, Languages & Automata
CS 488 Compilers
CS 499 Undergraduate Directed Study

CALIF STATE UNIVERSITY, NORTHRIDGE
Northridge, CA 91330
(818) 885-1200

Cal State Northridge's 350-acre campus is located 30 miles north of downtown Los Angeles. Students enrollment exceeds 25,000. The university is on a semester basis with two 6-week summer sessions. Faculty student ratio is about 1 to 19, while the libray contains over 800,000 volumes.

The Department of Computer Science offers BS and MS programs. Currently, there are 750 and 180 students enrolled in the programs respectively. Interested students should in November for the Fall Semester.

Within the BS programs, concentrations are available in the following areas: Applied Information Systems, Hardware Systems, Language Foundations, Mathematical Analysis, Mathematical and Logical Foundations, Office Automation, Scientific Programming, Software Engineering and Program Design, Statistics, System Analysis and Design, Theoretical Computer Science.

Computing facilities at Cal State Northridge include: CYBER 170/750 (NOS), PDP 11/70 (RSTS), PDP 11/45 (UNIX), Apple II+'s, supporting all popular high level languages plus Compass, Simula, Lisp, Snobol, Macro 11...etc. Usenet is accessible. Planned acquisition in near future includes a PDP 11/44.

The department has 21 full-time faculty. The Department seeks PhD's in computer science at the assistant and associate professor ranks.

Course Offering:

Undergraduate
100 Computers:Their Impact and Use
101 Introduction to Algorithms (2)
105 Computer Programming (1)
122 Intro to Digital Computer
132 Intro to Algorithms & Programming
165 Computer Graphics
182 Data Structures & Program Design
182l Program Design Lab (1)
194 Experimental Courses With Computers (1-4)
196 Selected Topics in Computer Science (1-4)
205 Advanced FORTRAN Program Lab (1-4)
222 Computer Organization
232 Concepts in Program Languages
242 Files and Data Bases
281 Advanced COBOL Programming (2)
281l COBOL Programming Lab (1)
294 Experimental Courses With Computers (1-4)
296 Selected Topics in Computer Science (1-4)
310 Automata, Languages and Computers
322 Intro to Operating Systems (2)
322l Operating Systems Lab (1)
325 Microprogramming Applications (2)
325l Microprogramming Lab (1)
332 Programming Language Semantics
380 Program Design Techniques
394 Experimental Courses in Computers (1-4)
396 Selected Topics in Computer Science (1-4)

399 Individual Study (1-3)
420 Principals of Operating Systems
424 Computer System Security
428 Distributed Teleprocessing
430 Database Design
431 Simulation Languages
440 Database Design
450 Societal Issues in Computing
461 Text Processing & Application
465 Computer Graphic Systems
465l Computer Graphic Systems Lab (1)
469 Intro to Artifical Intelligence
470 Numerical Methods for Computing
480 Software System Developement (2)
480l Software System Developement Lab (1)
494 Expermntl Courses in Computer Sci (1-4)
496 Selected Problems in Computer Sci (1-4)
497 Internship/Field Study (0-3)
499 Independent Study (1-3)

Graduate
505 Seminar in Project Development (1)
510 Data Structures & Algorithms
520 Computer System Architecture
530 Formal Semantics of Programming
580 Software Engineering
591 Advances in Computer Science

Cal State Sacramento's 288-acre campus supports 23,000 students with a faculty student ratio of 1 to 19, and a library containing 750,000 volumes.

The Department of Computer Science offers BS and MS in computer science. 750 students are currently enrolled in the BS and 150 in the MS program. Interested students should apply in November for the Fall Semester.

Within the BS program, one may choose one of three occupationally oriented specialty areas: systems software, data processing applications, and scientific applications. Likewise, concentration areas under the MS program include software engineering, computer systems, scientific and engineering applications.

Computing facility at the university includes a CDC Cyber 173 (NOS), PDP 11/45 (UNIX), PDP 11/70 (RSTS), IBM PC's, Atari 800s, Apple II+s, plus many other microcomputes. The Californis State University Systems network, Cyber 170/760 730, is also accessible.

With 21 full-time faculty members, the Department continues to seek individuals at all ranks. Computer scientists in Data Communication and Computer Network are particularly desired.

Course Offering:

Lower

001	Intro to Computer Science
005	Computers & Society
015	Programming for the Computing Sciences
016	FORTRAN Programming (2)
16A	FORTRAN Programming for Adv Students (2)
16S	Self-Paced FORTRAN (2)
022	BASIC Programming (1)
023	Adv BASIC Programming (1)
030	COBOL Programming
035	Assembly Language Programming
096	Experimental Offerings in C S (1-4)

Upper

0122	PASCAL Programming & Applications (2)
0126	Micro-Computer Programming (2)
0127	Minicomputer Programming (2)
0129	Intro to Statistical Packages (1)
0130	Computer Science: Theory & Practice
0134	Adv Data Structures & File Organization
0135	Systems Programming
0136	Programming Languages
0137	Machine Organization & Performance
0139	Operating Systems Principles
0140	Computing Models & Stuctures
0142	Adv Computer Organization (4)
0148	System Simulation
0151	Compiler Construction
0153	Intro Computer Graphics & Its Applctns
0155	Intermediate Computer Graphics
0158	Interative Techniques for Optimization
0159	Operating Systems Pragmatics
0170	Computer Systems Analysis

0171	Programming & Project Management
0172	Computer Systems Design
0173	Advanced COBOL
0174	Data Base Management Systems
0175	Data Communication Systems
190A	Senior Project: Part I (2)
190B	Senior Project: Part II (2)
0195	Field Work in Computer Science (1-3)
0196	Experimental Offerings in C S (1-4)
0199	Special Problems (1-3)

Graduate

209	Research Methodology (1)
210	Structured Software Design
215	A I & Heuristic Programming
216	Structural Pattern Recognition
220	Analysis of Algorithems
225	Optimization Methods
231	Programming Systems Management
235	Adv Simulation
237	Hardware-Software Spec Microprcssor System
240	Adv Computer Systems Analysis
244	Data Base Design
245	Performance Modeling & Measurement
250	Computer Security & Privacy
251	Principles of Compiler Design
255	Distributed Prcssng & Computer Networks
275	Data Communication System Design
295	Field Work (1-3)
296	Experimental Offerings in C S (1-4)
299	Special Problems (1-3)
500	Master's Thesis (2-5)
502	Master's Project (2)

SAN DIEGO STATE UNIVERSITY
San Diego, CA 92182
(619) 265-5200

San Diego State's 300-acre campus is 12 miles from the Pacific Ocean. Serving a student body of 32000 students, the university maintains a 770,000 volume library and a faculty student ratio of 1 to 20.

The Department of Mathematical Sciences in the College of Sciences, offers BS and MS in Computer Science. Currently, there are 650 enrolled in the BS program and 125 in the MS programs. Prospective students should apply in November for the Fall.

Computing facilities at SDSU include a CDC Cyber 750 (NOS), VAX 11/780 (VMS), PDP 11/44 (UNIX), several M68000 microcomputers (UNIX), and 40 Apples.

The Department seeks faculty at all ranks. Computer scientists in all areas will be considered.

Course Offering:

107	Intro to Computer Programming I	0580	Systems Programming II
107	Intro to Computer Programming II	0581	Small Computers
137	Intermediate Computer Programming I (4)	0582	Database Theory and Implementation I
137	Intermediate Computer Programming II (4)	0582	Database Theory and Implementation II
138	Higher Level Languages (1-2)	0583	Computer Simulation I
Upper Division		0583	Computer Simulation II
0371	Discrete Math w Computer Applications	0584	Interactive Computer Graphics I
541A	Numerical Analysis and Computation I	0584	Interactive Computer Graphics II
541B	Numerical Analysis and Computation II	Graduate	
0570	Data Structrures	690A	Theory of Computability & Algorithms
0572	Programming Languages	690B	Theory of Computability & Algorithms
0573	Automate Theory	691A	Formal Languages & Syntactic Analysis
0574	Intro to Computability	691B	Formal Languages & Syntactic Analysis
0575	Compiler Construction	692A	Computer Architecture & Prgmmng Systems
0575	Artificial Intelligence II	692B	Computer Architecture & Prgmmng Systems
0578	Algorithems and Their Analysis	0700	Applications of Computer Science
0580	Systems Programming I		

SAN FRANCISCO STATE UNIVERSITY
San Francisco, CA 94132
(415) 469-2141

San Francisco State's 130 acre-campus serves a population of 23,000 students with a faculty student ratio of 1 to 17, and a library that houses over half a million volumes.

The School of Science offers a BS and MS in computer science through the Department of Mathematics. In addition to the study of foundamental courses in computer science, the BS & MS programs require one of the these special emphasis to be selected: numerical analysis, software hardware systems, and information system design. Prospective students should apply in November for the following Fall.

The university maintains a Cyber 170/730 with 256,000 words (60-bit) memory, a PDP 11/70 for local timesharing, and has access to the California State University System's 170 730/760 in Los Angeles.

Course Offerings:

205	Intro to Programming: FORTRAN	690	Undergraduate Seminar
210	Intro to Programming: PASCAL	694	Cooperative Education
215	Programing Techniques	699	Special Study
300	Computer Language Survey		Graduate
310	Cmptr Orgnztn & Assembly Language Prgmng	710	Compiler Design
330	Discrete Math Structures for Cmptr Science	720	Operating Systems
410	Data Structures	730	Data Base Design
415	Operating Systems Principles	756	Microprogramming
510	Analysis of Algorithms I	810	Analysis of Algorithms II
520	Theory of Computing	856	Advanced Computer Architecture
600	Programming Language Design	890	Graduate Seminar
610	Sorting & Searching	897	Research
620	Natural Language Processing	898	Master's Thesis
630	Computer Graphics Systems Design	899	Special Study

SAN JOSE STATE UNIVERSITY
San Jose, CA 95192
(408) 277-2000

San Jose State's 134-acre campus is located 50 miles south of San Francisco. Students total over 25,000. Operating on a semester system with summer sessions, the university has a faculty student ratio of 1 to 20 and maintains a 715,000 volume library.

The department of Mathematics & Computer Science in San Jose State's School of Science offers a bachelor and a master of science programs in computer science. Currently, there are 500 enrolled in the bachelor's and 65 in the master's programs. In addition, the School of Engineering offers a BS in Engineering with an option in Computer Science. Call (408) 277-2207 for detailed information on that program.

The computing facilities at SJSU include: a CDC CYBER 170-760, CYBER 170-730, PDP 11/70 (RSTS/E), PDP 11/45 (UNIX), North Star Advantages plus various other microcomputers. Planned acquisition in the near future includes more micro and mini computers.

With 20 full-time faculty members, the Department continues to seek individuals at the assistant and associate professor rnaks. Applicants in all disciplines of computer science will be considered.

Course Offering:

44	Introductory Programming in BASIC	153	Concepts of Compiler Design
45	Intro to Computers & Programming	162	Probability and Computation
144A	Assembly Language (2)	242	Mathematical Concepts of Info Sciences
144F	FORTRAN (2)	254	Mathematical Theory of Computation
144L	LISP (2)	255	Design & Analysis of Computer Algorithms
144M	Micro Computer Systems (2)	256	Topics in Artificial Intelligence
144P	PASCAL (2)	257	Data Base Management Systems
145	Advanced Programming	258	Computer Communication Systems
146	Introduction to Data Structures	271	Mathematical Symbolic Logic
147	Machine Structures	280	Data Structures
149	Intro to Systems Programming	295	Graduate Seminar in Computer Mathematics

41

COLORADO

COLORADO STATE UNIVERSITY
Fort Collins, CO 80523
(303) 491-7201

Situated within the city of Fort Collins, the 833-acre main campus of Colorado State University has 19,000 students with a faculty student ratio of 1 to 18. Its William Morgan Library houses over one million volumes.

The Department of Computer Science of the College of Natural Sciences, offers BS, MS and PhD programs in computer science. In addition, the Department of Computer Information Systems of the College of Business offers an undergraduate concentration in information systems and a graduate program in Management Information Systems.

The CS Department consists of 10 full-time faculty members, whose research interests cover: firmware engineering, applicative languages, compilers and language theory, computational methods, parallel and vector processing, operating systems, system modeling, microprocessor applications, graphics, software engineering, and computer architectures.

Colorado State's computing facilities include a CDC Cyber 205 supercomputer, and two CDC Cyber 720's. Department maintains a VAX 11/750, VAX 11/730, HP 9845s and a wide variety of microcomputers.

Course Offerings:

110	BASIC & Personal Computing	486	Practicum
150	Intro to FORTRAN Programming	495	Independent Study
151	Intro PASCAL Programming	496	Group Study
192	Introductory Seminar	510	Computer Graphics
250	Fundamentals of Computer Orgnztn	514	Programming Methodology
350	Computer Architecture	520	Analysis of Algorithms
351	Data Structure	550	Advanced Data Structures
384	Supervised College Teaching	551	Principles of Operating Systems
403	FORTRAN Prgrmng & Computer Tchnq	553	Algorithmic Language Compilers
404	Advanced FORTRAN Programming	555	Database Systems
410	Intro to Computer Graphics	557	Computer Networks
414	Software Engineering	570	High-Level Language Architecture
420	Formal Languages & Automata	575	Parallel Processing
450	Concepts of Programming Systems	610	Cmptr Methods in Science & Engnrng I
451	Operating Systems	611	Cmptr Methods in Science & Engnrng II
453	Fundamentals of Prgrmng Languages	614	Performance Measurement & Evaluation
454	Introduction to Microprocessors	620	Theory of Computation
455	Computer System Design	651	Topics in Operating Systems
460	Numeric Digital Computing I	653	Advanced Compilers
461	Numeric Digital Computing II	670	Advanced Computer Architecture

692	Seminar	699	Thesis
695	Independent Study	795	Independent Study
696	Group Study		

UNIVERSITY OF COLORADO
Boulder, CO 80309
(303) 492-6301

The 600-acre Boulder campus of the University of Colorado serves a population of 22,000 students with a faculty student ratio of 1 to 17, and a library with 1.9 million volumes.

The Department of Computer Science offers MS and PhD programs which include the following areas of study: automata theory, programming languages, operating systems, business systems, and numerical analysis. In addition, students majoring in another department may also take enough hours in computer science to satisfy the minor requirement of their major department. Prospective students should apply through the Department of Computer Science. Deadlines for admission with financial aid: Feb 15 for the Fall Semester; admission without financial aid: April 1. For Spring admission, application should be completed by Oct 1. Contact the department's office for more information. Phone: (303) 492-7514.

University computing facilities on the Boulder campus include: a CDC Cyber 172, an IBM 370/145, DEC VAX 11/780, and several Novas. In addition, the department owns a VAX 11/780, plus several workstations dedicated exclusively to research.

The department has twelve full-time faculty and six associated faculty from electrical engineering. Areas of current strength include software engineering, numerical computation, theoretical computer science, and programming languages. Positions at the assistant professor rank exist. The department will consider background in all areas of computer science. Specialty in networks and operating systems, artificial intelligence, software engineering and numerical solution of partial differential equations would be particularly attractive. Faculty and their interests:

D A Baker (sftwr engnrng, specifctn methdlg, sftwr dsgn & evaluation, prgrmng envirnmnt & prgmng languages); R H Byrd (unconstrained & constrained optmztn, curve fitting, math prgrmng); A Ehrenfeucht (automata thry & logic); L D Fosdick (sftwr validation, analysis of algrthms, numerical math); H N Gabow (algrthms, complexity, graph thry & scheduling); P K Harter Jr (temporal logic, compilers, prgrmng languages); D M Heimbigner (dababases, operating systems); H F Jordan (hrdwr softwr interface, graphics, pseudo random sequences).

R King (data bases, operating systems); M G Main (automata thry, semantics distrbtd systems); L J Osterweil (combinatorial math, sftwr validation, graph thry & enumeration); R B Schnabel (unconstrained & constrained optmztn, soln of nonlinear equation, data fitting, numerical sftwr); J C Shultis (prgrmng languages, semantics, thry); W M Waite (prgrmng languae dsgn & translatn, sftwr portability, non-numeric tchnques).

Adjuncts and Courtesy Faculty: P T Boggs (numerical analysis, non-linear optmztn, non-linear systems of equations); B K Haddon (operating systems); G J Nutt (computer systems, performance evaluation & office automatn); W Riddle (prgrmng languages); G Rozenberg (automata thry & formal languages); P Swarztrauber (numerical soln of PDE); R Sweet (numerical analysis, math sftwr, numerical soln of PDE, sftwr for PDE, vector algrthms for PDE); H P Zeiger (data base dsgn); G Hachtel (spare matrices, computer aided dsgn, VLSI layout); W Hughes (system archtctr & dsgn, real-time system dsgn & performance evaluatn, computer system models, simulation of computer systems, hrdwr & sftwr support of computatnl parallelism, use of computer graphics in dsgn); M Lightner (computer aided dsgn, VLSI, optmztn, numerical analysis).

Course Offerings: (generally 3 semester units)

110	Elmntary Prgrmng for Scientists & Engnrs	562	Numerical Soln of Initial Value Prblms
210	Fundamentals of Computing I	563	Numerical Soln of Boundary Value Prblms
290	Honors Fundamentals of Computing	564	Numerical Linear Algebra
310	Fundamentals of Computing II	565	Numerical Methods for Optimization
401	Comparative Prgramming Languages	566	Numerical Methods for Data Analysis
413	Advanced Finite Math I	567	Intro to Approximation Theory
445	Data Structures	569	Numerical Methods for Nonlinear Optmztns
453	Assembly Language Programming	580	Operating Systems Practicum
459	Computer Organization	581	Data Management & File Systems
465	Intermediate Numerical Analysis I	582	Software Engineering
466	Intermediate Numerical Analysis II	583	Systems Programming
490	Selected Topics in Computer Science	584	Software Development Workshop
514	Advanced Finite Math II	611	Topics in Computer Graphics
531	Formal Languages	612	Topics in Operating Systems
540	Computer Decision Modeling	613	Topics in Programming Languages
545	Algorithms	614	Topics in Computer Systems
546	Theory of Automata	615	Topics in Formal Systems
553	Fundmntl Concepts in Prgrmng Languages	616	Topics in Data Processing
555	Non-Numeric Tchnques for Digital Cmptrs	617	Topics in Numerical Analysis
556	Translation of Programming Languages	665	Advanced Numerical Analysis
557	Operating Systems	700	Master's Thesis
558	Artificial Intelligence	701	Master's Reading Option
560	Numerical Analysis I	710	Doctoral Preliminary Seminar
561	Numerical Analysis II	800	Doctoral Research

UNIVERSITY OF COLORADO
Colorado Spring, CO 80907
(303) 593-3000

University of Colorado's 425-acre campus at Colorado Spring is located at the center of a rapidly growing high technology computer and electronics industry. Total student population exceeds 5,300. The university maintains a faculty student ratio of 1 to 19, a library that contains 170,000 volumes plus access to other University of Colorado campuses.

The Department of Computer Science at Colorado Springs offers bachelor in computer science, plus MS in CS through the univrsity-wide graduate school, that include all four campuses of the University of Colordo. Currently, only the Boulder campus has a Colorado Commission on Higher Education approved MS in CS. But the university-wide Graduate School concept permits the Colorado Spring's campus to offer MS in CS with Boulder. Interested students should apply through the Department of Computer Science before March 15 for the Fall Semester. For more questions, write or call the department: phone (303) 593-3426.

Computing facilities here include: a VAX 11/780 with four megabyte memory, PDP 11/70 with 1.75 megabyte memory, both connected by DECNET. Remote timesharing of the twin Cyber 720 computers is accessible. In addition, the College of Engineering maintains a PDP 11/35 running UNIX, a Hewlett-Packard 2100, twelve Apple IIs connected in a network, and three Hewlett-Packard 64000 developmental systems.

The Department has faculty positions open at all ranks. Applicants from all areas of computer science will be considered seriously. Background in operating systems, artificial intelligence, database systems, networks, software engineering, automated design/test tool would be particularly attractive.

Course Offerings:

101	Intro Computer Programming	460	Intro to Computer Graphics
105	Intro to Computers & Programming	465	Intro to Artificial Intelligence
110	Intro to Computer Science	470	Automata & Formal Language Theory
203	Intro to CS for Liberal Arts	480	Theory of Computation
220	Data Structures	485	Mathematical Programming
240	Microprocessors	531	Automata & Formal Languages
241	Microprocessor Lab	535	Topics in the Thr of Computation
250	File Structure & Database Design	540	Topics in Language & Compilers
300	Indep Study in Computer Science	545	Topics & Readings in Sftwr Engnrng
320	Programming Languages	553	Adv Concepts of Prgmng Languages
330	Assembly Language Programming	556	Compilers Construction
340	Discrete Mathematics	557	Operating Systems
350	Graph Theory	560	Numerical Analysis
400	Indep Study in Computer Science	561	Num Analysis II
410	Compiler Design	562	Num Soln of Initial Value Prblms
415	Numerical Analysis	563	Num Soln of Boundary Value Prblms
421	Computer Architecture Lab	581	Data Management & File Systems
430	Software Engineering	582	Software Engineering
440	Design & Analysis of Algrthms	591	Design & Analysis of Algorithms
450	Operating Systems	700	Master's Thesis

UNIVERSITY OF DENVER
Denver, CO 80208
(303) 753-2036

University of Denver is the largest private university in the Rocky Mountain West. Serving almost 9,000 students, its main campus is located in the residential area of Denver. The university has a faculty student ratio of 1 to 14, and a library with over 1.3 million volumes.

The Department of Mathematics & Computer Science offers a BS and MS in computer science. Currently, there are 200 and 150 students enrolled in the two programs respectively. Interested students should apply through the Office of Admissions or the Graduate School of Arts & Sciences.

Computing facilities at the university include: VAX 780, VAX 750, PDP 11/70, PDP 11/34, PDP 11/23 running RSX, UNIX, P-Code. The Math Lab has various microcomputers. Future acquisition includes another VAX 750.

UNIV OF DENVER

The department consists of 16 full-time faculty members. Openings exist at all ranks.

Course Offerings:

21-267	Computer Programming
21-269	Programming Minicomputers
21-320	Discrete Structures (4)
21-326	Data Processing with COBOL (4)
21-328	Theory of Data
21-330	Digital Computer Organization (4)
21-331	Introduction to Operations Research
21-332	Formal Languages
21-333	Theory of Automata I
21-334	Theory of Automata II
21-335	Programming Languages (4)
21-337	Data Structures (4)
21-338	Software Design Techniques
21-339	Seminar in Computer Applns (2)
21-342	Database Organization & Management
21-357	Introduction to Numerical Methods
21-380	Elements of Compiler Design
21-394	Intership in Computing
21-417	Numerical Analysis
21-419	Linguistics for Computer Scientist
21-421	Theory of Computation
21-423	Compiler Construction
21-428	Data Models (4)
21-436	Operating systems (4)
21-470	Adv Topics in Computer Science

CONNECTICUT

UNIVERSITY OF CONNECTICUT
Storrs, CT 06268
(203) 486-3137

University of Connecticut is a public university with a 2,800-acre campus, a population of 22,000 students, a faculty student ratio of 1 to 25, and a library containing over 3 million volumes.

The Department of Electrical Engineering and Computer Science offers BS, MS and PhD in computer science with current enrollment of 150, 40 and 10 students respectively. Because these programs are filled far in advance of the stated application deadlines (June 1 for the Fall and Nov 1 for the Spring). Prospective students should submit their applications to the Admissions Office as early as possible. For more specific information, write to Dept of Electrical Engineering & Computer Science: Box U-157C, Storrs, CT 06268.

Computer Science faculty includes: T L Booth, Y T Chien, D Jordan, C H Knapp, G N Raney, R E Cullingford, B W Lowell, H A Sholl, J C Cleaveland, I Greenshields, M Krueger, M Selfridge. Faculty openings exist at all professorial ranks.

Department facilities include: two VAX 11/780, a variety of PDP 11s and a microprocessor lab with extensive I/O interface and graphic displays. In addition, the university computer system features an IBM 3018 which is available for student use.

Course Offerings: (generally 3 units)

Undergraduate
101 Computers in Modern Society
110 Intro to Numerical Computations
111 Intro to Non-Numerical Computations 2
130 Fundamentals of Computations
207 Computer Science
210 Intro to Microprocessors
221 Performance Analysis of Computer Systems
235 Principles of Programming Languages
242 Sequential Networks & Digital Systems
244 Programming Language Translation
252 Digital Systems Design
253 Software Engineering
254 Intro to Discrete Systems
255 Principles of Data Base
256 Intro to Symbolic Computations
257 Numer Methods in Scientific Computations
258 Operating Systems
260 Introductory Laboratory

261 Digital Hardware Laboratory
265 Software Laboratory on Large Computers
267 Software Laboratory on Large Computers
267 Independent Laboratory Design
268 Microprocessing Laboratory
269 Computer Science Design Laboratory
282 Artificial Intelligence
293 Special Topics in Computer Science 1
295 Special Topics in Computer Science 1-4
299 Indepedent Study in Computer Design 1-4
Graduate
300 Special Topics in Computer Science
311 Seminar 1
320 Independent Study in Computer Science
325 Automated Design of Digital Systems
326 Probabilistic Methods in Digital Systems
327 Adv Software Engineering
340 Computer Architecture
342 Adv Digital Systems & Switching Theory

47

356 Interactive Computer Graphics
358 Adv Operating Systems
365 Fundamentals of Automata
366 Adv Automata Theory

367 Information & Digital Systems Laboratory
369 Pattern Recognition
383 Natural Language Processing

YALE UNIVERSITY
1502A Yale Station, New Haven, CT06520
(203) 436-0300

Yale University's 175-acre campus is the focal point of the intellectual and cultural life of New Haven, a town of 137,000, about 75 miles from New York City. Yale has about 10,000 students, maintaining a faculty student ratio of 1 to 7 and a library with over 7.5 million volumes.

The Department of Computer Science offers undergraduate and graduate (MS, M.Phil and PhD) programs in computer science. Currently, there are over 60 and over 80 students in the two programs respectively. 17 faculty, 15 research asociates, research assistants and postgraduate fellows serve the department. Prospective students should apply through the Admissions Office and the Department early in the Fall Semester for the following Fall. Early Action programs are available.

Computing facilities at Yale include: an IBM 370/158, IBM 4341, five VAX 11/750. The department lab operates a DEC 2060, a VAX 11/780, ten VAX 11/750, sixty Appolo Domain Workstations, a Floating Point Systems FPS-164 Attached Processor. In addition, forty Appolo workstations and a VAX 11/750 are used for education. Most of the VAX runs UNIX, several run VMS. Ethernet, Arpanet, Usenet, CSNet, Bitnet are accessible. Extensive word-processing facilities include two image laser printer, two NEC Spinwriters, and an OMNItech photocomposer.

Each graduate student office is equipped with at least one 9600 baud terminal connected to any computer via a central switching device, many even equipped with Apollo workstations. Unlimited access to computing facilities is therefore available to all graduate students.

Research of the department can be divided into four areas:

1. Artificial Intelligence focuses on the modeling of human thought processes that include natural language processing, models of memory and inference, representation of knowledge, problem solving, reasoning processes and learning. Faculty and research affiliates in this area include: R C Schank (natural language processing, models of memory & learning); D McDermott (representation of knowledge, reasoning about space & time, programming language, problem solving); E Soloway (cognition & programming, AI, learning, computer based tutoring systems); C K Riesbeck (natural languages, AI prgramming techniques, learning in complex domains); K Ehrlich (cognitive factors in programming, text understanding, reading); J A Galambos (human memory, language comprehension, AI, human factors, speech perception); R P Adelson (models of ideological belief systems); J Black (cognitive science, human story understanding)

2. Scientific Computing studies computer algorithms for scientific applications. Major emphasis is given both to theoretical analysis, such as rates of convergence, optimality and operation counts, and to programming considerations such as coding efficiency, numerical accuracy, gererality of application, data structures and machine independence. Faculty and research affiliates: M H Schultz (numerical analysis,

scientific computing); S C Eisenstat (linear and nonlinear algebra, partial diff equations, discrete math, concrete computational complexity); T F Chan (numerical analysis, ODE, PDE, linear algebra, continuous methods for nonlinear problems, computational fluid dynamics); W D Gropp (time-dependent PDE by adaptive methods, fluid dynamics, difference schemes, programming languages for scientific computation); C Douglas (PDE, linear algebra); H Elman (numerical linear algebra, math software); I C Ipsen (numerical analysis, VLSI, parallel computation); I Bernstein (applied plasma physics); R Dembo (nonlinear programming, optimization, nonlinear systems); R Jensen (computational applied plasma physics); A Maewal (computational mechanics); M Morf (signal, VLSI, architecture)

3. Systems Programming performs research in programming languages, programming in an interactive environment, highly-parallel computation and systems architecture, distributed systems and network topology. Faculty and research affiliates include: A J Perlis (conversational languages, automatic programming, software dynamics); J A Fisher (very long instruction word architectures, parallel processing, automated design of computers, microprogramming); L Johnsson (concurrent numerical algorithms, VLSI); M Chan (concurrent computation, models of computation, semantics, VLSI design, simulation and verification); D Gelernter (communications software, distributed programming languages & operating systems); P R Hudak (compilers, machine architecture, functional programming, semantics); C W Marshall (architecture, modeling, scientific calculation, digital signal processing); J Delosme (signal processing and estimation, VLSI design); A Ganz (embedded systems, software engineering); M Morf (signal processing, VLSI, architecture)

4. Theory of Computation investigates distributed computing, combinatorial computing, inductive inference and cryptographic protocols. Faculty and research affiliates: M J Fischer (distributed systems, algorithms & data structures, programming languages & software, theory of computation, complexity); D C Angluin (inductive inference, algorithms, complexity, theory of VLSI); D M Gusfield (combinatorial computing, optimization, algorithms, complexity, discrete math); D Lichtenstein (computational topology, combinatorics, algorithms, theory of computation); N Immerman (comoplexity, expressive power of logical theories)

Course Offerings:

521	Programming Languages & Their Processors	620	Software Engineering
522	Operating Systems	629	Semantics & Verification
525	Theory of Distributed Systems	640	Topics in Numerical Analysis
529	Parallel Computation	690	Independent Projects
530	Digital Systems	720a	Programming Languages Semantics
531	Computer Systems	720b	Programming Languages Semantics
535	VLSI Systems Design & Architectures	721	Transformational Programming
540	Numerical Computation I	722	Concurrent Systems
541	Numerical Computation II	729	Computer Arithmetic
560	Analysis of Algrthms & Complexity Thry	740	The Seminar Seminar
570	Natural Language Processing	761	Cryptographic Protocols
571	Knowledge & Understanding	762	Adv Topics in Theoretical CS
575	Problems in Artificial Intelligence	770	Adv Topics in Artificial Intelligence
577	Human Computer Communication Prblms	779	Seminar in Machine Learning

DISTRICT OF COLUMBIA

THE AMERICAN UNIVERSITY
Washington, DC 20016
(202) 686-2211

The American University, a private university affiliated with the Methodist Church, has 13,000 students, a faculty student ratio of 1 to 12, and a library with 400,000 volumes.

The Department of Mathematics, Statistics, and Computer Science offers undergraduate and master programs with current enrollment figures of 198 and 183 respectively. Apply through the Admissions Office. Deadline for financial aid is March 1.

The university has an IBM 4341 system and the IBM PC's. More IBM PC's will be acquired in the near future.

There are 25 full-time faculty in the department. A faculty position exists at the assistant professor rank. PhD's in Computer Science are welcome to apply.

Course Offerings:

166 Social & Cultural Implications of Computers	550 Discrete Structures
260 Intro Computing N (4)	560 Microcomputer Architecture
280 Intro Computer Science I (4)	565 Operating Systems
282 Intro Computer Science II (4)	566 Intro Compilers
282 Assembly Language Programming (4)	568 Artificial Intelligence
340 Data Structures & Algorithms	570 Data Management Systems
341 Organization of Programming Languages	582 Formal Language & Automata
390 Indep Reading in Computer Science (1-6)	584 Computer Graphics
392 Co-op Education Field Experience(3-9)	590 Indep Reading Course in C S (1-6)
460 Intro Numerical Methods	620 Design & Analysis of Algorithms
490 Indep Study in Computer Science (1-6)	646 Computer Network Design & Analysis
520 Graduate Survey of Computer Science I	690 Indep Study Project in C S (1-6)
521 Graduate Survey of Computer Science II	692 Co-op Education Field Experience (3-6)
540 System Organization & Programming	700 Seminar in C S (1-6)
541 Computer Architecture	797 Master's Thesis Seminar in C S(1-6)
546 Intro Computer Networks	

Howard University is a private university with 4 separate campuses in the DC area, a student population of 12,500, a faculty student ratio of 1 to 12, and a library with 1.25 million volumes.

A new bachelor's program, and a master's programs in computer science are offered. Current enrollment is 35 and 30 students for the two respectively. Prospective students should apply through the Office of Admissions by April 1 for the Fall Semester.

The university has an IBM 3033, HP 3000, plus many different microcomputers. There are 8 full-time members in the department.

Course Offerings: (generally 3 semester units)

CS 306-101	Intro Computer Science 1,2 (0)		542	Compiler Design
	164	Digital Computation (2)	551	Programming Methods I
	165	Elementary Computation	552	Programming Methods II
	201	Computer Fundamentals	556	Real Time Analysis
	303	Operating Systems I	603	Multivariate Analysis
	304	Operating Systems II	607	Data Structures
	307	Operational Languages	615	Programming Languages
	339	Methods of Computation	622	Switching Theory
	490	Senior Project	632	Data Base Management
Graduate			634	Systems Analysis II
CS 237-500	Computer Logic and Programming		637	Computer Logical Design
	522	Computer Graphics	652	Special Topics
	534	Systems Analysis I		

FLORIDA

FLORIDA STATE UNIVERSITY
Tallahannee, FL 32306
(904) 644-6200

Florida State University's 343-acre campus supports a student population with a faculty student ratio of 1 to 23, and a library with 1.4 million volumes.

The Mathematics & Computer Science Department offers bachelor's, master's, and PhD's programs in computer sciene. Currently, there are 804, 30, and 5 students enrolled in the three programs respectively. Prospective students should apply through the Math/CS department. Write to Admissions Office for current deadlines, early admission and concurrent enrollment programs.

There are 5 full-time faculty in the department. Openings exist at different levels (negotiable), with the following specialties particularly desired: computer architecture, software engineering, computer graphics, intelligent systems, data base management, computer network.

Computing facilities at Florida State include CDC 760 & 730 (NOS) and 12 S-100 micros. Future acquisition plan includes a VAX 11/750 and another Cyber 730.

Course Offerings: (generally 3 semester units)

			Graduate
COC 3400	Computers & Society	CAP 5621	Artificial Intelligence
COP 3100	Computer Programming I	CAP 5630	Pattern Recognition
COP 3101	Computer Programming II	CDA 5101	Computer Architecture
COP 3112	FORTRAN for Specialists	CIS 5114	Database Systems
COP 3120	Data Processing Using COBOL	COP 5116	FORTRAN for Graduate Nonspecialists
COP 3393	Intro to Computer Use 1	COP 5555	Programming Language Foundations
COP 3402	Assembly Language Programming	COP 5610	Operating Systems
COT 3132	Digital Networks	COP 5632	Software Engineering
MAD 3401	Numerical Analysis I	COP 5642	Thry of Parsing Trnslatn & Compiling
MAD 3105	Discrete Mathematics II	COT 5120	Thry of Automata & Formal Language
MAS 3103	Linear Algebra	COT 5316	Complexity of Algorithms
CDA 4102	Computer Organization	CS 265	Independent Lab Design
COP 4531	Software Project	CS 267	Software Lab on Large Computers
COP 4604	Software Project	CS 282	Artificial Intelligence

The 260-acre campus of this private university is located about 15 miles from downtown Miami. The university has a faculty student ratio of 1 to 13, and a library with 1.15 million volumes.

The Department of Mathematics & Computer Science offers BS & MS in computer science, and a PhD in Math & CS with computer option. Currently, 200 and 50 students are enrolled in the BS and MS programs respectively. In addition, the university offers programs in electrical and computer engineering, and management science & computer information systems. Contact respective departments for specific information.

There are 30 full-time faculty in the Department of Mathematics and Computer Science. Faculty openings exist at all ranks. Applicants in all areas of the field will be considered, theoretical computer scientists are of main interest.

The university runs a Univac 1100/81. The Hertz Computer Lab houses several mini/micro computers, including a PDP 11/44 time sharing system with UNIX and RSTS/E, plus several Apples.

Course Offerings: (generally 3 semester units)

MTH
220 Computer Programming II
320 Introduction to Numerical Analysis
120 Computer Pragrramming I
506 Symbolic Logic
516 Floating Point Computation
509 Discrete Structures
518 Interpreters and Compiler Theory
517 Data Structures
519 Programming Languages
520 Numerical Analysis I
521 Numerical Analysis II
523 Introductions to Filing Systems
522 Numerical Analysis III
524 Introduction to Probability Theory
525 Introduction to Mathmatical Ststistics
526 Time-Series Analysis

527 Theory of Automata
528 Combinatorics
EEN
114 Introduction to Computer Technology
322 PASCAL
224 Systems Programming
312 Microprocessors
314 Digital Systems Design I
414 Computer Organization and Design
511 Software Engineering
514 Microprogramming
521 Computer Operating Systems
554 Digital Systems Design II
MAS 223 Business Programming Languages
MAS 322 Analysis of Information Systems
MAS 522 Computer Simulation Systems
MAS 526 COBOL Applications and Implementation

Embry-Riddle Aeronautical is a private university with an 86-acre campus, 8,500 students, a faculty student ratio of 1 to 30, and a 52,000-volume library.

The Department of Computer Science offers an undergraduate program in computer science, which has 300 students currently. Prospective students should apply through the Department Chair. There are 8 full-time faculty in the department. The department seeks full-time faculty at the assistant and associate ranks. Individuals with background in operating systems, database management, and telecommunications are particularly desired.

Computing facilities here include an HP 3000, Prime 400, and the Apple II and TRS 80 microcomputers. Future plan includes the acquisition of many IBM PCs.

EMBRY-RIDDLE UNIVERSITY

Course Offerings:

101	Intro to Keyboard Operations	330	Systems Design & Documentation
102	Word Processing Concepts & Techniques	335	Intro to Computer Graphics
103	Word Processing File Orgnztns/Revisions	340	Computer Processing of Statistical Data
104	Word Processing Advanced Techniques	360	Adv FORTRAN with Aviation Applns
105	Intro to Computers in Aviation	370	Computer Organization
109	Intro to Programming with BASIC	372	Intro to Microprocessors
110	FORTRAN Programming	410	Data Structures
210	Scientific Programming	420	Operating Systems
216	Structured Programming	430	Numerical Analysis
218	COBOL Programming	436	Computer Graphics II with Aviation Applns
220	Digital Logic & Computer Operation	440	Database Management Systems
301	Intro to Discrete Structures	445	Interfacing
312	Assembly Language Programming	450	Real-Time Systems
318	Adv BASIC Programming with Aviation Appln	460	Telecommunication Systems
320	Adv COBOL with Aviation Applns	499	Special Topics in Computing

FLORIDA INTERNATIONAL UNIVERSITY
Miami, FL 33199
(305) 554-2311

Florida International is a public university with a student population of 11,000, a 350-acre campus in Tamiami and a 200-acre campus in Bay Vista, and a library containing over half a million volumes.

The Department of Computer Science offers BS and MS in computer science. Currently, 584 and 13 students are enrolled in the two programs respectively. The PhD program is at the planning stage. Prospective students should apply through the Admissions Office.

There are 10 full-time faculty in the department. Openings exist at all ranks. Background in operating systems and data bases are particularly desired.

Computing facilities here include: a Univac 1100/81, PDP 11/44, plus many Apples, Ataris and Motorola 68000-based microcomputers.

Course Offerings: (generally 3 semester units)

CAP 5721 Computer Graphics	COP 3122 Data Processing & COBOL
CDA 4101 Structured Computer Organization	COP 3172 Basic Programming for Business
CDA 4163 Data Communications	COP 3402 Assembly Language Programming
CDA 4171 Minicomputer Architecture & Applns	COP 3522 Programming Methodolgy
CDA 6166 Distributed Processing	COP 3530 Data Structures
CIS 3905 Independent Study	COP 4610 Operating Systems Principles
CIS 3932 Special Topics	COP 5506 Fund of Computer Science I (6)
CIS 4905 Independent Study	COP 5608 Fund of Computer Science II (6)
CIS 4932 Special Topics	COP 5540 Compiler Construction
CIS 5908 Independent Study	COP 6515 Structured Programming
CIS 5934 Special Topics	COP 6555 Survey of Programming Languages
CIS 6327 Stat Computer Performance Evaluation	COP 6614 Advance Operating Systems
CIS 6937 Sem:Contemporary Computer Science	COT 5320 Theory of Computation
CIS 6971 Thesis (10)	COT 6127 Theory of Formal Languages
COC 3300 Intro to Computers & Computer Applns	COT 6315 Analysis of Algorithms
COC 3400 Computer & Society	CRM 6121 Computer Management
COP 3112 Intro to Computers	

GEORGIA

GEORGIA INSTITUTE OF TECHNOLOGY
Atlanta, GA 30332
(404)894-4154

Georgia Tech's 300-acre campus is located in Atlanta, has a student population of 11,500, a library with over 1.3 titles and a faculty student ratio of 1 to 22.

The School of Information and Computer Science (ICS) offers BS, MS and PhD in information & computer science. Currently, there are 699, 178 and 35 students enrolled in these three programs respectively. Prospective students should apply through the Office of the Registrar; deadlines April 1 for in-state and Jan 1 for out-of-state students. Early Decision & Early Admission programs are available.

Computing facilities at Georgia Tech include: CDC 170/760 170/730, IBM 4341, three PRIME 550, two PRIME 400, one VAX 11/780, a HP 1000/45 Series F, an HP 3000/44, three IBM Series 1's, a Chromatics CG Color Computer, a HP 9845C Color Graphics Computer, two Three Rivers PERQ systems, a Symbolics 3600 LISP machine, an Ikonas RDS 3000, plus a microprocessor lab, and a Human Information Processing Lab. The NET/ONE is accessible. Future plan includes the acquisition of 4 additional VAX 11/780s.

There are 25 full-time faculty in the School. Faculty openings exist at all levels. The School seeks applicants in all areas of information & computer science, especially in the areas of: computer systems, artificial intelligence, VLSI, data communications, computer networking, and computer graphics. Faculty and their research interest:

R E Miller (theory of computation, machine organztn, parallel computation); L Chiaraviglio (theory, computer supported instruction); R A DeMillo (theoretical CS, software engineering, computer security); P H Enslow (distrbtd prcssng, ntwrks, compute systems, data communications, operating systems); J Gough Jr (semiotics, linguistics, philosphy of language); A P Jensen (large scale database systems performance, computer-aided instruction, small scale systems in instructional environments); J H Poore (computer-based education); V Slamecka (information systems); P Zunde (info science, info systems, system theory, pattern recognition)

A N Badre (human factors); P J Siegmann (evaluation and statistical tchnques for retrieval systems, documntn reprsntn methdlgy, appln of measures of information to dialogs); F E Kaiser (librarianship, info retrieval, indexing, literature searching, documntn)

J J Goda (prgrmng, prgrmng languages); M H Graham (theory of databases, logic database systems); N D Griffeth (databases, distrbtd systems, algrthms, human factors); K N King (theoretical computer sciene prgrmng languages, txt prcssng); J L Kolodner (AI, natural language prcssng, cognitive modelling); R J LeBlanc (prgmng language dsgn & implmntn, compiler portability, software engnrng tools); M S McKendry (operating systems, distributed systems, prgmng languages, compiler construction); B F Naylor (graphics, VLSI, computer-aided music); J Spinrad (algorithms, combinatorial complexity & optmztn, ntwrks, VLSI algrthms); W E Underwood (AI, intelligent robotics, expert systems, decision support systems).

Course Offerings:

1000	Information & Society 1-0-1	4652	Design Project II
1001	Computing Facilities 1-0-1	4653	Design Project III
1400	Intro to Algorithms & Compuiing	4754	Models of Human Information Processing
1401	Computer Programming & Problem Solving	4756	Human Factors in Software Development
1700	Digital Computer Organization & Programming	4801	Special Topics
2100	Programming & Problem Solvining Using Pascal	4901	Special Problems
2150	Intro to Discrete Structures	6100	Foundations of Information Science
2200	Data Structures	6114	Information Measures
2250	Technical Information Resourses 1-0-1	6116	Advanced Topics in Linguistics
2300	File processing	6117	Mathematical Linguistics
2601	Computer Organization & Programming I	6130	Philosophy of Mind
2602	Computer Organization & Programming II	6135	Theory of Communication
3110	Semiotics	6140	Systems theory I
3140	Intro to Discrete Systems	6141	Systems Theory II
3150	Intro to Mathmatical Logic	6144	Information Systems Design I,II
3155	Intro to Theory of Computing I	6146	Cybernetics
3300	Intro to Software Development	6152	Theory of Automata
3342	Intro to Computational Linguistics	6153	Theory of Compiling & Translation
3360	Intro to Artifiicial Intelligence	6155	Analysis of Algorithms
3400	Automatic Data Processing	6156	Complexity of Computation
3422	Survey of Programming Languages	6157	Advanced Theory of Computability
3500	Information Systems	6240	Orgnztn & Mngmnt of Information Industry
3510	Computer-Oriented Numerical Methods	6347	Computer-Aided Modeling 2-3-3
3602	Computer Organization & Programming III	6360	Artificial Intelligence
4110	Topics in Linguistics	6363	Pattern Reconition
4117	Intro to Mathmatical Linguistics	6370	Information Control Methods
4120	Intro to Information Processes I	6380	Computer Networks
4121	Intro to Information Processes II	6410	Computer Language Design
4136	Problem Solving	6412	Syntax Directed Compilation
4153	Computing Languages	6430	Computer Operating Systems
4155	Intro to Theory of Computing II	6431	Design of Computer Operating Systems
4240	Project Communication & Management	6435	Computer Systems Evaluation
4250	Literature of Science & Engineering 2-3-3	6450	Data Base Design
4305	Science Information Systems	6530	Graph Theory
4342	Natural Language Processing	6555	Queueing Theory & Applications I
4351	MIS Methodolgy	6556	Queueing Theory & Applications II
4370	Information Storage & Retrieval	6600	Advanced Small Scale Computer Systems
4380	Data Communications	6620	Advanced Computer Organization
4390	Computer Graphics	6750	Human Computer Interface
4410	Intro to Compilers	7000	Masters Thesis
4430	Intro to Operating Systems	7115	Phlosophy of Language
4450	Intro to Data Base Design	7999	Prep for Doctorial Qualifying Exams
4560	Elements of Information Theory	8111	Special Topics
4601	Computer Systems Laboratory I	8501	Special Problems
4602	Computer Systems Laboratory II	8999	Doctorial Thesis Preparation
4620	Microprogramming	9000	Doctorial Thesis
4651	Design Project I		

HAWAII

UNIVERSITY OF HAWAII
Honolulu, HI 96821
(808) 948-8207

University of Hawaii has a student population of 21,000, a faculty student ratio of 1 to 20 and a library with about 1.6 million volumes.

The Department of Information and Computer Science offers BS & MS in computer science. Currently, there are 250 and 50 students enrolled in the two programs respectively. BS students should apply through the Admissions and Records Office while MS applicants through the department. Application deadlines for the fall and spring semesters respectively: July 1 and Dec 1 for Hawaii students, June 1 and Dec 1 for students from the Mainland, and May 1 and Nov 1 for foreign students. MS deadlines are Mar 1 and Sept 1.

The university is equipped with an IBM 370, a DEC 20, HP 3000 and several INTEL 8086-based microcomputers.

Faculty positions exist for junior faculty committed to excellence in undergraduate and graduate teaching and research in computer science. Graduate faculty include: A Lew (software, computation system theory); N Abramson (info theory & coding, networks, satellite communication); W Gersch (math stat, time series, biomedicine); S Y Itoga (algoithms, complexity, formal languages); D Pager (compiler theory, computability, AI); W W Paterson (coding theory, prgmmng languages).

Course Offerings: (generall 3 semester units)

160 Intro to Computer Science I	EE 408 Advanced Scientific Computation
160L Intro to Computer Science Lab	EE 446 Info Theory & Coding
260* Intro to Computer Science II	EE 460 Switching Circuit Theory
266 Computer Org & Programming Techniques	EE 462 Computer System Design Project
267 Algorithms & Programming I	DS 351 Intro to Computers
367 Information System Technology	DS 352* Computer Systems & Appl in Orgnztns
368 Intro to Systems Programming	DS 451 Nonparametic Meth for Business Appln
443 Statistical Data Analysis	DS 455 Applied Regression Analysis
445 Intro to Random Processes	DS 485 Decision Analysis of Mngmt Info Systems
467 Algorithms & Programming II	ME 360 Computer Methods
477 Discrete Structures & Algorithm Analysis	Graduate
487 Modern Data Systems	367 Information System Technology
490 Software Systems Design	368 Intro to Systems Programming
491 Special Topics in Information Sciences	443 Statistical Data Analysis
499 Computer Project I	445X Intro to R&om Processes
EE 151 Intro Computer Programming Methods	467X Algorithms & Programing
EE 360 Digital Computer Structure	477 Discrete Structures & Algrthm Analysis
EE 407 Scientific Computation	487 Modern Data Systems

490 Software Systems Design
491 Special Topics
604X Computing Algorithms
620 Software System Theory
621 Theory of Formal Languages
622 Theory & Construction of Compilers
627 Information Structures
630 Info Processing in the Nervous System
641 Discrete State Stochastic Processes
644 Pattern Recognition
646 Parametric Meth in Time Series Analysis

650X Time Series Analysis
655 Applied Regression Analysis
661X The Theory of Automata
663 Theory of Computability
665X Operating Systems
670 Multivariate Analysis
671 Artificial Intelligence
675 Satallite Data Networks
680 Statistical Decision Analysis
686X Computer Simulation

IDAHO

BOISE STATE UNIVERSITY
Boise, ID 83725
(208) 385-1156

Boise State is a public university with an 120-acre campus, a student population of 12,000, a faculty student ratio of 1 to 19, and a library containing over 260,000 titles.

Information Science is one of the majors within the bachelor program in business administration. There are 400 students currently enrolled in the program. Prospective students should apply through the Admissions Office before August 15.

The department has 5 full-time faculty. Opening exists at assistant professor rank. Individuals with specialty in data base or software design are particularly desired. Computing facilities here include an IBM 4341, an HP 3000 and the IBM PCs.

Course Offerings:

210	Introduction to Information Sciences	405	Data Base Applications
220	Programming Techniques	420	Systems Analysis and Design
360	Programming Systems - COBOL I	430	Software Design
370	Programming Systems - COBOL II		

ILLINOIS

UNIVERSITY OF ILLINOIS AT CHICAGO
Chicago, IL 60680
(312) 996-4388

University of Illinois at Chicago is a public institution with 21,000 students. Operating on a trimester basis with 8-week summer sessions, the university maintains a faculty student ratio of 1 to 16 and a library with 1.15 million volumes.

The Department of Electrical Engineering and Computer Science (EECS) offers BS, MS and PhD programs, which currently enroll 733, 133, and 39 students respectively. All BS students are expected to acquire a common background in the fundamentals of computer science: programming, architecture, data structures, software design, theory of computation, and operating systems, plus a strong mathematics background in probability and discrete mathematics. MS students may pursue computer science (artificial intelligence, computer architecture, graphics, database management, information system, and software engineering) or electrical engineering (communications, control systems, design automation and robotics, digital systems and microprocessors, networks and solid-state electronics).

PhD students have opportunity to study and research in such areas of computer science: artificial intelligence, complexity, architecture, graphics, computer vision, database management, image processing, information retrieval, information systems, natural language processing, robotics, software engineering and theoretical computer science. They may also pursue such relevant areas in electrical engineering as: optical communications and waveguides, robotics, VLSI, solid-state device theory...etc. Prospective students should apply through Office of Admissions and Records. Contact that office for specific deadlines.

Computing facilities at the university include: PDP 11/70, and a PDP 11/45 running UNIX, Motorola 68000-based microcomputers. Future planned acquisition includes the VAX 11/780 system.

The Department seeks PhDs in Electrical Engineering or Computer Science. All areas of in the two fields will be considered. Background in computer architecture, design and commuications, would be highly desirable. Faculty of the department: W M Boerner, S K Chang, W K Chen, J C Lin, B H McCormick, T Murata, P Parzen, C K Sanathanan, L Siklossy, P L E Uslenghi.

R C Conant, T A DeFanti, M S Gupta, S R Laxpati, C Q Lee, R Priemer, A C Raptis, C T Yu.

S M Elnoubi, K Y Fang, R E Kent, S M Leinwand, G J Maclay, T G Moher, S Y OH, M Ouksel, S M Shatz, M Yousuf.

EECS Department Course Offerings: (a partial listing)

268	Intro to Programming Languages	391	Seminar
270	Data Structures	393	Special Problems
271	Digital Systems	396	Senior Design I
272	Computer Orgnztn & Programming	397	Senior Design II
274	Intro to Software Engineering		
292	Undergraduate Research		Graduate Courses
		405	Computer Instructional Systems
	Adv Undergraduate & Graduate Courses	406	Algebraic Semantics Prgrmng Languages
300	Intro to VLSI Design	407	Pattern Recognition II
301	Computer Architecture	408	Cybernetics II
302	File & Communication Systems	409	Pattern Recognition III
306	Languages & Automata	413	Active Network Synthesis
307	Pattern Recognition I	414	Adv Topics in Networks
320	Transmission Lines	415	Applied Graph Theory
332	Digital Communications	428	Integrated Optics
341	Instrmntatn for Cmptr Automatn	438	Information Flow in Systems
347	Integrated Circuit Engineering	470	Automata Theory
360	Automatic Control	472	Control System Simulation
370	Computer Systems	473	Advanced Data Base Systems
371	Digital Netowrks	474	Information Retrieval
372	Microprocessors	475	Artificial Intelligence
373	Data Base Systems	477	Computer Vision II
375	Artificial Intelligence	478	Computer Graphics II
376	Programming Language Design	491	Seminar
377	Computer Vision	492	Individual Study
378	Computer Graphics	493	Current Topics
379	Real-Time Data processing	495	Project Research
380	Physiological Applns Real-Time DP	499	Thesis Research

UNIVERSITY OF ILLINOIS
Urbana, IL 61801
(217) 333-1000

University of Illinois Urbana-Champaign 700-acre campus operates on a semester system with 8-week summer session, supporting a population of over 35,000 students with a faculty student ratio of 1 to 13 and a library containing over 9.6 million volumes. The Department of Computer Science Library itself maintains 195 journals, 10,000 books and 2,650 bound volumes of journals.

The Department of Computer Science offers a BS in computer science program in the College of Engineering. In addition, the Departments of Mathematics & Computer Science jointly offer a program in the College of Liberal Arts and Sciences for students interested in both mathematics and computer science. The Department of Electrical Engineering offers a program in the College of Engineering for students interested in EE & CS. There is also another program in the College of Liberal Arts & Science for students interested in teaching computer science in the secondary schools. Prospective undergraduate students should apply through Office of Admissions as early as possible.

Four graduate programs are offered by the department: PhD, MS, MS in the Teaching of Computer Science (MSTCS), and Master of Computer Science (MTS). MSTCS is a terminal degree for students who intend to teach computer science at undergraduate colleges, junior colleges, vocational technical colleges and high schools. MCS is also a terminal degree for those who wish to specialize in some application of computer science. For more information, write to: Department of Computer Science, University of Illinois at Urbana-Champaign, 1304 W Springfield Ave, Urbana, IL 61801.

The Computer Science Department here has been one of the premier research leaders in the world. Its Digital Computer Lab built the famed ILLIAC I in 1952. In 1957, plans were drawn to build ILLIAC II which would be 10 times faster than any computer then in existence. In 1963, ILLIAC ran at capacity. In 1964, its operating system was run. By 1966, it was operated on a time shared basis. As the department has grown in size with 32 faculty and 41 research projects, its activities and interests have become more diversified. Research is now carried out in all main facets of computer science and in many areas of application.

Computing facilities at the university include: a CYBER 175, VAX 11/780, and an IBM 4341, all housed in the Digital Computer Lab with the Department of /computer Science. In addition, two VAX 11/780 supply interactive UNIX time shared services, seven VAX 11/750 support graphics & network research. Each VAX 11/780 has four megabytes memory and share 1.2 gigabytes of disk storage and 160 communication ports.

A PRIME 650 which supports research in numerical software, fault-tolerant software systems and DBMS; a Ramtek 9400 and HP 3000 which support graphics and VLSI; a Xerox 1100 supports INTERLISP; two PDP 11/60 and two PDP 11/40 sharing six 28 megabyte disk drives and two 20 megabyte disk drives; a PDP 11/35 with two 20 megabyte disk drives, and a SUN workstation.

All VAX systems are networked via 10 MHz Ethernet that also ties the VAX 11/780 and several DCS personal workstations into the network. A 3 MHz Ethernet ties the Xerox 1100 and several personal workstations to the departmental VAX computer network.

More equipments will be purchased under NSF grants. Donation from computer companies will expand computing facilities continuously.

The research of the faculty are varied and evolving. The list of areas below is ongoing or has recently been completed: algorithm & data structure analysis, artificial intelligence, automata theory, automated theorem proving, biomedical computing, coding theory, combinatoral mathematics, compiler design, computational complexity, computer-aided design, computer-aided instruction, computer architecture, computer arithmetic, computer graphics, computer networks, data acquisition, electro-optical information processing, file processing, hardware design, image processing, information display systems, information retrieval, interactive programming, linear & nonlinear programming & optimization, microprocessor systems and applications, networks, operating systems, parallel computation, pattern recognition & machine learning, probabilistic computers, program transformation, program verification, programming languages, theory and practice, robitics, simulation, software engineering, reliability, and environments, special-purpose information processing, specification of software systems, structured programming, switching theory, VLSI design tools.

Faculty and their research interests: G G Belford (data mngmnt, distrbtd databases, reliable software, performance analysis); R H Campbell (operating systems, software engnrng, reliablty, software envrnmnt, prgmng language dsgn); N Dershowitz (prgm verification & devlpmnt, thry of computation); M Faiman (archtctr, logic dsgn & hardware, microprcssrs, interfacing & applns, educational labs); H G Friedman (operating systems, multiprgmng operating systems & languages, CAI); D D Gajski (system dsgn, multiprcssr & tessellated systems, dsgn automation); C W Gear (numerical analysis, soln of ODE, software, graphics, automatic prblm solvng systems, simulation & ntwrks).

M T Harandi (prgmng languages, compiler construction, translator writing systems, expert system, logic prgmng & applns in knowledge-based system, program spec & verification); S Kamin (thry software engnrng, data type spec, prgm verification, prgmng language semantics); C P Kruskal (parallel archtctr, sequential & parallel algrthms); W J Kubitz (d igital prcssor dsgns, VLSI design automation, hardware & technology); D J Kuck (coherent dsgns for numerical computation, file procssng, info retrieval); D H Lawrie (computer system organization, especially large systems & multiprocessors, language & system dsgn, ntwrks for large computation); C L Liu (appl combinatorial math & computational algrthms).

J W Liu (computer ntwrks dsgn, digital communctn, DBMS); R S Michalski (AI & info systems, computer inference, databases, knowledge-based systems, machine acquisition & reprsntn of knowledge, man machine interaction, decision thr, appln in medicine & agriculture); D Michie (expert systems, machine learning robotics, computer chess, cost benefit analysis of heuristics); M D Mickunas (languages, formal compiling methods, translator writing systems, mini micro software, opeating systems, networks); S Muroga (logic dsgn, CAD, switching thry, VLSI circuit logic dsgn, LP & integer prgmng); T A Murrell (logic & hardware dsgn engnrng applns, special purpose computers for industrial control); D A Plaisted (complexity involving sparse polynomials & integers, mechanical thrm proving, termination & confluence of systems of rewrite rules, graph algrthms).

W J Poppelbaum (hardware, averaging processors, intelligent displays, low-cost I/O, cognitive machines); S R Ray (image data analysis, algrthms & hardware devlpmnt of applns to biomedical image data, biomedical applns of microprocessors); E M Reingold (algrthms, data strctrs, probabilistic algorithms, combinatorial computing); J E Robertson (efficient and fast methods for digital arithmetic operations); Y Sagiv (database systems, relational databases, query optmztn, algrthms & data strctrs); A H Sameh (numerical analysis, numerical linear algebra & parallel computation); P E Saylor (numerical analysis, soln of PDE); R D Skeel (numerical analysis, diff equations); D L Slotnick (dsgn & appln of digital systems); J N Snyder (appln of digital computers in physics); D S Watanabe (numerical analysis, diff equations, math software, simulation of semiconductor devices).

Course Offerings:

101	Intro Computers for Appli to Eng & Phy Sci	331	Microprocessor Systems
102	Intro Computers & Appli to Architecture	333	Computer System Organization
103	Intro Computers & Appli to Soc & Behav Sci	335	Intro to VLSI System Design
105	Intro Computers & Appli to Bus & Commerce	337	Control Structure of Computers
106	Intro Computers for Nontechnical Major	338	Communication Networks for Computers
121	Intro Computer Science	339	Cmptr Aided Design for Digital Systems
196	Honors Course in Computer Science	341	Mechanized Mathematical Inference
221	Machine-Level Programming	342	Cmptr Inference & Knowledge Acquisition
225	Data Structures	346	Pattern Recognition & Machine Learning
264	Intro Structure & Logic of Digital Cmputrs	347	Knowledge-Based Programming
265	Logic Design Lab w Integrated Circuits	348	Intro to Artificial Intelligence
273	Intro Theory of Computation	355	Num Methods for Partial Diff Equation
281	Intro Computer Circuits	360	Scientific Appln of Minicomputers
282	Digital Circuits Laboratory	363	Integrated Circuit Logic Design
296	Honors Course in Computer Science	364	Intro to Computer Arithmetic
297	Special Topics in Computer Science	373	Combinatorial Algorithms
300	Advanced Computer Programming	375	Automata, Formal Lang, & Computations
310	Information Systems	376	Program Verification
311	Database Systems	378	Computer Appli to Problems in Mathematics
316	Interactive Systems for Instruction	381	Intro to Computer Memories & I/O
317	Computer-Assisted Instruction	384	Computer Data Acquisition Systems
318	Computer Graphics	385	Digital Computer Semiconductor Technology
323	Operating System Design	386	Information Display Systems
325	Programming Language Principles	389	Advanced Computer Circuits
326	Compiler Construction	391	Switching Theory
327	Software Engineering	392	Finite State Machines

397	Special Topics in Computer Science	463	Information Theory
400	Intro Auto Digital Computing f Grad Student	464	Topics in Digital Computer Arithmetic
405	Numerical Methods in Fluid Dynamics	465	Topics in Automata Theory
414	Engineering Applications of Linear Graphs	469	Intro to Coherent Optics & Holography
425	Topics in Compiler Construction	485	Topics in Computer Hardware
433	Theory of High-Speed Parallel Computation	491	Seminar in Computer Science
441	Computer Systems Analysis	492	Individual Project Study
445	Systems Modeling & Simulation	497	Special Topics in Computer Science
456	Coding Theory		

AUGUSTANA COLLEGE
Rock Island, IL 61201
(309) 794-7341

Augustana College is a private college with an 110-acre campus, a population of 2,200 students, a faculty student ratio of 1 to 17, and a library with 230,000 volumes.

The Department of Mathematics and Computer Science consists of 7 full-time faculty members. It offers a major in Computer Science/Mathematics which combines course work in pure mathematics, computational mathematics and computer science. Currently, there are 109 enrolled in the program. Prospective students should apply through the Admissions Office.

Augustana's Computer Center houses a DEC PDP 11/70 with 256K words of memory running RSTS/E, six Apple IIs, two Apple IIes, and a network that provides access to the Weeg Computing Center at the University of Iowa. Ten DEC Rainbow 100 microcomputers will be acquired in the near future.

Course Offerings

100	Intro to Computers & BASIC Programming	332	Operating Systems
200	Computing with FORTRAN	370	Data Structures
250	Programming with Business-Oriented Languages	371	Design & Analysis of Algorithms
330	Computer Architecture	380	Programming Language Principles
331	Assembly Language Programming	400	Independent Study

DePAUL UNIVERSITY
Chicago, IL 60604
(312) 321-7600

Depaul University is a Roman Catholic university with a total of 13,300 students, a 30-acre campus, a faculty student ratio of 1 to 21 and a 450,000-volume library.

The Department of Computer Science offers BS and MS in compter science. Within the BS program, students may choose one of the two concentrations: Computer Science or Computer Information Systems. Prospective students should apply through the Admissions Office. Deadline is July 1. Currently, there are 500 and 580 in the BS and MS programs respectively.

15 full-time faculty teach in the department. Faculty positions are open at all ranks. Recruitment interests extend to all areas of computer science.

The university runs a VAX (Cluster), two VAX 11/780, a VAX 11/750. The department has several PDP 11 and several microcomputers. VMS, PL/I, Datatrieve, SPSS...etc are available. Future plan includes the acquisition of another VAX 11/750.

Course Offerings:

110	Elements of Computer & Info Science	395	Computer Logic Design
145	RPG 11 Programming	396	Microprocessors
149	Programming with Basic	Graduate	
201	Business Computing	420	Discrete Structures
203	Cobol Programming	424	Adv Data Analysis
204	Adv Topics in Cobol	432	Computer & Info System Modeling
205	Fortran 77 Programming	442	Data Structures
210	Programming with PL/1	445	Computer Architecture
220	Programming with Pascal	446	Computer Operating Systems
225	Programming in C	447	Concepts of Programming Languages
230	Programming in Ada	448	Compiler Design
250	Computers & Human Intelligence	449	Design & Analysis of Algorithms
310	Principles in Computer Science 1	459	File Management & Organization
311	Principles of Computer Science 11	462	Data Communications
312	Assembly Language & Cmptr Organization	463	Computer Networks
320	Discrete Structures	469	Computer Graphics
323	Data Analysis & Statistical Software 1	475	Info Systems Design & Analysis
324	Data Analysis & Statistical Software 11	480	Artificial Intelligence
332	Computer & Info System Modeling	481	Pattern Recognition & Mchn Perception
342	Intro to File Processing	489	Queueing Theory w Computer Appln
343	Intro to Operating Systems	490	Theory of Computation
344	IBM Assembly Language Programming 1	491	Design & Analysis of Algorithms
345	Computer Architecture	492	Adv Topics in Algorithms
347	Concepts of Programming Languages	493	Automata Theory & Formal Grammars
349	Data Bases & Data Management	494	Sotware Methodologies
350	Design & Analysis of Algorithms	498	Digital Signal Processing
353	Vax Assembly Language Programming	545	Adv Computer Organization
354	IBM Assembly Language Programming 11	546	Operating Systems Design
360	On-Line Systems & Telecommunications	548	Adv Compiler Design
362	Principles of Data Communications	560	On-Line Systems & Telecommunications
•364	Adv Programming Techniques	562	Comm-Computer Network Dsgn & Analysis
365	Software Engineering	563	Protocols & Techniques for Data Networks
369	Computer Graphics	571	Software Maintenance
373	Computer Information Systems	572	Computer Security
374	Info Systems Analysis & Design 1	573	Data Bases & Data Management
375	Info Systems Analysis & Design 11	574	Adv Topics in Data Base
382	Legal Aspects of Data Processing	575	Topics in Info Systems
385	Numerical Analysis	586	Cmptnl Methods for Data Analysis
386	Adv Numerical Analysis	596	Topics in Info Systems
387	Op Research 1. Linear Programming	597	Topics in Data Communications
388	Op Research 11: Optimization Theory	598	Topics in Statistical Computing
394	Software Projects	599	Topics in Computer Science

ILLINOIS STATE UNIVERSITY
Normal, IL61761
(309) 438-2111

The 710-acre campus of Illinois State operates on a semester basis with 8-week summer sessions, serving a student body of 20,000 with a faculty student ratio of 1 to 18 while maintaining a 1.2 million library.

The Department of Applied Computer Science offers a BS in ACS, which has 1000 students currently. Designed to serve students who wish to apply computer and systems techniques to solve real world problems, the program allows majors to choose the Computer Information Systems Sequence or the Technical Systems Sequence. The first sequence prepares those who seek a position as a programmer or systems analyst in a commercial environment, while the second prepare those who are interested in math-based business or engineering applications. Prospective students should apply through the department before February 1 for the fall.

There are 16 full-time faculty in the department. The Department seeks faculty members at all ranks. Background in computer information systems would be particularly desirable.

Computer systems in use here include an IBM 3033 (MVS), Apples, TRS 80s and IBM PCs.

Course Offering: (generally 3 semester hours)

140	Intro to the Computer World	344	Discrete System Simulation
164	Intro to FORTRAN Programming	345	Applied Computer Modeling
168	Structured Prblms & the Computer	355	Microcomputer Appln & Design II
169	Information Processing Using PL/I	363	Intro to Systems Development
255	Microcomputer Application & Design	364	Software Design
265	Job Control Language	368	Topics in System Design
272	COBOL as a Second Language	372	External Data Structures
273	FORTRAN as a Second Language	376	Intro to Online Systems
274	PL/I as a Second Language	378	Database Processing
278	Data Structure	383	Principles of Operating Systems
281	Computer Systems Operation	385	Topics in Computer Science
283	Assembler Language Programming	390	Independent Study
288	Adv Assembler Language Programming	391	Directed Project in Appl CS
298	Professional Practice: Internship	398	Professional Practice: Internship

INDIANA

INDIANA UNIVERSITY
Bloomington, IN 47401
(812) 335-0661

Indiana University is a public institution whose 3200-acre campus, located in the wooded hills of Southern Indiana, supports 32,000 students with a faculty student ratio of 1 to 16, and a library with over 3.6 million titles.

The Department of Computer Science offers bachelor, master and PhD programs in computer science. Current enrollments in the three programs number 650, 250 and 30 respectively. Prospective students should apply through the Admissions or Graduate Admissions Offices.

Computing facilities at IU include: a CDC 172, 170/855, an IBM 4341, VAXs, PRIME, HP 3000, M 68000 and M6809-based microcomputers. Ethernet is accessible. Future plan includes more 68000 micros. In addition, the department has a VAX 11/780, several scientific workstations, and a digital hardware lab with logic design and PC board fabrication facilities.

The department seeks doctorates at the assistant professor rank. Applications for higher ranks will also be considered. Faculty and their research interests: J Barnden (AI, languages, formal semantics); C Brown (algorithms, compilers); J Buck (database & info systems, CS education); J Burns (theoretical CS, parallel & distributed systems, distributed data bases, graphics); W Clinger (semantics of prgrmng languages, AI, nondeterministic concurrent computation, logic); G Epstein (system design multiple valued logic, CS education); D Friedman (program methodology, formal semantics, AI, distributed computing, simulation languages, applicative languages, LISP).

S Hagstrom (hardware, lab automation, networking, operating system, software enginering, algorithms); S Higgins (CS education, number theory, modern algebra); D Hofstadter (AI, perception of pattern & style, self monitoring, self perception, philosophy of mind); S Kwasny (natural language understanding, AI, data structure, linguistics, data base systems); J O'Donnell (architecture, operating systems, VLSI design, prgmng languages).

F Prosser (Digital hardware, operating systems, CS education); P Purdom (analysis of algorithms, compiles); E L Robertson (thry of computation, complexity, hardware & software systems archtctr, data bases); M Wand (semantics of prgrmng languages, logic, algebra); D Winkel (digital design, architecture, assembly language, elementary architecture); D Wise (applicative prgmng, data structures, multiprcssng, archtctr & languages).

Course Offerings:

C201 Intro to Computer Programming (4)
S201 Intro to Computer Programming Honors (4)
C203 Cobol & File Processing
C251 Fndtns of Digital Computing
C252 Digital Computing Fndtns Nonmajors (1)
C301 Programming (1)
C302 PASCAL Programming (1)
C303 COBOL Programming (1)
C307 Applied Programming Techniques
C308 Systems Analysis (1)
C311 Programming Languages (4)
C355 Computer Structures (4)
C343 Data Structures (4)
C390 Individual Programming Laboratory
C398 Internship in Prof Practice 3-6cr
C421 Computer Organization
C422 Adv Computer Organization
C431 Assemblers & Compilers I
C432 Assemblers & Compilers II
C435 Operating Systems I
C436 Operating Systems II
C445 In Systems Design
C446 Information Systems Development
C451 Automata & Formal Grammars
C452 Theory of Computability
C455 Analysis of Algorithms I
C463 Artificial Intelligence I
C464 Artificial Intelligence II
C490 Seminar in Computer Science
C499 Honors Research
Graduate
C301 Fortran Prog (1)

C307 Applied Prog Tech
C311 Prog Lang (4)
C335 Comp Structures (4)
C343 DataStructures (4)
C421 Comp Org
C422 Adv Computer Org
C431 Assemblers & Compilers I
C432 Assemblers & Compilers II
C435 Operating Systems I
C436 Operating Systems II
C445 Information Systems Design
C446 Inform Sys Delep
C451 Automata & Formal Grammars
C452 Comp Theory
C455 Analysis of Algorithms I
C463 Artificial Intelligence I
C364 Artificial Intelligence II
C490 Seminar in Computer Science
C501 Computer Prgmng for Teachers (2)
C511 Adv Concepts in Programming Languages
C515 Logic & Program Verification
C521 Computer & Communication Architectures
C525 Logic Functions & Machine Theory
C531 Compilers III
C535 Operating Systems Theory
C546 Data Base Design Theory
C556 Analysis of Algorithms II
C561 Natural Language Understanding
C565 Computer Models of Learning
C567 Representation Issues for A I
C616 Seminar: Sematics of Prgmnng Languages
C690 Special Topics in Computing

PURDUE UNIVERSITY
West Lafayette, IN 47907
(317) 494-1776

Purdue is a public university with a 516-acre campus, a population of 33,000 students, a faculty student ratio of 1 to 15 and a library containing over 1.7 million volumes.

The Department of Computer Science, the oldest one in the US, offers BS, MS and PhD programs in which 908, 110 and 26 students are enrolled respectively. In addition, the department and the School of Management jointly offer a special Master's Program in Management Information Systems (MIS), which is a professional program for the analysis, design and management of complex information systems that aid decision making. Prospective students should apply through the department and complete their applications before Feb 1 for admission with support, or by March 1 for just admission alone.

Purdue's computing facilities include: the Cyber 205 supercomputer, CDC 6600, two CDC 6500, six VAX 11/780, three PDP 11/70, and the PDP 11/02 and Intel-8086 based microcomputers. ARPANET and CSNET are accessible. Future acquisition plan calls for more personal workstations.

There are 28 faculty members in the department. Each has own office terminal giving access to UNIX on the VAX systems, the Cyber 205 and the national networks. They actively pursue research in: operating systems, networks, programming languages, data base systems, software engineering, supercomputers, numerical analysis, and theoretical computer science. The department seeks computer scientists both at the junior and senior levels. For more information, write or call the department; Phone (317) 494-6004.

Course Offerings:

110	Intro To Computers	541	Data Base Systems
140	Intro To Data Processing (Basic)	542	Design of Data-Processing Systems
145	Intro To Data Processing (Fortran)	543	Discrete Systems Simulation
220	Programming I for Engineers & Scientists	544	Simulation & Modeling of Cmptr Systems
230	Programming I	545	Management Information Systems
300	Assembly Language Programming	546	Computer Modeling of Social Systems
320	Prgmng II for Engineers & Scientists	547	Info Storage, Retrvl & Ntrl Language
330	Programming II	548	Interactive Computer Learning Systems
380	Intro To Data Management	555	Cryptography & Data Security
402	Architecture of Computers	565	Programming Languages
403	Systems Programming	569	Intro to Robotic Systems
414	Numerical Methods	572	Heuristic Problem-Solving
415	Computational Methods for Diff Eq	574	Adv Computer Graphics
430	Data Structures	580	Algthm Dsgn Analysis & Implementation
440	Intro to File & Data Base Systems	582	Automata & Formal Languages
442	Applns of Computers in Business Systems	584	Thr of Computation & Cmptnal Complexity
444	Intro to Small Scale Computers	585	Mathematical Logic I
482	Intro to the Analysis of Algorithms	586	Mathematical Logic II
484	Intro to the Theory of Computation	590	Topics in Computer Sciences (1-5) cr.
490	Topics in C S for Undergrads (1-5)	613	Numerical Analysis in Function Spaces
Graduate		614	Num Soln of Ordinary Diff Equations
502	Compiling & Programming Systems	615	Num Soln of Partial Diff Equations
503	Operating Systsems	616	The Theory of Approximation
510	Elmnts of Sftwr Science & Sftwr Metrics	639	Tchnlgy of Cmptr Center & Sftwr Mngnt
512	Num Methods for Engineers & Scientists	643	Adv Simulation Design & Analysis
514	Numerical Analysis	660	Design of Translating Systems
515	Numerical Analysis of Linear Systems	661	Formal Compiling Methods
520	Computational Methods in Analysis	684	Adv Theory of Computation
535	Interactive Computer Graphics	690	Seminar on Topics in C S (0-5) cr
536	Data Communication & Computer Networks	698	Research M S Thesis
540	File Structures & Searching	699	Research PH D Thesis

Ball State is a public university whose 950-acre campus is about 60 miles from Indianapolis. The university has 19,000 students, a faculty student ratio of 1 to 20 and a library with over one million volumes.

Bachelor and master degrees in computer science are offered here with a current enrollment of 750 and 60 respectively. Apply through Admissions Office. Application period is open.

Twelve full-time faculty members serve the department. New faculty members are sought at the assistant and associate professor level. Main stream computer scientists are welcome to apply.

Computing facilities include: DEC 10, VAX 11/780, PDP 11/34 running Tops-10, VMS and RT-11, and the Apples. Future plan includes a PDP 11/60.

Course Offerings: (generally 4 quarter units)

120	Computer Proamming I	497	Software Engrng I - Systems Analysis
121	Computer Programming II	498	Software Engrng II - Design & Dvlpmnt
200	Intro.To Computer Info. Sys.		Graduate
203	Computer Science for Architects	524	Applied Combinatories
210	Business Application Programming	530	Machine Language & Systems Programming 1
220	Scientific Computer Programming	531	Machine Language & Systems Programming 2
225	Applications Programming Language I	532	Data Structures
226	Applications Programming Language II	533	Computer Hardware Systems
230	Machine Lang & Systems Programming 1	535	Computer Programming Languages
231	Machine Lang & Systems Programming 2	536	Database Design
232	Data Structures	537	Distributed Processing & Networks
305	Computer Assisted Instruction	538	Computer Graphics
324	Applied Combinatorics	540	Data Processing Techniques
333	Computer Hardware Systems	542	Computer Simulation Techniques
340	Data Processing Techniques	552	Secure Computer Systems
342	Computer Simulation	553	Cmptr Resource Performance Measrmnt
363	NumericalAnalsis	562	Numerical Analysis 1
435	Computer Promgraming Languages	563	Numerical Analysis
436	Database Design	572	Minicomputer Systems
472	Minicomputer Systems	576	Operating Systems
476	Operating Sysstems	578	Compiler Construction
		589	Rsrch Methods in Computer Science

IOWA

IOWA STATE UNIVERSITY
Ames, IA 50011
(515) 294-5836

Iowa State University is a public institution whose 1000-acre campus serves a population of 25,000 students. Operating on a semester system with 8-week summer sessions, the university maintains a faculty student ratio of 1 to 19, and a library with 1.45 millions of volumes.

The Department of Computer offers BS, MS and PhD programs in computer sciene. Current enrollment figures are 1000, 45, and 15 respectively.

University computing facilities include an NAS AS/7000, four VAX 11/780. The department maintains a VAX 11/780, two PDP 11/34. The university is planning an ambitious purchase program of microcomputers.

There are 16 full-time faculty in the department. Faculty positions exist at the assistant and associate professor ranks. Background in all areas of computer science will be considered. Individuals with specialty in computer systems organization, operating systems, architecture, programming methodology would be particularly desired.

Course Offerings:

102	An Intro to Computers & Their Applns (2)	432	Principles of Compiling
111	Computer Programming I	441	Computer Based Information Systems
112	Computer Programming II	452	Implementation of Operating Systems
170	Computer Applications & Impact	470	Computing Methods for Research Workers
172	Computer Programming in FORTRAN (2)	471	Cmptnl Lnr Algebra & Fixed Pt Iteration
175	Applied Computer Programming	481	Num Solution of Diff Eq & Interpolation
176	Computer Programming (4)	490	Independent Study (Credit Arranged)
200	Language(1)	495	Seminar (Credit Arranged)
201	Computer Programming in COBOL	Graduate	
202	COBOL Individualized Instruction (2)	501	Computer System Architecture
221	Intro Cmptr Org & Mchn Level Prgmnng (4)	507	Numerical Solution of Ordinary Diff Eq
260	Discrete Computational Structures	511	Prncpls of Algorithm Dsgn & Analysis (4)
290	Independent Study	509	Computational Methods of Linear Algebra
300	Cooperative Education (Credit Arranged)	521	Principles of Operating Systems
306	File Organization & Processing (4)	523	Implementation of Operating Systems
311	Data Structures & Algorithm Analysis	531	Theoretical Foundations
332	Principles of Programming Languages	532	Theoretical Foundations
375	Applied Information Processing Systems	541	Programming Languages
352	Intro to Operating Systems	542	Programming Languages
384	Computer Organization & Design I	551	Database Management Systems Design
385	Computer Organization & Design II	584	Digital System Organization
411	Software Engineering	585	Digital Systems Design

71

589 Advanced Digital System Architecture
590 Special Topics (Credit Arranged)
599 Nonthesis Research (Credit Arranged)
610 Seminar (Credit Arranged)

621 Advanced Topics in Operating Systems
641 Semantic Models for Prgmng Languages
699 Research

UNIVERSITY OF IOWA
Iowa City, IA 52242

University of Iowa's 1380-acre campus supports a population of 26,700 students with a faculty student ratio of 1 to 17, and a library of over 2.4 million titles.

The Department of Computer Science offers BA, BS, MS, PhD programs. Current enrollments are: 560 in the Pre-CS, 262 in the undergraduate CS major, 90 in the MS, and 20 in the PhD programs. Contact the Admissions Office for application deadlines and other information.

University computing facilities include an IBM 370/168, a network of six Prime 750/850s, two VAX 11/780s. The Department maintains a research lab that consists of: a VAX 11/780, PDP 11/23, HP2100, and a network of 3 HP 9836s supported by a lab manager and a full-time systems programmer. UNIX, Interlisp, and Ada are available.

There are 15 full-time members in the department. Faculty positions exist at all ranks. Members: T J Sjoerdsma, D A Alton, D L Epley, A C Fleck, R J Baron, K V Bhat, N Khabbaz, A Critcher, R Ford, D W Jones, C D Martin, R K Shultz.

Course Offerings: (generally 3 semester units)

Primarily for Undergraduates
  1 Survey of Computing
  7 Intro to Computing with FORTRAN
  9 Programming with COBOL
 16 Intro to Programming with Pascal (4)
 17 Programming with Pascal
 18 Computer Org & Assem Lang Prgmmng (4)
 19 Discrete Structures
 21 Data Structures
 23 Programming Language Concepts
 31 Digital Systems & Computers
 32 Intro to Systems Software
 55 Elementary Numerical Analysis
 96 Topics in Computer Science (arr.)
Graduate Service Courses
100 Intro to Computering with FORTRAN
106 Intro to Programming with Pascal
107 Programming with Pascal
108 Computer Org & Assem Lang Programming
109 Programming with COBOL
110 Programming with PL/1
111 Independent Study (arr.)
114 Computer Applns to Indvdlzd Instruction

Primarily for Computer Science Majors
115 Software Engineering - Applications
116 Operating Systems & Concurrent Prgmmng
118 Software Engineering - Systems
122 Advanced Computer Org & Architecture
123 Programming Language Foundations
125 Data: Abstractions, Types & Structures
127 Compiler Construction
135 Intro to Computation Theory
144 Design of Information Systems
145 Artificial Intelligence I
153 Design & Analysis of Algorithms I
167 Theory of Graphs
178 Computer Communications
Primarily for Graduates
216 Advanced Operating Systems
217 Topics in Programming Language Design
231 Advanced Theory of Computation
234 Topics in the Complexity of Algorithms
244 Topics in Information System Design
245 Artificial Intelligence II
247 Theory of Program Schemata
253 Design & Analysis Of Algorithms II
257 Formal Languages

KANSAS

KANSAS STATE UNIVERSITY
Manhattan, KS 66506
(913) 532-6250

Kansas State's 325-acre campus supports a population of 20,000 students. Operating on a semester basis with 8-week summer sessions, the university maintains a faculty student ratio of 1 to 19, and a library with over 900,000 volumes.

The Department of Computer Science offers BA, BS, and graduate degrees in Computer Science and Information Systems. The undergraduate CS program prepares students for careers in systems programming and analysis, scientific & engineering applications programming, management, and graduate study in computer science. The IS program prepares students for careers in business data processing, data base management, marketing and sales, management, and graduate study in information science.

On the graduate level, the department offers MS and PhD in computer science. The PhD is sponsored jointly by Kansas State and the University of Kansas. Completion of the doctoral degree requires 24 semester hours of course work beyond MS at KSU or KU. Students apply to one of the two schools, but are formally admitted to both universities. Inquire the department office for more information. There is no deadline for U S citizens. However, March 15 and Nov 15 are the deadlines for international students for the fall and spring semesters. Currently, there are 675, 160 and 10 students in the bachelor, master amd PhD programs respectively.

The Computing Center runs an National NAS/6130 OS/MVT with full range of software. The department has three Perkin-Elmer 32-bit machines, two Plexus Multi-user machines, two Pascal machines, five graphics systems, three Columbia MPC, and the Apple IIs. CSNET and ETHERNET are available. Future acquisition plan calls for a VAX 750.

There are 13 full-time in the department. Faculty openings exist at the assistant and associate professor ranks. Research interests here include: programming languages, language processors, data management systems, operating systems, software engineering, artificial intelligence, architecture, minicomputer networks, business and data base systems using minicomputers, graphics, simulation and modeling, distributed systems, information retrieval, and knowledge-based systems.

Course Offerings: (generally 3 units)

Undergraduate
100 Computing Appreciation
200 Fundamentals of Computer Programming (2)
201 FORTRAN Language (2)
202 PL/1 Language Laboratory (2)
203 APL Language Laboratory (2)

206 BASIC Language Laboratory (2)
207 PASCAL Language Laboratory (2)
211 FORTRAN Lab for Engineering Majors (1)
311 300 Algorithmic Processes
305 Computer Organization & Programming I
306 Operating Systems Laboratory

340 Software Engineering Project I (2)	761 Data Base Management Systems
341 Software Engineering Project II (2)	765 Systems Analysis for Business
362 Intro to Business Programming	780 Numerical Solution of Ord Diff Eqs (2)
397 Honors Seminar in Computer Science (1-3)	785 Numerical Solution of Partial Diff Eq (2)
405 Intro to Programming Languages	791 Intensive Cmptr Science: Concepts (1-3)
420 Operating Systems I	792 Intensive Cmptr Science: Data (4)
460 Data Structures	793 Intensive Cmptr Science: Systems (2)
499 Senior Honors Thesis (2)	798 Topics in Computeer Science
505 Computer Organization & Programming II	Graduate
561 Intro to Data Management Systems	800 Theory of Parsing
580 Numerical Computing	806 Semantics of Programming Languages
591 Computer Science Applications	820 Intro to Operating Systems Theory
658 Microcomputer Programming & Applns (2)	840 Adv Concepts in Software Engineering
662 Business Data Processing	860 Distributed Databases
665 Computer Installation Management	870 Automata & Computability I
670 Discrete Computationalk Structures	875 Automata & Computability II
680 Searching Procedures kj	890 Sp Topics in Computer Science (2-4)
690 Implementation Projects	897 Seminar in Computer Science (1-3)
697 Seminar in Computer Science (1-3)	898 Master's Report (1-2)
700 Translator Design I	899 Research in Computer Science (1-6)
710 Computer Simulation Experiments	900 Translator Design II
720 Operating Systems II	905 Theory of Programming Languages
725 Computer Networks	920 Contemporary Concepts in Prgmmng Systems
730 Artificial Intelligence	926 Computation Structures
736 Computer Graphics	930 Pattern Recognition & Image Processing
740 Software Engineering	940 Theory of Software Engineering
745 Software Development Management	960 Theory of Data Base Systems
750 Adv Computer Architecture Experiments	990 Research Topics (2-3)
755 Adv Computer Architecture	999 Research in Computer Science

UNIVERSITY OF KANSAS
Lawrence, KS 66043
(913) 864-3911

The University of Kansas is an educational and research institution with more than 26,000 students and 1,880 faculty. Classified by the NSF as a major university receiving substantial research support, the campus, located in an attractive area of rolling hills, woods and lakes, has been receiving over $35 million a year in federal research funds. Its library contains over 2.25 million volumes.

The Department of Computer Science offers BS, MS and in cooperation with Kansas State University, a PhD program in computer science. Application information can be obtained from the Department of Computer Science, 116 Strong Hall, The University of Kansas, Lawrence, Kansas 66045. (913) 864-4481.

Research & computing facilities include: a dual-processor Honeywell DPS-3 system (GCOS), a graphics lab equipped with a PDP 11/55 (UNIX) and Vector General 3400 graphics display system, an Interdata 85 mini, an Interdata 7/16 mini, and an well equipped microcomputer laboratory. Computer science students may also have access to the chemistry physics computer network, the Remote Sensing Lab's image processiing system and numerous other minicomputers. In addition to the popular programming languages, the list below is available: APL, ATMS, B, C, LEX, LISP, QED, ROFF, LEX, QED, ROFF, SIMSCRIPT, YACC..etc.

There are 13 full-time faculty in the department. Positions are open at the assistant and associate professor ranks. Applicants should have competence in at least one of the following: artificial intelligence, computer architecture, computer graphics, database systems and languages, distributed computing and networking, methodology and foundations of programming, operating systems, simulation and modelling. Faculty and their research interests:

Chair: V L Wallace, (operating system, graphics, man machine interaction, numerical & system analysis). Z Bavel (automata, algebraic thr of semigroups, formal language, computers & music); W G Bulgren (simulation, operating systems, queueing thry, computnl statistics, performance evaluation); J W Grzymala-Busse (automata, algebraic thry of semigroups, Petri nets, complexity, formal languages); E J Schweppe (persnl computers, micros, computer commnctn, interactive systems, concurrent processes, architecture, info structure, prgmng languages); S Y Sedelow (computnl linguistics & discourse anlys, intllgnt system & AI, info anlys, arts & humanities applns, comptnl stylistics); W A Sedelow Jr (language analysis, info systems, ntwrks, human factors, applns of computers & social implctns, history of info science & computing technlgies, cybernetics)

R Hetherington (numerical analysis); G Slutzki (algrthms, complexity, formal languages, automata, combinatorics, graph thry); A Tang (math semantics, recursive functn thry, descrptv set thry)

A G Akritas (dsgn & analysis of algrthms, symbolic & algebraic comptns, history of math, operations resrch); A D Bethke (algrthms, AI, prgmng, methdlgy); T Kamimura (formal language thry, automata thry, thry of computation, prgmng languages)

Course Offerings: (generally 3 semester units)

100 Programming Short Course (1)	690 Special Topics (1-3)
101 System Usage (2)	692 Directed Reading (1-3)
200 intro to Computing	710 intro to Automata Theory
210 Applied Boolean Algebra	711 Applied Boolean Algebra
211 Discrete Structures	716 Formal Language Theory I
300 Basic Programming Structures	717 Formal Language Theory II
350 Age of the Computer	722 Mathematical Logic
400 Computer Systems & Concurrent Processes	724 Computability Theory
410 Intro to the Theory of Computing I	726 The Meta Theory of Prgmng Languages
497 Computational Social Science	730 Artifical Intelligence
498 Honors Research (1-2)	735 Automated Theorem Proving
Graduate	742 Hstry of Computing Tchnlgy & Info Science
510 Intro to the Theory of Computing II	744 Social Issues in Computer Science
520 Intermediate Mathematical Logic	745 Human Factors in Computer-Based Systems
600 Computers & Programming (4)	748 Cybernetics
602 Information Processing through COBOL	750 The Computer as Instrumentation for Rsrch
610 Discrete Structures	in the Humanities & Social Sciences
632 Pattern Recognition & Pattern Generation	753 Computational Linguistics
650 Fundamentals of Symbol Processing (4)	754 Computational Semantics
660 Data Structures	755 Computational Stylistics
662 Programming languages	757 Information Systems
665 Compiler Construction	760 Operating Systems I
670 Computer Organization	761 Operating Systems II
675 Microcomputer Systems & Applications	762 Programming Structures
680 Numerical Calculus	764 Analysis of Algorithms
681 Numerical Analysis I	765 Syntactic Analysis & Compilers
682 Numerical Analysis II	766 Database Management Systems

768	Systems Simulation	823	Recursive Function Theory
770	Computer System Design	824	Abstract Computational Complexity
772	Computer Graphics	830	Advanced Artificial Intelligence
775	Computer System Simulation & Evaluation	881	Numerical Soln of Nonlinear Operator Eq
778	Computer Networking	882	Numerical Solution of Ord Diff Eq
780	Numerical Analysis of Linear Systems	883	Numerical Solution of Part Diff Eq
781	Numerical Functional Analysis	885	numerical Functional Approximation
785	Optmztn Thr: A Computational Approach	887	Computational Statistics
790	Advanced Topics (1-3)	890	Graduate Topics (1-3)
795	Seminar (1-3)	895	Research Seminar (1-3)
797	Special Problems (1-3)	898	Master's Rsrch Report (1-6) Seminar (1-3)
805	Computing in Business (2)	899	Master's Thesis (1-6)
810	Theory of Automata	998	Post-Master's Research (1-6)
816	Automata-Based Computational Complexity	999	Doctoral Dissertation (1-10)

KENTUCKY

UNIVERSITY OF KENTUCKY
Lexington, KY 40506
(606) 258-9000

University of Kentucky's 700-acre campus supports a population of 23,000 students. It has a faculty student ratio of 1 to 15, and a library with over 1.8 million volumes.

The Department of Computer Science offers bachelor and master's degrees in computer science. Currently, 1850 and 95 students are enrolled in the two programs respectively. Prospective students should apply through the Admissions and Registrar's office by June 1 for the fall and October 15 for the spring.

There are 15 full-time members in the department. Faculty positions exist at the assistant professor rank. Background in any area of computer science will be considered.

Computer systems in use here include: an IBM 3083, a DEC 10, two PRIME 850, VAX 11/750, two PDP 11/23, Compu Pro 8/16, ten North Star Horizons, two Genesis 5-100, Apple II+s, two TRS Model I, two Atari 800, an Atari 400, and TRS 80 Color Computer. Operating systems used: VM/CMS, Tops 10, Primos, RSX-11, UNIX, CP/M-80, CP/M-86, MP/M-86, Apple DOS, TRS DOS. Future acquisition plans call for more 68000 and 16032 micros.

Course Offerings: (3 units unless noted)

101	Computer Science I	530	Computational Methods
102	Computer Science II	532	Finite Precision Arithmetic
150	Intro to Algorithmic Processes	537	Numerical Analysis I
221	First Course in Computer Sci for Eng (2)	538	Numerical Analysis II
235	Logic for Computer Science	540	Systems Simulation
240	Intro to Discrete Computer Mathmatics	541	Advanced Compiler Design I
250	Computer Organization	550	Introduction to Coding Theory
270	File Processing	560	Non-Numerical Applns of Computers
321	Intro to Numerical Methods	570	Operating Systems Design
340	Discrete Structures in Computer Science	576	Theoretical Aspects of Computing
370	Data Structures	580	Algorithm Design
395	Independent Work in Computer Science	585	Intermediate Topics in Computer Science
415	Graph Theory	605	Advanced Information Processing
416	Principles of Operations Research I	612	Indep Work in Computer Science (1-3)
420	Compilers for Algorithmic Languages	615	Computer Architecture & Microprogramming
440	Foundations of Computing	620	Numerical Approximation & Curve-Fitting
450	Fundamentals of Programming Languages	622	Numerical Linear Algebra
460	Immigration into Computer Science	630	Num Evaluation of Transcendental Functns
461	Minicomputers	631	Error Analysis and Certification
470	Systems Software	641	Advanced Compiler Design II
472	Seminar	650	Problem Seminar
505	Data Base Management Systems	655	Design of Programming Languages
510	Discrete Computer Mathematics I		

University of Louisville's 170-acre campus serves a population of 21,000 students. Operating on a semester system with two summer sessions, the university maintains a faculty student ratio of 1 to 12, and a library with 910,000 volumes.

The Department of Applied Math & Computer Science offers BS and MS degrees with specialization in Applied Math & Computer Science. Currently, there are 500 and 100 in the two degree programs respectively. Prospective students may apply through the department Chair. For more information on application deadline or financial aid, contact the Admissions Office at (502) 588-6531.

Computer systems in use include: DEC 1090, IBM 370/165, DEC PDP 11/34s, 11/44s, five DEC LSI 11/03s, plus many Apples and DEC micros. Operating system used here include TOPS 10, RSTS 11, and RSX.

There are 20 full-time members in the department. Faculty positions are open at all ranks. Current research interests of the faculty include: operating system design, compiler design, database management systems, distributed processing, performance evaluation of mathematical software, software engineering, microcomputer systems, architecture, program testing, large-scale energy models, optimization, numerical analysis, statistical analysis, control theory, and simulation of engineering applications.

Course Offerings: (generally 3 semester units)

AMCS
110 COBOL Programming
210 Advanced COBOL Programming
301 Algorithms,Computers & Programming
302 Information Structures
303 Use of Selected Pgmmng Languages (1)
304 PL/I Programming (1)
305 Assembly Language Programming (1)
310 Logic Design
335 Design of File Structures
402 Programming Languages
410 Introduction to Discrete Structures
411 Engineering Analog Computation (1)
412 Computer Interfacing
420 Design of Operating Systems
450 Real-Time Data Processing Systems
488 Appl Math & CS Co-op Internship III (2)
500 Special Topics in Computer Science (1-6)
501 Combinations & Graph Theory
504 Automata Theory
508 Numerical Analysis I
509 Numerical Analysis II
510 Computer Design
520 Hybrid Computation
525 Microcomputer Design
530 Design of Compilers
540 Computer Control

545 A I & Heuristic Programming
550 Software Engineering
608 Advanced Operating Systems
610 Advanced Logic Design
611 Computer Architecture
612 Computer Communications
619 Design & Analysis of Computer Alogarithms
620 Evaluation of Computer Systems
621 Simulation of Continuous Systems
622 Simulation of Discrete Systems
625 Advanced Compiler Theory
627 Image Processing & Pattern Recognition
628 Interactive Computer Graphics
635 Text Processing

DPT
110 Digital Computation (2)
210 Assembly Language Programming
231 Algorithms, Computers & Programming
232 Information Structures
250 Data Processing Project I
312 Discrete Structures
335 Data Base & File Systems
420 Operating Systems
450 Data Processing Project II

ECS
102 FORTRAN Programming (2)
200 Programming Languages (1)

LOUISIANA

LOUISIANA STATE UNIVERSITY
Baton Rouge, LA 70803
(504) 388-1686

LSU is a public university whose 300-acre campus at Baton Rouge serves a population of 29,000 students. Operating on a semester system with 9-week summer terms, the university has a faculty student ratio of 1 to 26, and a library with over a million volumes.

The Department of Computer Science offers BS in computer science, MS in system science and PhD in computer science. Current enrollments in these three programs are 400, 77 and 10 respectively. Prospective students should apply through the Department of Computer Science at LSU or call the department chair at (504) 388-1495 for more specific information.

Computing facilities at LSU include: IBM 3033, Data General Eclipse S/140, two PDP 11/23, DEC VAX 11/780, six Cromenco S-100 Z80-based micro systems. Operating systems in use: UNIX on the VAX, MVS on the 3033. Future acquisition plan includes a $1.5 million academic computer network.

There are 23 full-time members in the department. Faculty positions are open at all professorial ranks. The department is looking for a senior theoretician, and individuals with specialty in languages, artificial intelligence, operating systems, compilers, or distributed systems. Faculty and their research interests:

D A Buell (query formulatn & query prcssng, computnl number thry, factorization, primality testing, cryptographic applns); P P Chen (entity-relationship model & applns in systems analysis & data mngmnt); G R Cross (pattern recogntn, image prcssng, AI, exploratory data analysis, computer performance); C M Hanchey (computer science education); T Y Hou (prgmng languages, sequential concurrent control structures used to synchronize parallel processes).

S S Iyengar (simulation modeling, data structures, OR, algrthms); J B Jones (numerical analysis, algrthms); L P Jones (formal languages, automata, formal languages, applied math); D H Kraft (modeling of info storage & retrieval systems, applns of OR methods towards info systems analysis & design); W G Rudd (simulation of agricultural ecosystems, assembly language prgmng); J M Tyler (operating system, numerical analysis); L J Waguespack Jr (system archctr, dsgn of secure system, sftwr engnrng, DBMS, very high level languages).

Course Offerings:

4100	Intro Operating Systems & File Mngmnt	7402	Database Management Systems
4101	Programming Languages	7444	Knowledge Engineering
4103	Operating Systems	7481	Information Retrieval Systems
4304	System Programming	7500	System Modeling & Simulation
4310	Communications in Computing	7560	Computational Methods
4321	Minicomputers	7700	Special Topics in Computer Science
4330	Programming Methodology	7799	Reading in Computer Science
4351	Compiler Construction	9000	CS Dissertation Research
4354	Computer Graphics		
4355	Appl Intrctv Graphics CAD		Relevant ECE Courses
4360	Sequential Machines	4130	Graph Theory
4362	Adv Numerical Mthds & FORTRAN	4700	Special Topics Computer Engineering
4365	System Reprsntatn & Basic Cybernetics	4730	Structr & Dsgn of Digital Computers
4368	Comptatnl Tchnqs in Linear Prgrmng	4770	Real Time Computing Systems
4402	Intro to Database Mngmnt Systems	4790	Strctr of Computations & Computers
4444	AI & Pattern Recognition	7640	Info Thry, Coding & Cryptography
4890	Intro to Theory of Computing	7650	Computer Communication
7001	Computing Principles I	7700	Adv Topics in Computer Engineering
7002	Computing Principles II	7710	Adv Digital Logic
7030	Computer-Based Info System analysis	7720	Digital Systems Architecture
7080	Computer Organization	7730	Digital Image Analysis
7135	Software Systems Development	7740	Image Analysis
7200	Thry of Computing I	7750	Machine Recgntn of Patterns
7201	Thry of Computing II	7760	Reliable Dsgn of Digital Systems
7300	Algrthm Design & Analysis	7790	Strctr of Computatns & Computers II

UNIVERSITY OF SOUTHWESTERN
LOUISIANA, Lafayette, LA 70504
(318) 264-6000

The University of Southwestern Louisiana has over 125,000 students. Located 140 miles west of New Orleans, Lafayette is the hub city of the French speaking Louisiana, offering a large number of cultural and recreational activities. Operating on semester system with 9-week summer sessions, the university has a faculty ratio of 1 to 21, and a library with half a million volumes.

The Department of Computer Science offers bachelor, master, and PhD degrees in computer science. Currently, there are 1012, 113 and 46 students enrolled in these three programs respectively. Undergraduates should apply through the Admissions Office 30 days before semester begins, while graduate students through the Graduate School; deadlines May 1 and Nov 1 for the Fall and Spring semesters.

Research and computing facilities available here include: Honeywell 3-CPU HIS 68/60 Multics with 8 megabyte internal memory, two VAX 11/780 , four TI 990/12, two PDP 11, five color graphics system, and several Intel Development Systems (micros).

There are 15 full-time members in the department. Faculty positions exist at all ranks. Background in operating systems, DBMS, programming languages, and performance measurement would be of great interest to the department. Faculty and their interests:

T R N Rao (computer system orgnztns, fault-tolerant computers); B R Shriver (computer systems orgnztns, microprgmng, operating systems, dataflow archtctrs & languages); T M Walker (prgrmng languages, simulation, operating systems).

W D Diminick (DBMS, info storage & retrieval systems, software monitoring, performance evaluation, interactive graphics); W R Edwards (thry of computation, AI) P Carr (prgmng languages, sftwr engnrng); T R Cousins (DBMS, MIS); C J T Linn (memory mangmnt, operating systems, multiprcssrs); K M Kavi (cmptr systems orgnztn, fault-tolerant systems); C J T Linn (memory mangmnt, opeating systems, multiprcssrs); J L Linn (compiling, operating systems, architecture, formal languages); E Lisboa (data systems, distrbtd data base systems); J E Urban (sftwr engnrng, specification languages, sftwr reliability, prgrmng languages)

Course Offerings:

150 Intro to Computing for Majors	515 Prin of Computer Graphics
151 Honors Intro to Computer Science	516 Cryptography & Data Security
208 Intro Fortran Programming for Engineers	530 Prin of Computer Systems Organization
250 PL/Programming I	532 Computer Arithmatic
251 PL/Programming II	533 Distributed Computing Systems
300 Computers & Modern Society	540 Prin of the Theory of Computation
301 Computing for the Natural Sciences I	541 Automata Theory
302 Computing for the Natural Sciences II	542 Formal Languages
303 Computing for the Social Sciences I	543 Complexity Theory
304 Computing for the Social Sciences II	550 Prin of Programming Systems & Languages
305 Computing for Commercial Applications I	551 Compiler Design
306 Computing for Commercial Applications II	552 Real-Time Software System
307 Buisness Data Processing	553 Software Methodology
351 Assembler Programming	555 Prin of Operating Systems
352 Scientific Programming	560 Prin of Computer-Based Information Systems
353 Commercial Programming	561 Information Storage & Retrieval
360 Data Structure Concepts	562 Data Base Management Systems
400 Intro to Computer Science for Educators	563 Computer Facility Operations
405 Fundamental Prncple of Computer Prgmmng	590 Special Project (1-6)
410 Social & Legal Implications of Computers	591 Scholarly Paper (1-3)
411 Intro to Simulation	599 Thesis Research & Thesis (1-6)
415 Intro to Computer Graphics	614 Fault-Tolerant Computing
418 Nonnumeric Programming	619 Adv Topics in Computer Science
430 Intro to Computer Architecture	630 Adv Computer Structure
431 Minicomputer Systems	639 Adv Topics in Computer Architecture
440 Intro to the Theory of Computation	641 Adv Automata Theory
450 Intro to Programming Languages	642 Adv Formal Languages
451 Intro to Compiler Systems	643 Recursive Function Theory
453 Intro to Software Methodology	649 Adv Topics in the Theory of Computation
455 Intro to Operating Systems	650 Language Processing for Distrib Systems
460 Intro to Computer Information Systems	651 Adv Compiler Design
461 Intermediate Computer Info Systems	653 Adv Software Methodology
497 Special Projects	655 Adv Operating Systems
498 Special Projects	659 Adv Topics in Computer Software Systems
511 Prin of Simulation	660 Evaluation & Admnstrtn of Info Systems
512 Prin of Artificial Intelligence	662 Info Systems for Minicomputers & Ntwrk
513 Prin of Computer Communications & Networks	669 Adv Topics in Computer Info Systems
514 Prin of Information Theory & Coding	

UNIVERSITY OF NEW ORLEANS
New Orleans, LA 70148
(504) 286-6000

University of New Orlean's is a public institution that supports a population of 16,000 students with a faculty student ratio of 1 to 23, and a library with 1 million titles.

An undergraduate degree in computer science is offered here with a current enrollment of 300 students. Prospective students should apply through the Office of Admissions.

There are 7 full-time faculty members in the department. Faculty openings exist at all ranks. Background in operating systems, networks, data communicatins, or data base systems would be most desirable.

Computer systems in use: DEC 10, VAX 11/780, PDP 11s, LSI 11s, Zenith Z-100s and many other microcomputers. Operating systems available: TOPS 10, VMS, RT-11, and RSX-11. Future acquisition plan calls for more VAX 11/780s and VAX 11/750s.

Course Offerings: (generally 3 semester units)

1060	Intro to Programming I	4271	Adv Math Programming
1069	Intro to Programming II	4302	Computer Architecture
2120	Structures of Algorithms	4310	Minicomputer & Microcomputer Systems
2125	Data Structures	4311	Computers Ntwrks & Telecommunications
2271	Mathematical Programming	4401	Principles of Operating Systems I
2450	Machine Strctr & Assembly Lang Prgrmng	4402	Principles of Operating Systems II
2460	System Programming Concepts	4501	Programming Language & Structures
2601	Data Processng & File Management	4502	Semantics of Prgrmng Languages
3090	Undergraduate Seminar	4601	Data Base Management Systems
3301	Computer Organization	4611	Systems Analysis & Sftwr Dsgn
4097	Problems in Computer Science	4750	Adv Prgrmng for Social & Life Sciences
4101	Analysis of Algorithms	4920	Computers in Scientific Research
4102	Intro to Thry of Computation	4990	Special Topics in Computer Science
4103	Formal Language & Automata	6750	Computer Applications in Education

MAINE

UNIVERSITY OF SOUTHERN MAINE
Portland, Maine 04103
(207) 780-4141

The University of Southern Maine is a public institution serving 8,500 students with a faculty student ratio of 1 to 18, and a library with half a million volumes.

A bachelor and a master degree programs are offered by the Department of Mathematics and Computer Science, in which 400 and 12 students are currently enrolled. There are five full-time members in the department. Faculty positions exist at the assistant professor rank. Background in all area of computer science, except numerical analysis, will be considered. Undergraduates should apply through the Admissions Office, while graduates through the Department; deadlines: Oct 1 for the Spring and Mar 1 for the Fall Semesters.

Computing facilities here include an IBM 4341, VAX 11/750, several LSI-11s, PDP 11/24, IBM 4331, 16 Apple+s, 5 Apple IIe's, 14 Commodore 64s, 1 Commodore Super Pet, 11 IBM PCs, 1 Osborne I, and 62 TI 99/4As. The BITNET is accessible.

Course Offerings:

100 Intro to Computer Science
160 Intro to Programming: FORTRAN
161 Algorithms in Programming
230 Programming in COBOL and RPG
234 Computer Prgrmmng for Elementary Teachers
240 Programming in PL/1
250 Intro to Computer Systems
280 Discrete Structure
350 Systems Programming
355 Computer Architecture
358 Data Structures
360 Concepts of Higher Level Prgmmng Languages
370 Topics in Computer Science
374 Numerical Analysis I
375 Numerical Analysis II
380 Intro to Theory of Computing

450 Operating Systems
458 Advanced Data Structures
469 Intro to Compiler Construction
472 Artificial Intelligence
497 Independent Study in Computer Science
Graduate
550 Advanced Operating Systems
552 Computer Ntwrk & Distributed Processing
555 Advanced Computer Architecture
558 Database Management
565 Software Design & Development
569 Struct of Assmblr, Intrprtrs, & Compilers
570 Seminar: Adv Topics in Computer Science
580 Theory of Computation
582 Design & Analysis of Algorithms

MARYLAND

JOHN'S HOPKINS UNIVERSITY
Baltimore, MD 21218
(301) 338-8171

John's Hopkins is a private university with 3,200 students, a faculty student rate of 1 to 10 and a library with over two million volumes.

The Department of Electrical Engineering & Computer Science offers BES, BA, MSE, and PhD programs. Currently, there are 225, 20 and 40 students enrolled in the two bachelors, master and 'PhD programs respectively. Prospective students should apply through the Admissions Office; deadlines: Jan 1 for freshman and Mar 1 for graduate students.

The department maintains modern, well-equipped instructional laboratories, a machine shop, darkroom, and an instrument calibration and repair center. Computing facilities include a VAX 11/780 running VMS, two VAX 11/750s running UNIX, PDP 11/45, and several Intel 8085 and Mot 6800-based micros. The IBM 4341 in the Homewood Computer Center is available. The department's Graphics Lab houses a variety of devices, including color and high-resolution monochrome graphics Tektronix terminals, plotters, and a Versatec hard-copy unit. Tektronix graphics terminals, plotters and Versatec hard copy unit.

Computer science research activities include: analysis of algorithms, artificial intelligence, computational complexity, computer vision and computer graphics. Computer engineering research includes work on computer structures with emphasis on mini-micro processors, parallel & distributed processing, fault-tolerant computing, and interconnection networks. Computer science faculty in the department and their interests:

F Davidson (quantum optics, optical coherence, optical commnctns); W C Gore (info thry, error-correcting codes, communctn systems); W H Huggins (circuit & system thry, signal represntatn, computers); S R Kosaraju (applied complexity thry, dsgn of algrthms, parallel prcssng, VLSI thry); G M Masson (digital system thry, fault tolerant computing, interconnection networks); G G L Meyer (thry of iterative algrthms, comptnl methods, fault tolerant computing); V D VandeLinde (info & control processes); R Melville (analysis & applns of algrthms, data structures); J O'Rourke (computer vision, graphics, comptnl geometry); M J Post (comptnl geometry, database security).

Associated faculty: D Entwisle (sociology, social resrch, computers); G E Mitzel (systems & communications); S G Tolchin (data base systems & computer networks); G V Trunk (Pttrn recgntn, detection & estimation).

Course: (a partial listing of department offerings)

8 Intro to Computer Programming	327 Compiler Theory & Design
37 Intro to Computers (Minicomputers)	337 Intro to Artificial Intelligence
38 Intro to Operating Systems	342 Software Tools
42 Digital System Fundamentals	350 Computer Ntwrk Architectures & Protocols
45 E E & Computer Science Laboratory	372 Computer Organization
46 E E & Computer Science Laboratory	373 Faulty Analysis
49 Microprocessor Laboratory	381 Microwaves
50 Advanced Microprocessor Laboratory	611 Graduate Seminar Artificial Intelligence
72 Intro to Computational Models	637 Seminar VLSI Theory
307 Design & Analysis of Algorithms	638 Seminar VLSI Theory
308 Design & Analysis of Algorithms	651 Seminar Documnt & Txt Prcssng Using Cmptrs
311 Lasers & Optical Information Processing	675 Computer Interconnection Structures
312 Lasers & Optical Information Processing	689 Coding Theory
315 Systems	690 Coding Theory
319 Theory of Iterative Algorithms	695 Seminar in Coding Theory
320 Theory of Iterative Algorithms	696 Seminar in Coding Theory
322 Data Base Systems	

UNIVERSITY OF MARYLAND
College Park, MD 20742
(301) 454-5550

University of Maryland's 300-acre campus supports a student population of 28,000 with a faculty student ratio of 1 to 16, and a library with 1.6 million volumes.

The Department of Computer Science offers bachelor, master and PhD programs in computer science. Currently, there are 1800, 150 and 75 students enrolled in them respectively. Prospective student should apply through the Admissions Office; deadline Feb 1 for graduate and April 30 for undergraduates.

Computer systems in use include: Univac 1100/82, IBM 4341, VAX 11/780, PDP 11s plus several microcomputers. Operating systems available include VM/CMS and UNIX. CSNET is accessible. Future plan calls for more VAX 11/780 and 11/750s.

There are 30 full-time members. Several faculty positions exist at the assistant professor ranks. However, qualified individuals may be considered for higher ranks. Background in any area of computer science will be considered. Faculty and their interests:

A K Agrawala (dsgn & evaluation of computer systems, ntwrks); W F Atchison (CS education, computability thry); V R Basili (softwr engnrng, analysis of process & product); Y Chu (archtctr, microprgmng, sftwr engnrng, microprcssrs); H P Edmundson (thry of computng, math and comptnl linguistics); L Kanal (machine intllgnce, pttrn recgntn, computer vision); H D Mills (sftwr engnrng); J Minker (AI, knwldg-based systems, database thry); A Rosenfeld (automation, computer vision, robotics); G W Stewart (numerical analysis); R T Yeh (sftwr engnrng).

R H Austing (CS education); L Davis (image prcssng, AI, pttrn recgntn); J D Gannon (prgmng language, sftwr engnrng); R G Hamlet (computability, prgmng language thry, sftwr engnrng); D O'Leary (numerical analysis); H Samet (code optmztn, list prcssng tchnques); B Shneiderman (human factors, interactive systems); S Tripathi (operating systems, performance evaluation); M V Zelkowitz (compiler & language dsgn, program measrmnt, sftwr engnrng).

85

M Elsanadidi (computer ntwrks, modeling & analysis); R Fontecella (numerical analysis); B Jacobs (database mangmnt, recursion thry, math logic); D Nau (AI, thry of computing); D Perlis (AI, thry of computing); I V Ramankrishnan (systems, theory); J Reggia (expert systems, cognitive modeling, computnl neurolinguistics); G Ricart (computer systems); N Roussopolous (database systems, dsgn methdlgy, data semantics & evolution); A U Shankar (performance evaluatn, verifctn, protocols); C Smith (thry of computation, inductive inference); M Weiser (sftwr engnrng, prgrmng methdlgy, cognitive issues).

Course Offerings:

103 Intro to Computing for Non-Majors
110 Introductory Computer Programming (4)
112 Computer Science I (4)
120 Intermediate Computer Programming (4)
122 Computer Science II (4)
211 Assembly Language Programming
220 Intro to File Processing
250 Intro to Discrete Structures
311 Computer Organization
330 Organization of Programming Languages
386 Independent Work Study: Field Work (1)
387 Independent Work Study: Analysis (2)
390 Honors Paper
400 Intro to Computer Languages & Systems
411 Computer Systems Architecture
412 Operating Systems
415 Systems Programming
420 Data Structures
424 Database Design
426 Image Processing
430 Theory of Language Translation
432 Compiler Writing
434 Human Factors in Computer & Info Systems
435 Software Design & Development
450 Elementary Logic & Algorithms
451 Design & Analysis of Computer Algorithms
452 Elementary Theory of Computation
455 Elementary Formal Language Theory
460 Computational Methods
470 Numerical Mathematics: Analysis

471 Numerical Mathematics: Linear Algebra
475 Combinatorics & Graph Theory
477 Optimization
498 Special Problems in Computer Science (1-3)
612 Computer Systems Theory
620 Prblm Solving Meth in A I
630 Theory of Programming Languages
640 Computability & Automata
720 Information Retrieval
723 Computational Linguistics
725 Mathematical Linguistics
730 Artificial Intelligence
733 Computer Prcssng of Pictorial Information
737 Topics in Information Science
740 Automata Theory
745 Theory of Formal Languages
750 Theory of Computability
770 Adv Numerical Linear Algebra
772 Numerical Solution of Nonlinear Equations
782 Modeling & Simulation of Physical Systems
798 Graduate Seminar in Computer Science (1-3)
799 Thesis Research
818 Adv Topics in Computer Systems (1-3)
828 Adv Topics in Information Processing (1-3)
838 Adv Topics in Programming Languages (1-3)
840 Adv Automata Theory
858 Theory of Computing (1-3)
878 Adv Topics in Numerical Methods (1-3)
899 Dissertation Research

TOWSON STATE UNIVERSITY
Towson, MD 21204
(301) 321-2112

Towson State is a public university whose 325-acre campus supports a population of 16,000 students with a faculty student ratio of 1 to 19, and a library with 374,000 volumes.

A bachelor's degree in computer science is offered by the Department of Mathematics and Computer Science. Currently, there are 400 students and 10 full-time faculty members in the program. Faculty openings exist at the assistant professor rank. Background in graphics, artificial intelligence, and operating systems would be most desirable.

Computer systems in use include a VAX 11/780 (VMS), Apples, TRS 80s, Commodore 64s, Compupolor. The network Maryland State College Information Center (MUCIC) is accessible through Decnet. Future plan calls for upgrading the VAX 11/780 to an 11/782.

Apply through the Registrar's Office. For more information, call the Department Office at (301) 321-2633 or 321-3091.

Course Offerings:

101 Computers and Society
201 Intro to Information Systems
212 Intro to Business Programming
235 Fundamentals of Computing
236 Structured Programming
280 Assembly Language Programming
306 Structured Programming for the Sciences
335 Advanced Business Programming
336 Data Structures and Sorting Techniques
338 Computer Organization
339 Operating Systems Principles
355 Survey of Programming Languages
367 Discrete Structures
383 Design and Analysis of Algorithms
397 Practicum in Computer Science

411 Systems and Design
415 Implementation of Programming Languages
417 Intro of the Theory of Computing
431 Selected Topics in Computer Science
437 File and Data Structures
441 Computer Systems Performance Evaluation
457 Database Management Systems
461 Artificial Intelligence
471 Computer Graphics
499 Honors Thesis in Computer Science
501 Computers in Secondary Education
507 Computers in Education
511 Computer Simulation
513 Hardware and Software in Microcomputers

MASSACHUSETTS

BOSTON UNIVERSITY
Boston, MA 02215
(617) 353-2000

Boston University is a private institution that supports a population of 28,500 students, with a faculty student ratio of 1 to 14, and a library with 1.4 million titles. The Boston location offers a rich opportunity for employment or research in the nearby high technology industry.

In January 1983, the Computer Science Division of the Mathematics Department became a department. Experiencing rapid growth, the department is slated to move into the university's new Science & Engineering Center in Spring 1984. The department offers BA, MA and PhD in computer science. Currently, there are 25 enrolled in the BA/MA program, and 6 in the MA/PhD program.

Eleven full-time faculty members serve the department. Strong in theoretical concepts of computer science, recent hiring has added strength in artificial intelligence and databases. Research interests of the faculty include: automata theory, artificial intelligence, complexity theory, database systems, dynamic logic, programming methodologies, operating systems, software engineering, graphics and cryptography.

The department seeks faculty at the assistant or associate professor level. Individuals in core computer science areas or MIS development will be of special interest to the department.

Computing facilities include an IBM 3081, VAX, PDP 11/34, PDP 20/60, plus personal computers and interactive graphics systems.

Course Offerings:

CS 119 Intro to Computers
   120 Computer Languages
   191 Intro to Computer Science I
   192 Intro to Computer Science II
   193 Intensive Intro to Computer Science
   291 Assembler Language
MA 293 Discrete Mathematics I
MA 294 Discrete Mathematics II
   391 Non-numeric Languages
   392 Concepts of Programming Languages
   393 Intro to Computer Graphics
   394 Intro to Formal Languages
   395 Analysis of Algorithms
   396 Computability and Complexity
   401 Senior Distinction Project I
   402 Senior Distinction Project II

   495 Topics in Computer Science
   496 Advanced Assembler Language
   497 Computer Organization
Graduate
MA 531 Intro to Logic and Computer Science
   532 Foundations of Mathematics
   574 Intro to Data Base
   577 Automata Theory and Formal Languages
   578 Cryptography and Cryptanalysis
   579 Systemms Software
   590 Computer Creativity
   591 Compiler Design Theory
   592 Operating Systems
   593 Natural Language Processing
   594 Artificial Intelligence
   596 Computer Science Consulting Seminar

597	Software Engineering	796	Database Systems
598	Data Communications	798	Interactive Computer Graphics
691	Computers in Scientific Research	799	Compiler Construction
792	Advanced Topics in Computer Science	892	Computer Science Seminar (3,3)
793	Advanced Programming Languages	996	Directed Study in Computer Science
795	Advanced Operating Systems Theory		

HARVARD UNIVERSITY
Cambridge, MA 02138
(617) 495-1551

Harvard is a private university established in 1636. Operating on a semester basis with summer sessions, the university has a total of 16,000 students, a faculty student ratio of 1 to 10, and a library with over 10 million volumes.

The Division of Applied Sciences offers bachelor, master and PhD programs in computer science. Currently, there are 125, 3 and 23 students enrolled in these programs respectively. Courses offered in other departments of the Faculty of Arts and Sciences are open to graduate students in the Division without cross-registration. In addition to courses at Harvard, a student may enroll in courses offered at the Massachusetts Institute of Technology if they do not duplicate the material covered in Harvard Courses. Prospective undergraduate students are suggested to apply through the Admissions Office by November 15, deadline December 1. Graduate students should apply through the Graduate School of Arts and Sciences, deadline December 31. For more information on admission and financial aids, contact the Academic Office, Pierce hall 212, Harvard University; Phone (617) 495-2833.

Harvard maintains two PDP 11/70s, two VAX 11/750s, two VAX 11/780s; the department has a VAX 11/780 and a network of Apollo high performance micros. Within the auspices of the Graduate School of Arts and Sciences, the Center for Research in Computing Technology was organized to teach and conduct research in computer science, and to provide expertise in computer science to the university community. The Center has also established the Harvard Fund for Information Science to provide seed money for innovative projects. For more information, call the Center Director's Office at (617) 495-4117.

In addition, Harvard's Graduate School of Design operates the Laboratory for Computer Graphics and Spatial Analysis. For more information on the Lab, call (617) 495-2526.

Faculty members in the Division of Applied Sciences who have research interest in computer related topics include: T C Bartee (cmptr ntwrks; microprcssrs, data base mangmnt systems); W H Bossert (cmptr eductn, interactive cmptr, video disk technlgy); T E Cheatham (extensible languages, prgrm develpmnt & maintenance envrnmnts, symbolic evaluation of prgrms & prgrm optmztn); U O Gagliardi (archtctr issues of geographically & locally distrbtd computing systems); Y C Ho (info structr & incentive decision prblms, discrete event dynamical systems & queueing thry).

H J Komorowski (PROLOG prgrmng language for rapid prototyping); H R Lewis (logic, decision prblms, complexity, parallel & probabilistic computatn, cmptr modelling in secondary school physics eductn); M O Rabin (complexity of computatns, randomizing algrthms, concurrent computatns, transactn protection protocols, decidability); L G Valiant (comptatnl complexity thry, distrbtd & parallel computatn).

Junior or senior faculty positions in computer science exist. Applicants with research

89

interests in computer systems or experimental computer science would be very desirable.

Course Offerings:

10	Intro to Programming	181	Intro to Knowledge Based Systems
11	Computers, Algorithms and Programs	Graduate	
121	Intro Formal Systems and Computation	207r	Intro to the Theory of Computation
124	Data Structures and Algorithms	224r	The Complexity of Computations
137	Information Theory and Data Processing	226r	Efficient Algorithms
141	Intro to Digital Computers	228	Intro to Formal Systems
150	Intro to Computer Programming	252r	Advanced Programming Languages
152	Intro to Programming Languages	254r	Programming Methodologies
161	Operating Systems Architecture	256r	Seminar: Software Engineering
163	Theory and Construction of Compilers	265r	Theory of Database Management
165	Database Management Systems	270	Technology of Logic Programming
175	Intro to Computer Graphics	281	Topics in Machine Intelligence
180	Intro to Artificial Intelligence		

MASSACHUSETTS INSTITUTE OF TECHNOLOGY
Cambridge, MA 02139
(617) 253-4791

MIT's 135-acre campus is close to the center of a large metropolitan area that contains more than 50 schools including Harvard, Radcliffe, Boston University, Brandeis...etc. The concentration of academic, cultural, and intellectual activities is one of the largest in the country. The school has a student population of 9,000, a faculty student ratio of 1 to 4, a library with holdings of 1.9 million volumes, and more than 19,000 journals and periodicals.

The Department of Electrical Engineering & Computer Science (EECS) offers BS in Computer Science & Engineering, MS in EE & CS, the degree of Electrical Engineer (more course work than MS), PhD, and Doctor of Science. Undergraduates should apply through the Admissions Office; deadlines: November 1 for early action; January 1 for regular application. For more specific information: write or call EECS Undergraduate Office, (617) 253-7329. Graduate students may request application forms and financial aid from the Director of Admissions, or from the Graduate Office, Dept of EECS. All prescribed forms must be completed by January 14. A brochure on Research and Graduate Study in EE & CS may be obtained from the Graduate Office, Dept EECS, Room 38-444, MIT, (617) 253-4605.

Graduate study in computer science is centered in the EECS department, where about 30 faculty members actively pursue research in many areas of computer science, supported by professional staffs and students, plus computers whose range and capacity are unmatched at most of other American universities. Most of the research in the Department is carried out in the following labs:

1 Artificial Intelligence Lab.

The A I Lab consists of 140 members including 12 faculty members, 5 academic staff, 50 research and support staff, and 60 graduate students conducting research activities funded by the DARPA, System Development Foundation, Office of Naval

Research, Air Force Office of Sponsored Research, NSF, Atari, DEC, IBM, and Martin Marietta. Current research includes work on computer robotics and vision, expert systems for electronic design, music cognition, language and learning, intelligent supercomputing, common-sense reasoning, intelligent apprentices, natural language understanding and computer architecture. The Lab's facilities include a large 2060 system and 25 LISP Machines, a new Gaussian convolver and a TV frame memory that feature extraordinary flexibility and speed, a Micro-net based on the INTEL 8031 now being used in a contro system for a rectilinear arem, a linear-array-based stereo camera, a laser depth finder, a control system for stepping motors, and a Lisp-Machine control system for the Unimation Puma 600 robot arm. For more information on the Lab, contact Artificial Intelligence Laboratory at 545 Technology Square, MIT.

2 Lab for Computer Science.

The Lab consists of 300 members, mostly from EECS, organized into 16 groups to study: (1) knowledge based systems that include clinical decision making, mathlab, message passing semantics groups; (2) machines, languages and systems that include structure, communications, functional languages and architecture, information mechanics, programming methodology, real time systems, distributed systems groups; (3) theoretical foundations in computer science that include theory of computation and VLSI design tool groups; (4) computers and people that include educational computing, office automation, programming technology and societal implications groups. The Lab uses over 100 computers interconnected through local area networks and to other research institutions through the ARPANet. These include DEC 2060s, PDP 10s, DEC 1090s, VAX 11/780s, VAX 11/750s, ALTOs, NUs, Apollo Domains, LISPs, IBM PCs, Apples, and numerous large personal computers. For more information, contact the Lab at (617) 253-2145.

In addition, there are (3) Lab for Information and Decision Systems, which studies communication science & systems, systems and control science, computation and information systems; (4) VLSI Research, which studies submicron structures, semiconductor materials and devices, VLSI design automation, and highly parallel architecture; (5) Research Lab of Electronics, which studies, among other topics, audio signal processing, image processing, pattern recognition, small computers and their languages, programming, digital system engineering, speech, hearing linguistics, sensory aids; and (6) Lincoln Lab, which provides unusual opportunities for electrical engineering research in computer systems, digital signal processing, solid state devices, air traffic control, optical communications, lasers...etc.

Research interests of the EECS faculty members are divided into six broad areas. Faculty members in Area II (computer science) and Area III (electronics, computers and systems): H Abelson (complexity of VLSI & distrbtd cmptr educatn); R B Adler (VLSI technology & device modeling); J Allen (natural language procssng, archtctr, dsgn of custom ICs, CAD tools); Arvind (multiple processor archtctr, functional prgmng languages, distrbtd systems); A B Baggeroer (acoustics, signal prcssng, array prcssng, oceanogaphic data systems); D P Bertsekas (computer ntwrk communctn, distrbtd algrthms, optmztn).

R C Berwick (natural language prcssng, language acquisition & parsing, AI, learning including inductive interence, complexity analysis); F J Corbato (operating systems, archtctr, ntwrks & user interfaces); R Davis (AI, expert systems, hrdwr trouble shooting, distribtd prblm solvng); J B Dennis (language dsgn, system orgnztn, data driven computer systems); M L Dertouzos (personal computers, distrbtd systems, graphics); D J Edell (microelectronics & fabrication technlgy); P Elias (info thry applied to data prcssng prblms); R M Fano (educatnl computing); E Fredkin (physics of computatn, conservative logic, info mechanics)

R G Gallager (data commnctn ntwrks, distrbtd algrthms, info thry); D K Gifford (large scale systems, languages & semantics, archtctr & hardwr dsgn); L A Glasser (IC archtctr & implmntn, CAD, ultra high-speed optical & electronics devices); S Goldwasser (encryption, cryptography, operating systems, complexity thry, VLSI dsgn, graph algrthms); L A Gould (control dsgn algrthms & softwr for micro-controlled systems); J V Guttag (appln of formal spec to prgm devlpmnt, term rewriting systems, prgmng languages); R H Halstead (systems & languages for centrlzd & distrbtd comptng, architctr for multiprcssr systems, VLSI archtctrs & dsgn tools); M Hammer (office automation, database mangmnt, MIS); F C Hennie (thry computn & algrthms, automata, relatnl database applns).

C E Hewitt (procedural embedding of knwldg, concurrent comptatn, proving properties of prcdures, knwldg-based systems, mssge passing semntcs, elctrnc office systems); B K P Horn (machine vision, adv automatn, manuipulation, visual percptn, reprsntn of objects & space, robotics); J G Kassakian (energy conversion & microprcssr controls); J L Kirtley (computer control of energy systems, local area ntwrks); J H Lang (digital & distrbtd control systems, special-purpose digital control prcssrs, appln to rotating machines & flexible structures); F F Lee (data acquisition & real time systems).

C E Leiserson (VLSI thry, algrthms, systolic computatn, graph thry); J C R Licklider (graphical prgmng, computer commnctns, info policy); J S Lim (image prcssng, speech prcssng, thry of digital signal prcssng); B H Liskov (prgmng mthdlgy, prgmng languages, distrbtd systems); T Lozano-Perez (robotics, algrthms spatial reasoning, reprsntn of objects & space, computnl geometry, AI); N Lynch (thry of distrbtd computing, formal models, algrthms dsgn, complexity, verifictn, distrbtd data mangmnt, synchrnztn, resource allocation, reliability, complexity thry); R G Mark (clinical applns of instrmntn & data procssng, real time arrhythmia analysis, cardiovascular physiology).

A R Meyer (logic of prgrms, semantics, complexity, combntrl algrthms, automata, recursive fnctns, decision prcdures in logic); S Micali (randomness, cryptography computatnl number thry, combntrl optmztn & graphy thry); M L Minsky (AI, children's thinking & education, robotics & machine vision, reprsntn of knwldg, strctr of personality, natural language, musical concepts); J Moses (algebraic manipulation, knwldge-based systems for home computers); B R Musicus (algrthms for stochastic estimation & digital signal prcssng, VLSI archtctr for signal prcssng, system dsgn); R S Patil (AI, modeling behavior of experts in clinical medicine, LSI circuits, dsgn building, knwldge-based tools for hrdwr dsgn spec & analysis). P Penfield Jr (IC dsgn automation, computer-aided circuit dsgn & analysis, APL language extensions); D P Reed (engnrng of sftwr systems, decntrlzd systems, simplified devlpmnt of complex softwr systems, data commnctns ntwrks, adv personal cmptrs).

J F Reintjes (applns, info storage & retrieval systems, wide-band commnctns); R L Rivest (cryptography, complexity, algrthms, VLSI dsgn aids, VLSI routing & placement algrthms, combinatorics, number theoretic algrthms); J H Saltzer (local data commctn ntwrks, coordination of parallel activities with recovery from failure); S D Senturia (integrated sensor tchnlgy & applns, properties of polyimides and of thin dielectrics for VLSI); J H Shapiro (optical commnctns for local area ntwrks); W M Siebert (appln of communication & systems thry to physiological systems); A C Smith (transport in semiconductor devices, quantum & statistical limitations on device size).

H I Smith (fabrication of submicron strctrs & devices, microlithography, microscopy, X-ray optics, semiconductor thin films for microelectronic devices); C G Sodini (MOS device physics, analog circuits); H A Spang (control system dsgn, robotics); D H Staelin (signal prcssng, remote sensing from satellites, video bandwidth compression & image prcssng); K N Stevens (speech communication, acoustics of speech production, perception, physiology); G J Sussman (AI, learning, prblm solvind & prgrmng, computatnl performance models for intelligent behavior); P Szolovits (applns of AI technqs to medical decision making, effective reprsntatn of knwldge & natural languages).

R R Tenney (distrbtd control of physical systems, distrbtd prblm solviig, modelling knwldge & info transfer, applns to power systems, command & control, robotics); R D

Thornton (motors & motor control systems, computatnl systems for electronic circuits & machines, integrated machines); D E Troxel (applns of digital systems, image prcssng, graphics); J Weizenbaum (social implctns of computers, teaching of computatn, computer counterculture); M V Wilkes (archtctr, relation between power, size and speed, capabilities & their relation to prgrmng languages).

A S Willsky (signal procssng, spatially distrbtd random data, aggregatn & hierarchical mthds for large-scale systems); P H Winston (AI, learning); J Wyatt (analog behavior of digital IC); R E Zippel (LSI dsgn & dsgn tools, modeling of expert dsgn, archtctrs for distrbtd prcssng, algebraic manipulation, knwldg based systems, AI); V W Zue (speech prcssng, recgnitn, analysis & synthesis, speech communctn, acoustic characterization of continuous speech, speech training aids for the deaf, lexical access).

Course Offerings:

Courses offered by EECS dept:
(a Partial Listing)
001 Structure & Intrprtatn of Cmptr Prgms
004 Computation Structures
032 Computation Structures
033 Computer Systems Engineering
034 Artificial Intelligence
035 Computer Language Engineering
036 Problem-Solving Paradigms
045 Cmputablty Automata & Formal Languages
046 Intro to Algorithms
074 Intro to telecommunications

Undergraduate Lab Subjects
100 EE & CS Lab
101 Intro Electronics Lab
111 Intro Digital Systems Lab
114 Real-Time Computing & Control Lab
115 Microcomputer Project Lab
150 Intro to Microelectronic Technology
151 Semiconductor Devices Project Lab
161 Modern Optics Project Lab
162 Image Transmission Systems Project Lab
163 Strobe Project Lab
170 Lab in Software Engineering

Adv Undergraduate & Graduate by Area
Systems Science & Control Engineering
263 Data Communication Networks
264 Queueing Theory with Applications
291 Seminar in Systems, Commnctns & Control

Electronics, Computers & Systems
301 Solid State Circuits
302 Feedback Systems
311 Telephony
312 Acoustics
333 Electronic Circuits
343 Digital Speech Processing
361 Image Processing
371 Intro to VLSI Systems
372 Design & Analysis of VLSI Circuits

Probabilistic Systems & Communication
441 Transmission of Information
451 Principles of Communication
452 Stochastic Filtering & Detection
454 Adv Topics in Optical Communctn Rsrch
455 Marine Data Systems

Bioelectrical Engineering
523 Computers and Patient Care
541 Speech Communication
542 Lab Physiology, Acoustics, Speech Prcptn
543 Natural Language Processing
551 Sgnl Prcssng Auditory System: Physiology
552 Sgnl Prcssng Auditory System: Perception

Solid-State Material & Devices
720 Semiconductor Devices
721 Contemporary Digital MOS Circuits
732 Physics of Solids II
763 Applied Superconductivity
772 Integrated Circuit Devices & Processes
773 Topics in Semiconductor Device Research
774 Physics of Microelectronic Fabrication
775 Design of Analog MOS LSI
776 Plasma Procssng in I C Fabrication
777 Implantable Microelectronic Instrmntatn
791 Spec Topics in Solid State & Applns

Computer Science
801 Machine Vision
802 Robot Manipulation
821 Concepts in Modern Prgrmng Languages
823 Computer System Architecture
824 Artificial Intelligence
830 Program Semantics & Verification
835 Thry of Concurrent Systems
837 Data Base Management Systems
840 Theory of Computation
845 Topics in Computer Systems Research
847 Dataflow Computer Systems
851 Algorithms
856 Algebraic Manipulation

863	Natural Language & Cmptr Reprsntn of Knwldg	922	Advanced Industrial Practice
866	Machine Vision	925	Engineering Internship
867	Robot Manipulation	929	Undergraduate Thesis Presentation
868	Topics in Artificial Intelligence	930	Management in Engineering
871	Knowledge-Based Applns Systems	931	Development of Invention & Creative Ideas
875	Cryptography & Cryptanalysis	933	Telecommunication Technology & Policy
880	Perspectives on Computers & Society	936	Entrepreneurship
891	Special Topics in Computer Sciences	951	Graduate Industrial Prachice
		961	Intro to Resrch in EE & CS
	Special Subjects	962	Special Studies in EE & CS
901	Invention & Patents	971	Special Subjects in EE & CS
910	Special Studies in EE & CS	980	Teaching EE & CS
911	Special Subjects in EE & CS	991	Research in EE & CS
921	Industrial Practice		

UNIVERSITY OF MASSACHUSETTS
Amherst, MA 01003
(413) 545-0222

The University of Massachusetts is the largest state university in New England. Its 1100-acre campus at Amherst is situated in one of most picturesque sections of New England. The University has a student population of 24,000, a library with over three million volumes, and a faculty student ratio of 1 to 20.

The Department of Computer & Information Science (COINS) offers BS, MS and PhD programs. Currently, there are 120 enrolled in the bachelor's and 126 in the graduate programs respectively. Prospective students are suggested to apply through the department and to complete their applications by March 1 for the Fall semester.

The COINS Research Computer at the University is equipped with: two VAX 11/780 with 4MB memory each, three VAX 11/750s with 2MB memory and Floating Point Accelerator, DEC Ethernet interface, seven VAX 11/750s with 2MB plus 3COM Ethernet interface, one LSI 11/23 with 256KB, one LSI 11/03 with Rhino Robots RX1 Robot Arm, two Color SUN workstations with 2MB memory running UNIX, 10 GIGI Graphics processors, and 18 VT125 graphics terminals, twenty one Apple & AIM 8-bit microcomputers. Anticipated acquisition in the near future includes: two to ten SUN workstations, one to three Symbolics 3600 class LISP machines, four to six LSI-11 with disks, twenty five DEC personal computer, one Digital Recording Color camera, one Floating point accelerator for the VAX 11/780, one to two gigabytes of additional memory for the VAX 11/780s, ten megabytes of additional memory for the VAX 11/750s and eight megabytes for the VAX 11/780.

Operating systems in use here include: VAX VMS, Eunix overlay (UNIX emulator) for the VAXs, RT-11 for the LSIs. Database systems include CDD, Datatrieve and DBMS for the VAXs. Graphics software include D13000, DIGR, FPP, GRLIB, GUS and REGIS. In addition, networks CSnet, DECnet and Localnet are available. Future software addition includes a Berkeley UNIX on the VAX 11/750s, network software linking the LISP machines and the SUNs to the VAXs, and a relational database management systems.

Research activities of the faculty: Content addressable memories (Foster); Database management & info retrieval (Croft, Orenstein, Stemple); Distributed computation, concurrent software systems, dynamically structured parallel systems (Kohler, Lesser, Stankovic, Stone, Wileden); Machine architecture (Foster, Stone); Operating systems

(Foster, Graham, Wogrin); Performance (Graham, Wogrin); Program Verification and validation (Clarke, Wileden); Program synthesis, theory of computation (Moll); Programming languages semantics (Arbib, Manes).

Adaptive network simulation and neural modeling (Arbib, Barto, Kilmer, Spinelli); Artificial Intelligence, machine vision (Hanson, Lesser, Riseman); Computational strategies in learning and education (Peelle, Rissland, Selfridge, Soloway); Instrumentation for biological research (Spinelli); Neurophysiology of visual systems, visual system modeling, visuomotor coordination (Arbib, Spinelli); Structure of mathematical knowledge, test case generation (Rissland); Computational linguistics (Arbib, Lehnert, McDonald, Moll).

Visual and tactile control of robots (Arbib, Hanson, Riseman); Computational epistemology (Rissland, Selfridge); Software development environments, programming methodology, programming languages (Clarke, Graham, Wileden); Office information systems (Croft); Human factors of computer languages (Stemple); Adaptive control (Selfridge); Algebraic analysis of concurrent systems (Avrunin, Wileden); Knowledge representation and natural language (Lehnet, McDonald).

Faculty and Affiliated Faculty: M Arbib, A Barto, L Clarke, W Croft, C Foster, R Graham, A Hanson, W Lehnert, V Lesser, D McDonald, R Moll, J Orenstein, K Ramamritham, E M Riseman, E Rissland, D N Spinelli, D Stemple, J Wileden, C Wogrin, S Zeil.

P Abrahams, G Avrunin, F Edwards, C Hutchinson, W Kilmer, W Kohler, E Manes, H Peelle, A Prince, T Roeper, O Selfridge, E Soloway, J Stankovic, H Stone, D Towsley, E Williams.

Course Offerings:

102	Computers & Society	583	Artificial Intelligence
121	Intro Pblm Solving w Computers	591S	Software Engineering
123	Intro Pblm Solving w Computers (majors)	591T	Natural Language
201	Assembly Language Programming	791T	Cntrl & Meta-Cntrl in Pblm Solvng Systems
250	Intro to Computation	791U	Cryptanalysis
287	Data Structures	791V	Neural Modelling
306	Real Time Programming	791W	Computational Epistemology
320	Programming Methodology	791X	Software Testing
501	Fundamentals of Computation	791Z	How to Build a Relational Database System
502	Fundamentals of Systems Programming	791A	Protection in Object Oriented Systems
503	Fundamentals of Cybernetics	791B	AI Programming Techniques
510	Translator Design	791C	Image Underst&ing Systems
535	Computer Architecture	791D	Networks & Software Development
545	Information Systems	791E	Visuomotor Coordination in Frog & Toad
572	Neurobiology	791F	Purpose Driven Software

BOSTON COLLEGE
Chestnut Hill, MA 02167
(617) 969-0100

Boston College is a private Catholic college with a 200-acre campus, 15,000 students, a faculty student ratio of 1 to 16, and a library with one million volumes.

The Department of Computer Science offers an undergraduate degree in computer science. Currently, there are 11 full-time members in the department and 200 students enrolled in the program. Faculty positions exist at the assistant professor rank. Prospective students should apply through the Admissions Office before February 1.

Computing facilities here include a VAX computer system running VMS, and the Apple IIe's. More microcomputers will be purchased in the near future.

Course Offerings: (generally 3 units)

022	Intro to Computer Science	Graduate	
299	Independent Study	707	Computer Information Systems
350	Structured Programming	802	Management Information Systems
365	Systems Analysis	803	Analysis & Design of Mngmt Information
400	Business Systems	804	Aspects of Design of Top Mngmt Info Systems
404	Machines and Languages	821	Applications Programming I
406	Data Structures	822	Applications Programming II
452	Assembly Language	Math Department	
455	LISP	060	Intro to Computer Programming
456	Artificial Intelligence	061	Intro to Computer Programming
460	Compilers	460	Intro to Structured Programming
465	Database Systems	461	Adv Computer Programming Techniques
470	Operating Systems	462	Internal Machine Structure
480	Topics in Computer Science	463	Algorithms: Design and Analysis
670	Technology and Culture		

BRANDEIS UNIVERSITY
Waltham, MA 02154
(617) 647-2878

Brandeis is a private university whose 250-acre campus is 10 miles from Boston, serving a population of 3,400 students with a faculty student ratio of 1 to 10, and a library with 820,000 volumes.

An undergraduate concentration in computer science is offered here, which currently enrolls 150 students. There are 5 full-time faculty members in the departent. Faculty positions are open at assistant and full professor ranks. Background in systems, artificial intelligence or programming languages would be most desirable.

Computing facilities include two VAX 11/780 running UNIX 4.1. CSNET is accessible.

Prospective students should submit their completed applications through the Admissions Office before February 1.

Course Offerings:

2a	Introduction to Computers	20a	Discrete Mathematics
5a	Machines, Languages, & Minds	21b	Fundamental Computational Structures
13a	Intro Computer Programming in BASIC	24a	Assembly Language Programming
14a	Intro Computer Programming in FORTRAN	31a	Computer Structures & Organization
16a	Intro Computer Prgmng for Social Sciences	32a	Logic Circuits & Computer Design Lab
18b	Intro Data Structures & Pascal	33b	Numerical Methods

35a	Lisp & A I Programming	80a	Topics in Artificial Intelligence
43a	Computer Architecture I	84a	Topics in Programming Languages
43b	Computer Architecture II: Networks	86a	Topics in Computer Systems
45a	Programming Environments	95a	Directed Research
51a	Natural Language Processing	96a	Directed Projects
60a	Language Computnal Perspctve: Structure	97a	Tutorial in Computer Science
64a	Advanced Data Structures	98a	Readings in Computer Science
68a	Formal languages & Automata	99	Senior Research

FRAMINGHAM STATE COLLEGE
Framingham, MA 01701
(617) 620-1220

Framingham State College is a public college with a 71-acre campus, 3,200 students, a faculty student ratio of 1 to 18, and a library with 200,000 volumes.

A bachelor's program in computer science is offered here. Currently, there are four full-time faculty and 200 students enrolled in the program. Prospective applicants should apply through the Admissions Office before March 1.

Computer systems in use here include CDC Cyber 170, PDP-11, Prime 400, and the IBM PC's.

Course Offering:

150	Introduction to Computer Science	466	Theory & Implementation of Compilers
152	Computer Science I	467	Data Base Management Systems
252	Computer Science II	470	Computer Algorithms & their Analysis
261	Computer Org & Assem Language Prgmnng	472	Computer Graphics
261	Computer Org & Assem Language Prgmnng	363	Minicomputers
254	Cobol Prog with Comm Apps I,II (3,3)	475	Microcomputers
271	Data Structures	477	Computer Networks
355	Computer Architecture	479	Design of Digital Computers
357	Programming Languages	404	Seminar in Cmptr Science Related Area
361	File Structures	371	Simulation with Digital Computers
362	Software Engineering	490	Directed Study
465	Operating Systems	495	Internship in Computer Science

SMITH COLLEGE
Northampton, MA 01063
(413) 584-2700

Smith is a private women's college whose 125-acre campus supports a population of about 3,000 students with a faculty student ratio of 1 to 10, and a library with 950,000 volumes.

An undergraduate program in computer science is being offered. Prospective students are urged to apply early and submit their completed application to the Admissions Office by February 1.

Computing facilities include a VAX 11/780 and a VAX 11/750 running VMS, plus IBM PCs, Apples, and the Aim 65 microcomputers.

The program is supported by three full-time faculty members. Faculty positions are open at the assistant professor rank. Computer scientists with expertise in any area of computer science will be considered.

Course Offerings:

115a	Intro to Computing & Computer Prgrmng	290a	Intro to Artificial Intelligence
115b	Intro to Computing & Computer Prgrmng	301a	Special Studies
201b	Microcomputers & Assembly Language	301b	Special Studies
212b	Data Structures	330	Topics in Information Systems
240	Computer Graphics	362b	Systems Programming
250a	Foundations of Computer Science	380b	Adv Topics in Programming Languages
262a	Intro to Operating Systems	390b	Seminar in Artificial Intelligence
270	Topics in Programming Languages		

WELLESLEY COLLEGE
Wellesley, MA 02181
(617) 235-0320

Wellesley College is a private women's college with a 500-acre campus bordering on Lake Waban, surrounded by woodlands, hills, meadows, ponds, and miles of footpaths. The college supports a population of 2,200 students with a faculty student ratio of 1 to 11, and a 600,000-volume library.

An undergraduate program in computer science is being offered here, supported by a DEC 2060 computer system with access to other computers in New England. In addition, Wellesley has a cross registration program with MIT, thereby increasing the resources and curricular options available to both students and faculty. Prospective students should apply through the Admissions Office, deadline February 1.

Faculty position exists at the assistant professor rank. Computer scientists from all fields will be considered.

Course Offerings:

110	Intro to Programming & Computation	302	Artificial Intelligence
120	Computer Science & Its Applications	310	Math Foundations of Computer Science
230	Info Structures $ Algrthms Tchnques	349	Seminar: Topics in Computer Science
240	Organization of Computer Systems	350	Research or Individual Study
301	Thry of Programming Languages	370	Thesis

MICHIGAN

MICHIGAN STATE UNIVERSITY
East Lansing, MI 48824
(517) 355-8332

Michigan State University is a large public university with a 5,300-acre campus, a population of 43,000 students, 2,300 faculty members, and a library with 2.7 million volumes.

The Department of Computer Science offers BS, MS and PhD programs in computer science. Within the BS program, there are two areas of study emphasized. The first is the various types of artificial languages, including instruction and communication codes, problem oriented languages, and the formal language of mathematical logic. The second is the design of the information processing system itself, the logical design as related to individual processor components, and system architecture as related to designs for enhanced operating characteristics. For the graduate program, students are expected to have some background in assembly and higher level languages. However, a degree in engineering is not required for admission. Students are suggested to apply before January. Check Office of Admissions and Scholarship for specific deadlines.

The university's Computer Lab operates a CDC Cyber 170 Model 750. The department's Image Processing and Pattern Recognition Lab contains two Harris H500 superminis, a Spatial Data Systems image digitizer and analyzer, a PDP 11/34 with interactive graphics. The Artificial Language Lab is equipped with minis, micros, a speech recogition system and various special electronics for the enhancement of communication projects. Several other computer systems are available in the College of Engineering and elsewhere on campus. Through the MERIT network, access is available to the computer systems at University of Michigan, Wayne State university, and Western Michigan University.

Faculty's research and teaching interest include: artificial intelligence, automata theory, clustering and scaling algorithms, advanced computer systems, mathmatical theory of languages, operating systems, pattern recognition, image processing, computer networking, switching theory, performance measurement techniques, large data base theory, and the theory of algorithms. Members of the Department:

H G Hedges; J R Burnett; R C Dubes; A K Jain; J Kateley Jr; C V Page; R J Reid; D J Weinshank; J B Eulenberg; L H Greenberg; H D Hughes; M G Keeney; H E Lee; G C Stockman; B L Weinberg; J J Forsyth; L M Ni; S Pramanik; R G Reynolds.

Course Offering:

120	Computer Prgmng for Engnrs & Scientists	809	Computer Arithmetic Algorithm
251	Algorithms & Computing I	813	Logic Design Methodologies
252	Algorithms & Computing II	815	Archtctr of Computational Systems
301	FORTRAN Lab	818	Intro to Robotics
311	Assembly Language & Machine Orgnztn	822	Digital Image Processing
312	Generative Coding & Info Structures	827	Switching Theory
313	Intro to Systems Programming	831	Theory of Formal Languages
321	Intro to Discrete Structures	832	Theory of Formal Languages II
322	Intro to Theory of Computing	841	A I & Adaptive Systems
412	Computer Communications	842	A I & Adaptive Systems II
414	Inteactive Computer Graphics	876	Performance Measurement Tchnques
416	Digital Design	881	Operating Systems Theory I
417	Digital Design Lab	882	Operating Systems Theory II
423	Computer Architecture	884	Large Data Base Theory
447	Digital Filtering	890	Special Topics
451	Design of Language Processors I	899	Master's Thesis Research
452	Design of Language Processor II	906	Advances in Pattern Recognition
453	Design of Language Processors III	911	General Automata Theory I
490	Selected Topics	912	General Automata Theory II
495	Independent Study	913	General Automata Theory III
801	Independent Study	921	Advanced Computer System I
805	Clustering & Scaling Algorithms	922	Advanced computer Systems II
806	Fundmntls of Pattern Recognition	999	Doctoral Dissertation Research

WAYNE STATE UNIVERSITY
Detroit, MI 48202
(313) 577-3577

Wayne State is a public university with 33,000 students, a 180-acre campus located in the Cultural Center of Detroit with access to numerous high-technology companies in the southeast Michigan, a faculty student ratio of 1 to 18, and a library with 1.9 million volumes.

The Department of Computer Science offers BS in Computer Science, BA with a Major in Information Systems, Minor in Computer Science for Liberal Arts Major, Certificate in Computer Science, MA, MS, and PhD in Computer Science. Currently, there are 400, 95, 14 students enrolled in the bachelor's, master's, and PhD programs respectively. Prospective students should apply through the Department of Computer Science, 532 Mackenzie Hall, Phone : (313) 577-2477.

University Computing facilities include 2 AMDAHL 470 V/8 systems. The Department operates an Intelligent Systmes Lab (ISL) and a Digital Systems Lab (DSL). ISL supports research in artificial intelligence, computer vision, computer graphics and pictorial databases. The DSL facilitates the design and construction of microprocessor-based devices. The two labs contains a PDP 11/23, a PDP 11/44, a COMTAL VISION ONE/20 Image Processing System, a VAX 11/780, plus an assortment of micros such as: the IBM PCs, ONTEL/AMIGO, the MITS, Altair 680b and Altair 8800b which are based on the Motorola 6800 and Intel 8080 MPUs respectively, other peripherals such as function generators and logic analyzers, as well as a Tektronix 8500 microprocessor development system supporting both 8 and 16 bit microprocessors. In addition, the Merit Computer Network connects the university's computers to the computing facilities of the University of Michigan, Michigan State University and Western Michigan University. Telenet, MTS, UNIX are used. MEGAFRAME will be acquired in the near future.

The Department consists of 16 full-time faculty supported by 50 part-time instructors and graduate assistants. Openings exist at all levels. Applicants from all areas of computer science will be consired. Background in operating systems, computer networks, computer graphics, software methodology, and information management systems would be of particular interest to the Department. Current research areas of the faculty include: advanced modelling and design methodology, artificial intelligence, computer vision, brain modelling and evolutionary algorithms, pictorial database management, digital signal processing, program correctness and semantics, numerical analysis, and multiple processor architectures. Members of the faculty and their interests:

C Briggs (operating systems, security, numerical mthds); M Conrad (modeling of biological systems, brain models & intelligence, macromolecular computers, thry of adaptable systems, ecological & evolutionary prblms); K Culik (prgrmng languages, their thry & applns, correctness of prgrms, compilers, thry of computation & algorithms, parallelism & concurrency, thry & reprsntatn of knowledge, math & computatnl linguistics, graph thry & applns); M Farhang (database mangmnt systems, inter-process communication, data strctrs, file orgnztns, formal languages & automata thry).

C Friedlander (syntactic pattern recgntn, biological signal prcssng, formal languages & automata thry); W Grosky (database mangmnt, data strctrs & algrthms, AI, formal languages); R Hill (computer vision, knowledge based systems, distrbtd prblm solving); S Jayaramamurthy (pttrn recgntn & image prcssng, computer vision, digital signal prcssng); R Kampfner (computatnl modeling, biological info prcssng, learning & adaptive systems, info systems analysis & dsgn); R Rada search thry, theoretical AI, evolutionary prgrmng, data strctrs, & computer applns in medicine).

M Rahimi (AI, combinatorics, computer aided instruction, commnctn prostheses, AI); B Romberger (operating systems, databses, AI, prgrmng languages, educatnl uses of computers); I Sethi (image analysis, pttrn recgntn, sequential decision algrthms & microprcssr applns); N Tsao (analysis & implmntatn of numerical & non-numerical algrthms); S Wolfson (numerical mthds, computer systems); B Zeigler (modeling & simulatn, sftwr system dsgn mthdlgy, thry in computer & system science).

Course Offering: (generally 3 semester units)

100 Intro to Computer Science	503 Computers in Statistical Data Analysis
102 Computer Science I (4)	504 Intro to Programming (4)
105 Computer Science Lab for Engineers (1)	505 Computers in Scientific Applications
202 Condensed Intro to PASCAL (2)	506 Adv Concepts in Computer Science (4)
203 Computer Science II (4)	511 Adv Software Development
206 Intro to Digital Computing with FORTRAN	513 Information Systems Analysis
207 Intro to Programming with PL/I (4)	514 System Design & Implementation
208 Computer Concepts for Engineers (4)	515 Administration of Computer Centers
209 Computers & Mankind (2-3)	518 Intro to Modeling & Simulation
210 Intro to Business Data Processing	519 Comput. Modeling of Complex Systems
320 Survey of Higher Level Languages	520 Principles of Prgmmng Languages (4)
370 Intro to Data Structures	521 A I Prgmmng w LISP (2)
413 Systems Concepts & Implications (4)	531 Computer Organization (4)
441 Intro to Computer Systems (4)	537 Mini-Microcomputers (4)
450 Intro to Theoretical Computer Science	541 Computer Operating Systems (4)
460 Intro to Numerical Methods	542 Data Communications
470 Intro to File Structures	571 Database Management Systems I
495 Prof Practice in Computer Science (1)	572 Survey of Database Management Systems
501 Computers & Research	575 Direct Access Storage Devices
502 Computers & Business Research (2)	590 Directed Study (1-4)

612 Computers & Medicine	723 Auto Optmztn of Programs by Compilers
618 Simulation Languages & Methodology	724 Program Verification
619 Computational Modeling Laboratory	725 Extensible Languages
621 Structure of Compilers I	731 Computer Architecture
622 Structure of Compilers II	732 Fault-Tolerant Computer Architecture II
632 Fault Tolerant Cmptr Architecture I (4)	740 Adv Design of Operating Systems
638 Microprogrammed Computer Design (4)	742 Computer Networks
640 Design of Operating Systems	745 Parallelism in Computation
652 Automata Theory	751 Theory of Computation
658 Analysis of Algorithms	752 Theory of Adaptable Systems
661 Computational Algorithms: Analysis	754 Computer Graph Structure
662 Computational Algthms: Linear Algebra (4)	771 Adv Database Management Systems
663 Computational Algorithms: Optimization	773 Adv Data Structures
671 Database Management Systems II	775 Techniques of Data Management
680 Artifical Intelligence I	780 Deduction Systems
682 Intro to Adaptive Systems	782 Adaptive Systems II
683 Intro to Pattern Recognition	783 Adv Pattern Recognition
685 Analysis of Natural Language	786 Computer Vision
686 Digital Image Prcssng & Scene Analysis	788 Seminar in Natural Computing
687 Computer Graphics	790 Directed Study (1-5)
688 Principles of Natural Computing	813 Advanced Topics in Computer Science (2-4)
699 Topics in Computer Science (1-4)	819 Seminar in Advanced Modeling Concepts
711 Design of Adv Software Systems	840 Modeling & Measurement of Computer Systems
713 Information Systems Analysis & Design	850 Computer Science Seminar (1-4)
719 Theory of Modeling & Simulation	852 Seminar in Adaptability Theory
720 Formal Grammars & Syntactic Analysis	871 Seminar in Databases
722 Formal Definition of Semantics	880 Artifical Intelligence II (2)

NORTHERN MICHIGAN UNIVERSITY
Marquette, MI 49855
(906) 227-2650

Northern Michigan is a public university with 8,500 students, a 300-acre campus, a faculty student ratio of 1 to 20, and a library with 1 million volumes.

An undergraduate program in Computer Science/Data Processing is offered jointly by the School of Business & Management, and the Department of Mathematics. Several options are available: Business Data Processing major, Computational Mathematics Major, Data Processing Major, Data Processing/Computing Minor. Prospective students should contact the Department of Mathematics, or the Business School for more information. Application deadline for financial aid is Feb 1.

Computing facilities include an IBM 4341, PDP 11, Apple, IBM PC, plus other microcomputer systems. A Corvus network is available.

Course Offering:

DP 103 Intro to Data Processing (2)	DP 316 System Analysis & Design Workshop II
DP 105 Computer Systems for Problem Solving (2)	CS 331 Microcomputer Architecture I (2)
DP 110 Principles of Data Processing	CS 332 Microcomputer Architecture II (2)
CS 120 Intro to Computing	CS 333 Electronic Instrmntatn: Interfacing (2)
DP 125 Structured COBOL	DP 440 Info & Decision Support Systems I (2)
DP 210 Intro Data Processing Operations JCL/OS	DP 441 Info & Decision Support Systems II (2)
CS 221 PL/1 (2)	Graduate
CS 222 FORTRAN IV (2)	CS 320 Computer Org & Assembly Language Prgmng
DP 223 RPG II (2)	CS 340 Combinatorial Computing
DP 225 Advanced Structured COBOL	CS 410 Telecommunications & Teleprocessing
CS 240 Computational Models & Problem Solving	CS 420 Data Structures
CS 295 Sp Topics in Computer Science (1-4)	CS 440 Computer Graphics
CS 297 Drcted Studies in Computer Science (1-4)	CS 495 Sp Topics in Computer Science (1-4)
CS 298 Drcted Studies in Computer Science (1-4)	CS 496 Sp Topics in Computer Science (1-4)
DP 310 Intro to System Design & Analysis	CS 497 Drctd Studies in Computer Science (1-4)
DP 315 System Analysis & Design Workshop I	CS 498 Drctd Studies in Computer Science (1-4)

THE UNIVERSITY OF MICHIGAN
Ann Arbor, MI 48109
(313) 764-7433

The University of Michigan, Ann Arbor, is one of the largest public universities in the nation. Its 2550-acre campus has a population of 45,000 students, a faculty student ratio of 1 to 17, and a library systems with close to 6 million volumes.

The Department of Computer & Communication Sciences (CCS), a unit of the College of Literature, Science, and the Arts, offers an undergraduate program while the Horace H Rackham School of Graduate Studies offers graduate programs in computer and communication sciences. For more information, contact the Department at 221 Angel Hall, Phone: (313) 764-8504. The College of Engineering offers MSE in Computer Aided Design; MSE and MS in Computer, Information and Control Engineering (CICE); a Professional degree: Computer, Information and Control Engineer, CICE. Contact the CICE Program Office at 1520 East Engineering , Phone (313) 764-9387 for more information. In addition, the Electrical and Computer Engineering Department offers undergraduate and graduate programs in computer engineering. Interested students should contact that department at 2500 East Engineeing, Phone: (313) 764-2390. As for doctoral programs in computer science, a students becomes an applicant for the doctorate when admitted to the Horace H Rackham School of Graduate Studies and accepted in a field of specialization. Contact the Graduate School for more information about the doctorate program in computer science and admission details.

The central computer system is the AMDAHL 470/V8 running under the operating system Michigan Terminal system (MTS). In addition, the Engineering Library, one of the 25 libraries in the University Library systems, contains half a million volumes and subscribes to 3,000 serial titles.

Course offering:

Computer & Communication Sciences
274 Elementary Programming Concepts
301 Special Topics
374 Programming & Computer Systems
380 FORTRAN Programming Language
381 ALGOL Programming Language
384 SNOBOL Programming Language
385 LISP Programming Language
387 Spec Courses Various Prgrmng Languages
400 Foundtn of Cmptr & Commnctn Sciences
469 Histroy of Computers
476 Data Structures
478 Intro to Software Architecture
494 Computer Programming
495 Machine Orgnztn & Data Structures
500 Special Study
501 Special Topics
510 Digital & Analog Systems
522 Thry of Automata
524 Intro to Adaptive Systems
525 Man as an Info Processing System
526 Foundamentals of Modelling
532 Theory of Parsing
541 Thry of Natural Language Structure
544 Logic, Grammar, & Info Processing
550 Foundations of CCS Math
565 Artificial Intelligence
569 Computer Structures
572 Prgrmng Languages & Software Systems
573 Operating Systems
574 Simulation Languages & Techniques
575 Compiler Construction
577 Algrthms & Computational Complexity
580 Informational Aspects of Biology
590 Computational Logic

Computer, Information & Control Engineering
     (a Partial Listing)
424 Signal Transmission for Cmptrs & Commnctns
460 Structure of Digital Computers
461 Prgrmng Languages & Data Structures

464 Cellular Computers & Image Processing
465 Computer Graphics Applications
466 Digital Design Lab
467 Switching & Sequential Systems
468 Thry of Languages & Computation
469 Applns of Real-Time Computer Systems
478 Interactive Computer Graphics
479 Intro to Sftwr Architecture
482 Analog Computation
505 Simulation for Large Scale Systems
507 Artificial Intelligence
509 Intro to Robotics: Thry & Practice
565 Logical Dsgn of Digital Computers
567 Automata Theory
568 Reliable Computing Systems
569 Digital Computer Arithmetic
573 Computer Operating Systems
575 Compiler Construction
577 Data Management Systems
578 Geometric Modeling
580 Hybrid Computation
665 Systems Design of Digital Computers
675 Compiler Construction Lab
679 Formal Aspects of Sftwr Archtctr
760 Special Topics in Computer Systems

Electrical & Computer Engineering
     (a Partial Listing)
270 Computer Prgrmng & Algorithms
271 Assembly Language Programming
364 Data Structures
365 Digital Computer Engineering
366 Digital Computer Engineering Lab
367 Algebraic Foundtn of Cmptr Engnrng
424 Signal Transmssn Cmptrs & Commnctns
434 Digital Commnctn Signal & Systems
462 Computer Circuits & Devices
514 Semiconductor & IC Modeling for CAD
574 Integrated & Fiber Optics
587 Digital Integrated Circuits

UNIVERSITY OF MICHIGAN, FLINT
Flint, MI 48503
(313) 762-3300

The University of Michigan, Flint, is a public university with 4,600 students, a 42-acre compus, a faculty student ratio of 1 to 18, and a library with 125,000 volumes.

The Department of Computer Science offers BS in Computer Science, and a joint program with the Psychology Department, BS in Computer Science & Psychology. Undergraduate enrollment in the department is 800. Prospective students should apply through the Admissions Office at 254, CROB. For more information, call the department at (313) 762-3121.

Computer systems in use include an AMDAHL 5860 (MTS); Burroughs 1830, and the IBM PCs. A CORVUS Network for the IBM PC will be acquired in the near future. The MERIT network provides access to computing facilities to other major universities in Michigan.

There are 7 full-time faculty in the department. Openings exist at the assistant professor level.

Course Offering: (generally 3 semester units)

121	Using a Computer System I (1)	365	Micro-Computer Architecture (4)
122	Using a Computer System II (2)	375	Adv Prblm Solving & Prgmmng Concepts (4)
175	Problem Solving and Prgmmng Concepts (4)	377	Systems Programming
265	Computer Logic Design (4)	395	Cooperative Practice in Computer Science
270	Data Processing	422	Foundations of Computer Science
271	Computer Prgmmng for Scientific Problems	444	Simulation & Modeling
274	Intro to Programming	446	Artifical Intelligence
275	Intermed Prblm Solving & Prgmng Concepts (4)	465	Computer Architecture
277	Intro Computer Org & Assembly Languages (4)	470	Modeling & Anlysis for Admnstrtv Decisions
280	COBOL Language Laboratory (1)	474	Intro to Numerical Analysis
284	PL/1 Language Laboratory (1)	477	Operating Systems
285	FORTRAN Language Laboratory (1)	480	Data Base Design
286	Computer Language Laboratory (1)	481	Compiler Construction I
290	Computer Applns in the Health Sciences	482	Compiler Construction II
320	Computers & Society	491	Advanced Directed Study
321	Discrete Structures	492	Topics in Computer Science

WESTERN MICHIGAN UNIVERSITY
Kalamazoo, MI 49008
(616) 383-1950

Western Michigan is a public university with a population of 19,000 students, a 400-acre campus, a faculty student ratio of 1 to 18, and a library with 1.7 million volumes.

The Department of Computer Science offers bachelor's and master's programs in which 480, and 85 students are enrolled respectively. Prospective students should apply through the Department. Application deadlines: Graduate financial aid, Feb 15; Spring Admission, Mar 1; Graduate Assistantship, Mar 15; Fall Admission, July 1; Winter Admission, Nov 1; undergraduate scholarships, Feb 15; undergraduate loan, Mar 15.

Computer systems in use include a DEC 10, VAX 750, VAX 780, plus microcomputers from Apple, Digital, ...etc. The MERIT provides access to facilities at Univerity of Michigan, Michigan State, and Wayne State Univeristy. There are 14 full-time faculty in the Department.

Course Offerings: (generally 3 semester units)

Graduate

105 Intro to Computers	506 Scientific Programming
106 BASIC for Engineers (1)	527 Theory of Computer Graphics
111 Computer Programming I	542 Data Base Management Systems
112 Computer Programming II	544 Software Systems Development
215 File Processing with COBOL	599 Indep Study in Computer Science (1-3)
223 Computer Organization	603 Studies in Computer Science
224 Assembly Language	625 Computer Structures
306 Introductory Programming: FORTRAN (2)	631 Advanced Data Structures
309 Introductory Programming: ALGOL (2)	632 Analysis of Computer Algorithms
331 Data Structures and Algorithms	643 Advanced Data Base Management Systems
342 Software and File Systems	655 Advanced Operating Systems
485 Programming Languages	680 Mathematical Theory of Formal Languages
499 Senior Seminar (1)	681 Compiling Theory and Practice
	682 Artifical Intelligence

MINNESOTA

UNIVERSITY OF MINNESOTA
Minneapolis, MN 55455
(612) 373-2144

The University of Minnesota, Twin Cities, is a public university with a 280-acre campus in Minneapolis, and a 70-acre in St Paul, supporting a total of 47,000 students with a faculty student ratio of 1 to 13 and a library system with 4.1 million volumes.

On the undergradate level, a BA in computer science can be obtained from the College of Liberal Arts (CLA), and a BS from the Institute of Technology (IT). Both curricula are designed to provide students a broad base in the foundation subjects offered by the Computer Science Department. On the graduate level, MS and PhD programs in computer and information science are offered. Currently, there are 700 in the undergraduate , 70 in the master's, and 40 in the PhD programs. Prospective students should apply through the offices of Undergradate Admissions or Graduate School appropriately. Application deadline for undergraduate financial aid is March 1. For graduate financial support, apply through the Admissions and Awards Committee, Computer Science Department, 136 Lind Hall. Contact the department for more specific information.

Computing facilities in use include: Cyber 74, 172 (NOS), VAX 11/780 (UNIX), PDP 11/60, the Apple and IBM PC microcomputer systems. CSNet is available. Future planning calls for the establishment of a major research software lab.

The Department consists of 18 full-time members. Faculty positions exist at the assistant and the full professor ranks. Background in software, systems, or large scale computation is particularly desired. Members and their interests:

J B Rosen (math prgrmng, numerical mthds); W D Munro (numerical analysis, machine arthmtc); V Berzins (sftwr engnrng); W E Boebert (sftwr mangmnt, distrbtd systems); D L Boyd (operating systems); S Bruell (operating systems, performance evaluation, queueing ntwrk models); T H Chan (computatnl complexity, prgrm verification); K Frankowski (compilers & assemblers, algebraic manipulation, math of computations); W Franta (operating system dsgn & simulatn, distrbtd prcssng, prformance evaluation).

H A Freeman (database computers, distrbtd prcssng); H Gyllstrom (compiler dsgn); A R Hevner (database systems, distrbtd systems, operating systems); M A Holly (computer graphics); O H Ibarra (thry of computation, thry of algrthms, computatnl complexity); M J Kascic (numerical methds for PDE); J A Larson (database mangmnt systems, interactive systems, data strctrs); K J Maly (prgrmng languages, language prcssrs, data strctrs); E H McCall (linear & integer prgrmng, numerical analysis).

S K Sahni (dsgn & analysis of algrthms, parallel computing, data strctrs); G M Schneider (computer ntwrks, data communctns); M L Stein (machine arithmetic, orgnztn of prgrmng systems); W B Thompson (scene analysis, pttrn recgntn, AI); K J Thurber (computing system archtctr).

Members of graduate CIS faculty from other departments: E Ackerman (biomedical applns); F N Bailey (analysis of systems, interactive computing); G B Davis (MIS); L C Gatewood (physiological control systems, medical information); R P Halverson (dsgn of hardwr, implmntatn of higher level languages); R Y Kain (system archtctr); L L Kinney (system archtctr); K S P Kumar (systems analysis, stochastic control); E B Lee (control thry); P Patton (data structrs, language analysis); M B Pour-El (math logic, automata, recursive thry); H F Weinberger (ord & partial diff equatns).

Course Offerings: (generally 4 quarter units)

1100 Intro FORTRAN Programming I (2)	5299 Problems in Machine Design (1-4)
1101 Intro FORTRAN Programming II (2)	5400 Intro AutomataTheory
3001 Perspectives on Computers & Society	5401 Intro Formal Languages
3101 A FORTRAN Intro Computer Programming	5499 Prblms in Comptnal Thr & Logic (1-4)
3103 Intro Prgmng Languages & Prob Solving	5501 Artificial Intelligence
3104 Intro Programming & Problem Solving	5502 Intro Operating Systems
3105 Fundmntl of Algorithms & Languages I	5503 Intro Compilers
3106 Fundmntl of Algorithms & Languages II	5521 Pattern Recognition
3107 Intro Structure & Prog of Comp Systems	5702 Principles of Database Systems
3131 FORTRAN Laboratory (2)	5703 Database System Design
3134 PASCAL Laboratory (2)	
3400 Discrete Structures of Computer Science	Graduate Offerings
5001 Theory & Appln of Linear Prog Algorithms	8101 Computer System
5002 Computational Methods for Nonlinear Prog	8102 Modeling & Analysis
5101 Structure & Prog of Software System I	8201 Math of Computers & Control Devices
5102 Structure & Prog of Software System II	8299 Seminar: Machine Design (1-3)
5103 Structure & Prog of Software System III	8301 Computation of Spec Functions & Formulas
5104 System Simulation	8303 Computational Methods for
5105 Theory of Machine Arithmetic	Initial & Boundary Value Problems
5106 Structure of Higher Level Languages	8401 Algorithms I - Design Techniques
5107 Computer Graphics I	8402 Algorithms II
5117 Computer Graphics II	8499 Seminar: Cmputnl Theory & Logic (1-3)
5121 Intro Data Structures	8505 Optimization in Compilers
5122 Advanced Data Structures	8511 Adv Concepts in Artificial Intelligence
5199 Problems in Language & Systems (1-4)	8599 Seminar: Nonnumeric Computation (1-3)
5200 Continuous System Simulation	8699 Seminar: Control Science (1-3)
5201 Computer Architecture	8701 Advanced Topics in Database Systems
5211 Data Communications & Cmptr Networks	8799 Seminar: Information Science (1-3)

MOORHEAD STATE UNIVERSITY
Moorhead, MN 56560
(218) 236-2161

Moorhead State is a public university with 6,200 students, a 105-acre campus, a faculty student ratio of 1 to 23, and a library with 275,000 volumes.

The Computer Science Department offers bachelor's and master's programs in which 390, and 18 students are enrolled respectively. Prospective students should apply through the Office of Admissions before Aug 15 for the Fall Quarter. Deadline for financial aid is April 16.

Computing facilities include a VAX 780, 25 Apple II's, and remote access to Univac 1100/80, and the University of Minnesota's Cyber 72.

The department consists of 10 full-time members. Faculty positions exist at the assistant and associate professor ranks.

Course Offering: (mostly 4 quarter units)

110 Intro to Microcomputers (3)	352 System Software (8)
120 Computers & Society (2)	370 Advanced Data Structures
130 BASIC Programming with Microcomputers (3)	380 Intro to Systems Software
140 FORTRAN Fundamentals	410 Theory of Language Translation
145 Business Data Processing	450 Numerical Analysis I
155 COBOL Programming	469 Internship (3-16)
160 Topics in Programming Languages (2)	480 Seminar in Computer Science (1)
201 Intro to Computers & Programming I	490 Spec Problems in Computer Science (1-6)
202 Intro to Computers & Programming II	500 Fundamental Structures (3)
204 Assembly-Languages Programming	502 Automata & Formal Languages (3)
220 Computers & Programming Systems	504 Algorithm Analysis (3)
230 Computers in Education (2)	511 Compiler Design Theory II (3)
245 Systems Analysis & Design	515 Operating Systems II (3)
250 Numerical Methods	521 Database Systems I
255 Advanced COBOL Programming (2)	522. Database Systems II
280 Statistical Analysis of Data (2)	525 Analysis of Computer Systems (3)
285 Computer Simulation Models	530 Advanced Computer-Based Education (3)
300 Ethc & Soc Concerns of Cmptr Scientsts (3)	531 Author Languages (3)
305 Logical Design of Computers I	532 Design Principles for CAI Systems (3)
306 Logical Design of Computers II	540 Software Engineering I (3)
315 Data Structures	541 Software Engineering II (3)
325 Microprocessors	580 Seminar in Computer Science (1)
330 Survey of Programming Languages	590 Advanced Topics in Computer Science (1-3)
350 Intro to Computers & Programming (8)	597 Individual Study (1-3)
351 Fndmntl Computer Design & Organization (8)	599 Thesis in Computer Science (6)

UNIVERSITY OF MINNESOTA, DELUTH
Duluth, MN 55812
(218) 726-8000

The University of Minnesota, Duluth, is a public university with a 240-acre campus, a population of 6,500 students, a faculty student ratio of 1 to 13, and a library with 245,000 volumes.

The Deparmtment of Mathematical Science offers a bachelor's program in computer science. A new master's program is pending. Interested student should apply through the Admissions Office, or contact the Deparmtment: Phone: (218) 726-8254. Deadline for financial aid is Mar 1 for the Fall Quarter.

Computing facilities available include a local CDC 171-6 (local), remote access to a CRAY computer, Cyber 730, VAX; microcomputers from Apple, Terak, Xerox, and the IBM PCs. A local timeshare network and the University of Minnesota Network are available. The department will purchase additional micros in the near future.

UNIV OF MINNESOTA, DELUTH

There are 22 full-time members in the department. Several positions exist at the assistant or associate professor ranks. Doctorate in Computer Science or related field with substantial computer science background is desired.

Course Offerings:

1001	Computer and Society	5526	Data Structures
1501	Fortran Programming	550	Numerical Analysis
1502	Pascal Programming	551	Numerical Linear Algebra
1515	Microcomputers & Their Applications	552	Numerical Methods in Physics
1520	Programming and Algorithms	5540	Comparative Programming Languages
150	Basic Programming	5542	Computer Architecture
1550	Workshop	554	Operating Systems
1970	Special Topics	5500	Workshop
505	COBOL Programming	5715	Microcomputer Systems
510	Intermediate Fortran	5725	Algorithms
515	Machine Assembly Language & Systems	574	Operating Systems
520	Programming and Algorithms	5745	Database Management System Design
521	Intro to System Software 4	5755	Thr of Prgmmng Lang, Trnsltn & Compiling
52	Machine Languate and Organization	5765	Automata, Cmputblty, & Formal Languages
55	Introduction to Computer Graphics	5775	Arificial Intelligence
540	Database Management Systems	5950	Independent Study
941	Seminar for Majors 1	5970	Special Topics
970	Special Topics	5980	Honors Project
950	Independent Study		

MISSOURI

UNIVERSITY OF MISSOURI, ROLLA
Rolla, MO 65401
(341) 341-4164

The University of Missouri, Rolla, is a public university with 7,000 students, a 70-acre campus, a faculty student ratio of 1 to 14, and a library with 420,000 volumes.

The Department of Computer Science at UMR offers BS, MS, and PhD programs in which 750, 100, 15 students are enrolled respectively. Prospective students should apply through the Admissions Office. Application deadlines for financial aid is March 1 for the Fall Semester. Graduates should apply through the Department for teaching and research assistantship. For more information, contact the department, the Admissions Office, or Office of the Dean of Arts and Sciences.

The University's computing facilities include: an IBM 4341 M2, an IBM 4331 K2, an IBM 3705 Communication Controller, a COMTEN 3650-II Communications Processor for local timesharing and access to the University of Missouri Computer Network. The University-wide computer network has 2 AMDAHL 470/V8 systems. The Computer Educational Services Lab contains a Data General Eclipse S/230, an Intecolor 8051 micro, and a TRS 80. Graphics equipment include numerous graphics terminals, a Teckronix 4954 Digitizing Tablet, numerous digitizing tablets, a Calcomp 1051 Drum Plotter with 907 Controller, a Calcomp 936 drum Ploter, and several Tektronix 4662 digital plotters. The department has a Microdata M1621, an IDI Vector Display Scope, an IMSAI 8080 micro, a PET, a TI 9900, a microcomputer network consisting of 10 IMSAI's, and a Microdata Reality system.

There are 14 full-time faculty members in the department. Openings exist at all levels. Applicants for junior positions should have broad teaching and research interests within one or more of the following: artificial intelligence, operating systems, languages, analysis of algorithms, and information systems. Members and their interests:

T B Baird (operations research, business applns); J K Byers (scheluling, reliability modeling); A DeKock (data base mangmnt systems, reliable sftwr, AI); B B Flachsbart (large scale mangmnt info systems); B E Gillett (parametric integer prgrmng, simulation, regression analysis); J W Hamblen (computer education); C Y Ho (robotics international finance, portfolio thry); R E Lee (graphics, computer center mangmnt).

T L Lo (operating systems performance modeling); J R Metzner (macro prgrmng systmes, foundational aspect of parallel algrthms). T Moges (operations rsrch); T Moges (operations rsrch); L D Peterson (optimiztn of diff equations); J B Prater (data strctrs, file systems sftwr, sftwr science); H D Pyron (numerical analysis); J R Rao (ntwrk dsgn, CAD CAM, distrbtd graphics); T F Reid (database dsgn, real time system); A K Rigler (math modeling, applns, operations rsrch).

T J Sager (formal languages, compilers); D C St. Clair (math prgrmng, database dsgn implmntatn in maintenace, operations rsrch); P D Stigall (micro & mini digital systems dsgn); R M Strandberg (basic systems sftwr, operating system performance); M C Vidalon (AI); F G Walters (numerical mthds, operations rsrch); G W Zobrist (interactive graphics, database mangmnt, flow ntwrks).

111

Course Offerings: (generally 3 semester units)

1	Intro to Computer Science
63	Computer Programming Lab
73	Basic scientific Programming
74	Job Control Language-System
83	Intro to Machine Language Programming
101	Special Topics
163	Block Structured Language Programming
168	Business Data Processing Techniques
183	Assemby Language Programming
199	CO-OP Training
200	Special Topics
202	CO-OP Training
210	Seminar
218	Intro to Numerical Methods
253	Data Structure & Logic
260	Intro to Operations Research
264	Special Purpose Languages
268	Adv Business Data Processing Techniques
293	Assembler Level Software Systems
300	Special Problems
301	Special Topics
303	Software Systems Survey
310	Seminar
313	Interactive Computer Graphics
324	Multifunction Operating System
328	Numerical Analysis I
329	Numerical Analysis II
333	The Structure of a Compiler
339	Information Processing & Retrieval
345	Intro to Robotic Systems
349	Data Base Systems
353	Abstract Structures
359	Designing Information Systems
360	Methods of Optimization
361	The Structure of Operating Systems
362	Determistic Operations Research Survey
364	Prblstic Operations Research Survey
365	Linear Programming
366	Regression analysis
368	Digital Simulation

376	O R Tchnques for Managerial Decisions
379	Software Development
383	Architecture of Assemblers & Machines
388	Computer Center Management
390	Undergraduate Research
400	Special Problems
401	Special Topics
409	Num Soln of Part Diff Equations
410	Seminar
414	Network & Distributed Computing
428	Matrix Computation
430	Formal Languages & Syntax
431	Fault-Tolerant Computing I
432	Fault-Tolerant Computing II
433	Theory of Compiling
441	Math Logic & Computability
445	Robotic Sensors & Controls
447	A I and Pattern Recognition
469	Queueing Theory
461	Analysis of Operating Systems
465	Integer Programming
466	Nonlinear Optimization
467	Nonlinear & Geometric Programming
470	Game Theory & Applications
483	Macro Systems & Extensible Languages

Course under Consideration:

439	Document Retrieval Systems
440	Pattern Recognition Theory
450	Formal Automata Theory
453	Combinatorics & Analysis of Algorithms

EE

61	Circuit Analysis I
211	Digital Systems Design
312	Digital System Design Lab
313	Microcomputer System Design
315	Digital Computer Design
412	Switching Theory
413	Adv Switching & Automata Theory
415	Adv Topics Digital Cmptrs System Design

Northwest Missouri State is a public university with 5,000 students, a 175-acre campus, a faculty student ratio of 1 to 20, and a library with 320,000 volumes.

The Department of Computer Science offers a bachelor's program and an MS in School Computer Studies. The two programs have 300, and 80 students respectively. Apply through the Admissions Office. Application for financial aid should be completed before April.

Computing facilities include a VAX 11/780, DEC Rainbow and Apple II microcomputes, 14 graphics terminals, and access to the AMDAHL computer systems through the University of Missouri Network. The department consists of 7 full-time members.

Course Offering: (generally 3 semester units)

150	Introduction to Computers	
240	Assembler Programming	Graduate
247	Fundamentals of Computer Science	544 Automata, Computability & Formal Languages
248	Beginning COBOL Programming	545 Concepts & Theory of Programming Languages
249	FORTRAN Programming (2)	546 Design & Analysis of Algorithms
275	Computers in the Elementary School (2)	552 Computer Graphics (2)
343	Scientific Simulation and Models	640 Elementary Computer Concepts
345	Computer Design Fundamentals	642 Computer-Aided Instruction
347	Data Structures	644 Microcomputer Systems in the School
348	Advanced COBOL Programming	647 Fundamentals of Computer Science
440	Compiler Techniques	648 COBOL
445	Computer Subsystems Design	649 Advanced Programming Languages
446	Operating System and Data Systems	657 Data Structures
494	Seminar in Computer Science (1)	694 Sem: Computers, Society & Social Values (2)
495	Specialized Languages in C S (1)	695 Research in Computer Science Education
		698 Advanced Independent Study

UNIVERSITY OF MISSOURI, ST. LOUIS
St. Louis, MO 63121
(314) 553-5451

The University of Missouri-St Louis is a public university with 12,000 students, a 115-acre campus, a faculty student ratio of 1 to 25, and a library with 370,000 volumes.

The Department of Mathematical Sciences offers a bachelor's program in which 500 students are currently enrolled. Prospective students should apply through the Office of Admissions. Application for financial aid should be completed by March 1.

Computing facilities include an AMDAHL V7, an AMDAHL V8, a Series/1 mini, the IBM PC and Intel-based microcomputers. BITNET, EDUNET are available to provide access to the University of Missouri Network. The department consists of 6 full-time members.

Course Offerings: (generally 3 semester units)

UNIV OF MISSOURI, ST. LOUIS

MONTANA

UNIVERSITY OF MONTANA
Missoula, MT 59812
(406) 243-6266

The University of Montana supports a population of over 9,000 students with a 200-acre campus, a faculty student ratio of 1 to 20, and a library with 680,000 volumes.

The Department of Computer Science offers BS and MS programs in which 400 and 20 students are currently enrolled. In the BS program, in addition to the general computer science emphasis, students may choose software systems emphasis, business systems emphasis, or scientific applications emphasis. Prospective undergraduates should apply through the Admissions Office or through the Graduate Committee, Department of Computer Science. April 15 is the deadline for admission to the Fall Quarter. Contact the department for more information, Phone: (406) 243-2883.

University's computing facilities include a DEC-20 (TOPS 20) system. The departments operates a VAX 11/750 (UNIX), Commodor PET, and Motorola 68000-based microcomputer systems. Starnet and Ethernet are available.

The Department consists of 7 full-time members. Openings exist at the assistant and associate professor levels. Background in software engineering, programming languages, or artificial intelligence would be particularly desired.

Course Offering:

101	Introduction to Programming (4)	373	Computer Simulation
102	Intro to Computer Science	374	Applications of Digital Computers
103	FORTRAN Programming	375	Intro to Numerical Methods (4)
150	Algorithmic Process (2)	381	Switching Theory & Logical Design
171	Elements of Computational Algorithms (4)	395	Special Topics
172	Elements of Computational Algorithms	398	Cooperative Education Internship
173	Elements of Computational Algorithms	401	Adv Programming (4)
195	Special Topics	402	Adv Programming (4)
200	Computer Organization	403	Adv Programming (4)
201	Machine/Assembly Language Programming (4)	421	Analytic Models in Operating Systems
202	Machine/Assembly Language Programming (4)	422	Data Communications in Computer Systems
212	COBOL Programming & Data Processing	423	Elements of Computer Graphics
299	Undergraduate Seminar	451	Computers & Society
301	Programming Languages	452	Computer Applications In Education
302	Data Structures	470	Analysis & Design of Business Systems
303	Compiler Theory	471	Appl Analysis & Dsgn of Business Systems
305	Computer Methods in the Natural Sciences	473	Large Scale Computer Models (4)
306	Computer Methods in the Natural Sciences	474	Large Scale Computer Models
307	Computer Modeling in the Natural Sciences	475	Computer Simulation of Business Systems
312	Adv COBOL Prgmmng & Business Applns (4)	481	Adv Logic Design
313	Dvlpmnt of Computerized Bsnss Systems (4)	485	Microprocessors
314	Data Base Management Systems	487	Microprocessor Applications
371	Intro to Discrete Structures	491	Adv Topics in Computer Science
		499	Seminar

115

NEBRASKA

UNIVERSITY OF NEBRASKA
Lincoln, NE 68508
(402) 472-3601

The University of Nebraska is a public university whose 560-acre campus serves a population of 25,000 students with a faculty student ratio of 1 to 18, and a library with close to 1.2 million volumes.

The Computer Science Department offers BS, MS and PhD programs in which 875, 70 and 15 students are enrolled currently. The PhD degree is offered within the framework of the interdisciplinary engineering. In addition, a computer science PhD option is also offered through the Department of Mathematics. Prospective students should apply through the Admissions Office. No deadline is specified.

Computer systems in use include: IBM 370/158, VAX 11/780 and many microcomputers. There are 15 full-time members in the department. Faculty positions exist at all ranks.

Course Offerings: (normally 3 semester units)

101	Intro to Digital Computers (1)	420	Language Structures
103	Making It Count (2)	422	Programming Language Concepts
110	Intro to Data Processing	425	Compiler Construction
150	Intro to FORTRAN Programming	430	Computer Architecture
151	Computer Orientation (1)	435	Switching & Finite Automata Theory
155	Intro to Computer Programming	436	Microcomputer Applications
230	Computer Organization	441	Approximation of Functions
231	Assembler Language Programming (2)	450	Systems Programming (5)
235	Intro to Discrete Structures	455	Numerical Methods
237	Intro Computer Applns in Business (4)	460	Operations Research
252A	COBOL Programming (1)	470	Computer Graphics
252B	Interactive Computing - APL (1)	496	Special Topics in Computer Science
252D	FORTRAN Programming (1)	498	Computer Problems
252E	Job Control Language (1)	910	Formal Languages
252G	PASCAL Programming (1)	922	Very High-Level Lang & Prog Systems
252P	PL/I Programming (1)	930	Adv Cmptr Archtctr for Modular Systems
252S	Stat Packages for Social Scientists (1)	932	Fault Tolerant Computing
300	Intro to Computing in Social Sciences	935	Mathematical Theory of Automata
310	Information Structures (4)	950	Advanced Operating Systems
336	Digital Laboratory (1)	955	Cmptr Performance Model w Queueing Thr
340	Numerical Analysis I (4)	965	System Simulation
400	Computers and Society	970	Pattern Recognition
412	Data Base Organization & Management	990	Advanced Topics

Creighton is a private university whose 85-acre campus supports a population of 5,800 students with a faculty student ratio of 1 to 14, and a library with 460,000 volumes.

A bachelor's program in computer science is offered here. 300 students are currently enrolled in the program. Prospective students should apply thrugh the Director of Admissions at least one month prior to the start of semesters.

Computing facilities at Creighton include a dual Univac 1100/60s, and many Apple IIes. Additional microcomputers will be purchased in the near future. Currently, there are 11 full-time faculty members in the department.

Course Offerings: (normally 3 semester hours)

107	BASIC Programming Language (3)	511	Intro Compiler Design
111	COBOL Programming Language I	523	Applied Linear Algebra
112	COBOL Programming Language II	527	Data Structures & Algorithm Analysis
113	FORTRAN Programming Language	530	Intro Artificial Intelligence
117	PASCAL Programming Language	533	Organization of Programming Languages
121	Computer Programming I	537	Discrete Structures
122	Computer Programming II	543	Numerical Analysis
201	Intro Microcomputer Orgnztn & Programming	553	Intro Systems Programming
303	Intro to Computer Systems	557	Intro Data Communications
307	Intro Computer Organization	563	Database Management Systems Designs
313	Intro File Management	573	Operating Systems Structure & Design
493	Directed Independent Readings	577	Computer Architecture
495	Directed Independent Study	585	Automata, Computability, & Formal Languages

NEVADA

UNIVERSITY OF NEVADA
Reno, NV 89557
(702) 784-6865

The Reno campus of the University of Nevada supports a population of 11,000 students with a faculty student ratio of 1 to 21, and a library with over 710,000 volumes.

The Department of Electrical Engineering and Computer Science is the only department in the state that offers a bachelor and master's degrees in computer science. Currently, there are 100 and 20 in these two programs. Interested students should apply through the Office of Admissions and Records. No deadline is specified.

There are 12 full-time members in the computer science program. Faculty positions exist at all ranks. Background in all areas of computer science will be considered.

Computing facilities at UN Reno include: a Cyber 730, two Harris 8000, two DEC 11/45, Three DEC 11/35, VAX 750 and many micros including the HP85s.

Course Offerings:

Electrical Engineering Dept.

131	Computer Techniques I (2)
132	Computer Techniques (2)
231	Computerized Matrix Algebra (1)
333	Computer Logic & Architecture
533	Computer Logic & Architecture
335	Computer Programming & Organization
535	Computer Programming & Organization
336	Computer Programming Languages
536	Computer Programming Languages
337	Cmptr Acquaintance for Bio Sciences
537	Cmptr Acquaintance for Bio Sciences
339	Computer Acquaintance (1)
405	Microprocessor Laboratory (1)
430	Num Methods in Electrical Engineering
630	Num Methods in Electrical Engineering
431	Digital Computer Design
631	Digital Computer Design
435	Microprocessors
635	Microprocessors
436	Cmptr Systems & Systems Programming
636	Cmptr Systems & Systems Programming
437	Computer Graphics
637	Computer Graphics
731	Advanced Switching Theory
732	Theory of Finite Automata
733	Advanced Microprocessors

Mathematics Dept.

183	Introduction to Computer Science
283	Computer Mathematics
385	Computer Programming & Organization
585	Computer Programming & Organization
386	Computer Programming Languages
586	Computer Programming Languages
387	Computer Logic & Architecture
587	Computer Logic & Architecture
480	Computer Applications in Education
680	Computer Applications in Education
483	Numerical Methods I
683	Numerical Methods I
484	Numerical Methods II
684	Numerical Methods II
485	Computer Data Structures
685	Computer Data Structures
486	Prncpls of Computer Operating Systems
686	Prncpls of Computer Operating Systems
487	Computer Database Management Systems
687	Computer Database Management Systems
489	Topics in Computer Science (1 to 3)
689	Topics in Computer Science (1 to 3)
703	Computability & Complexity
709	Topics in Advanced Computer Science

NEW HAMPSHIRE

DARTMOUTH COLLEGE
Hanover, NH 03755
(603) 646-1110

Dartmouth is a private college with a 175-acre campus, a population of 5,000 students, a faculty student ratio of 1 to 12, and a library containing over 1.5 million volumes and more than 15,000 subscriptions to periodicals.

The Computer and Information Science (CIS) Program offers undergraduate and graduate degrees. Currently, there are 100 in the bachelor's and 40 in the MS and 1 in the PhD programs. Prospective students should apply through the Admissions Office; deadlines: March 1 for the graduates and Jan 1 for the undergraduates. Matriculation into the CIS program is possible only in September at the beginning of the Fall term. In addition, the School of Engineering offers undergraduate and graduate programs in Engineering Science which allow students to specialize in EE and Computer Science.

Computing equipments at Dartmouth include: two Honeywell DPS systems, a dyadic processor 66/DPS-3 and DPS 8/44, a Prime 750 for large computational tasks; a VAX 750 (UNIX) for computer science instruction and research. Microcomputers such as the DEC LSI 11s, IBM PCs, Apples, and Teraks are available. They can be attached to the campus-wide Kiewit Network, which provides access to services based on the UNIX time-sharing system and on the IBM 4341 computer. The Dartmouth Time-Sharing System, the seventh version, includes extensive graphics capabilities. More personal computers will be acquired in the near future.

There are 10 full-time members in the program. Dartmouth is in the process of expanding its academic programs in Computer Science and Computer Engineering. One or two positions exist at the assistant professor rank, one at the full rank. Background in software systems is particularly desired. Faculty and their interests:

S J Garland (stfwr dsgn, prgrmng mthdlgy, verifctn tchnqs); T E Kurtz (language dsgn, educatnl computing, statistics); W Y Arms (educatnl computing, graphical sftwr, library automation, ntwrks, distrbtd editng); R P Bigelow (law & tchnlgy, social implctns); L P Chew (theoretical computer science); B Ives (mangmnt of computing, dsgn of man-machine interfaces, diffusion of scientific knowledge); I F Jackson (info mangmnt & control); J G Kemeny (user friendly systems, social implctns); P D L Koch (prqmnq languages, operating systems); A M Kratzer (ntwrks, architctr, VLSI); D L Kreider (logic, recursion thry, linguistics, complexity thry); G P Learmonth (self-adaptive tchnqs, OR, quantitv analysis)

Course Offerings:

111	Organizations and Data	157	Topics in Systems Design
112	Algorithms and Data Structures	161	Data Base Systems
122	Software Design and Developement	162	Programming and Operating Environments
123	Computer System Organizations	167	Readings in Computer & Information Systems
131	System Analysis	173	Networks and Distributed Processing
134	Project Management	176	The Ethical & Social Impact of Computing
154	Management of Computing	177	Independent Projects
155	Quantitative Methods fo Decision- Making	179	Professional Communications

119

NEW JERSEY

PRINCETON UNIVERSITY
Princeton, NJ 08544
(609) 452-3060

Princeton is a private university with a 2200-acre campus, a population of 6,000 students, a faculty student ratio of 1 to 7, and a library containing over 3 million volumes.

The Department of Electrical Engineering and Computer Science (EECS) offers bachelor's, MSE and PhD programs. Currently, 240, 25 and 60 students are enrolled in these three programs respectively. Prospective students should apply through the Admissions Office before January 1.

The major academic areas within the department are: computer science, computer enginering, information sciences and systems, electronic materials and devices. The Computer Science area is concerned with fundamental properties of digital information processing systems, with an emphasis on algorithms and their implementation, and design of computer systems, both hardware and software. Research activities in computer science include: theory of algorithms, asynchronous sytems, discrete optimizations, and pattern recognition. Research in the Information Science & Systems area include: estimation and detection, stochastic processes, optimization of stochastic systems, adaptive and learning systems, mathematical systems theory, nonlinear filtering, computer commnication, data communication, digital and optical signal processing.

Computing facilities available include: an IBM 3081, one VAX 11/780, eight VAX 11/750 using UNIX, HP F1000, HP 2116, HP 2116, HP 2100 and numerous Terak microcomputers.

There are 23 full-time members in the department. Positions exist at all levels. All qualified candidates will be considered. Background in architecture, hardware, microprocessors, programming languages, operating systems, or computer graphics would be of particular interest. Faculty and their interests: (a partial listing)

F S Acton (numerical computation, prgrmng tchnqs); B W Arden (operating systems, archtctr); B W Dickinson (system thry, communication thry); D P Dobkin (geometric complexity thry, graphics algrthms, VLSI); H Garcia-Molina (database systems, distrbtd prcssng); P Honeyman (database systems, VSLI circuits); A Kahn (semiconductors surfaces & interfaces); A S LaPaugh (complexity thry, VLSI design); R J Lipton (theoretical computer science, softwr engingeering); B Liu (communication thry, signal processing); A W Lo (computer organization, computer components); J C Seed (medical computer systems); K Steiglitz (algrthms, digital signal prcssng0; W H Surber (computer aided design); D C Tsui (physics of thin film and interfaces).

Course Offerings:

103	Intro Computers & Programming	498	Senior Independent Work
118	Intro Digital Computing & Application	311	Electrical Aspects of Energy
119	Intro Digital Programming	317	Computer Structure
211	Intro Signals, Circuits, & Microcomputers	318	Principles of Computer System Organization
212	Principles of Applied Electronics	320	Compiling Techniques
217	Intro Programming Systems	383	Electronic Devices & Circuits
283	Intro Electrical Engineering	384	Digital Electronics & Systems
284	Intro Discrete System	385	Engineering Analyisis
286	Physical Foundations of E E	386	Physical Principles of Electronic Devices
202	Intro Energy & its Impact on Environment	390	Linear Systems Theory
206	Intro Engineering Dynamics	398	Junior Independent Work
215	Intro Nuclear Science & Nuclear Issues	400	Computer Applications to Medicine
221	Thermodynamics	418	Microcomputer Hardware & Software
483	Microwave Electronics	420	Design of VLSI Systems
484	Feedback Systems	423	Theory of Algorithms
485	Signal Analysis & Communication System	424	Optimization Techniques
486	Digital Commnctns: Technq, Systems & Ntwrks	425	Database Systems
487	Theory of Automata & Computation	426	Computer Graphics
489	Materials & Solid State Device laboratory	481	Intro Solid State Electronics
490	Solid State Devices	482	Digital Signal Processing
495	E E & Computer Science Seminar		

NEW MEXICO

NEW MEXICO INSTITUTE OF MINING
& TECHNOLOGY
Socorro, NM 87801   (505) 835-5424

The New Mexico Institute of Mining and Technology, also known as New Mexico Tech, is a public institute serving a populatin of 1,300 students. The Institute has a faculty ratio of 1 to 15 and a library containing over 90,000 volumes. The 320-acre campus is located on the Rio Grande in a broad valley surrounded by mountains and desert. The mild and sunny climate, the national forests, and Tech's 18-hole golf course make the area ideal for outdoor enthusiasts.

The Computer Science Department offers BS MS and PhD programs. Currently, 160, 24, and 6 students are enrolled in them respectively. Two options are available in the BS program, one one systems programming and theoretical computer science, the other on scientific applications programming. Prospective students should apply through the Office of Admissions; deadline: Aug 15 for the Fall and Dec 15 for the Spring.

The Tech Computer Center operates a DEC 2060 and a graphics lab. The Systems Programming and Software Development Lab runs a VAX 11/750 (UNIX) which is also used as Tech's node in the PhoneNet portion of NSF's CSNet. The Microcomputer Lab has several LSI/11 and Motorola 6802 micros, supported with a cross asembler and simulator on the DEC 2060. Object code produced by the cross asembler can be downloaded into one of the micros via a local network developed at the Institute. Intel Microprocessors and Mostek memory chips are available for student projects. Real time control applications and high speed data handling are done on a SEL 32/77, a 32-bit minicomputer capable of handling an input rate of four megabytes per second. It can be used for real time acquisition of radar data and analysis of lightning data.

Faculty positions are open at the associate professor level. All areas will be considered. Background in computer architecture, and/or operating systems, and possibly numerical analysis would be particularly desirable. Faculty and their interests:

R T Duquet (data structures, simulation, commercial applications software, scientific data bases); T Hintz (microprocessors, architecture, interface of local networks with packet switching networks); R M McGehee (applied numerical analysis, fluid dynamics); E Runnion (system programming, microcomputers); A M Stavely (software design and analysis tools, programming languages, concurrent processing); G Smith (operating systems, simulation, psychology of programming); K Taghva (theory of computation, formal language theory, programming languages, functional programming); F Thomason (microprocesors control and interface, S-100 bys and networking) .

Course Offering:

100	Digital Computer Programming (2)	102	Practicum in COBOL (1)
106	Digital Computer Programming II (2)	201	Practicum in Macro 20 Assembly Language (2)
111	Intro Systematic Programming (2)	202	Practicum in Macro 11 Assembly Language (2)
112	Intro Computer Systems (4)	203	Practicum in APL (1)
212	Non-Numeric & Symbolic Computation	205	Practicum in PASCAL (1)
221	Intro Systems Programming (4)	301	Practicum in GASP (1)
307	Intro Computer Programming & Numer Methods	302	Practicum in C (2)
325	Principles of Operating Systems	303	Practicum in SNOBOL (1)
328	Software Consturction	304	Practicum in LISP (1)
330	Data Communications	305	Practicum in Computer Graphics (1)

Graduate Offerings

341	Theory & Design of Digital Machines	500	Directed Research (CR to Be Arranged)
342	Formal Languages & Automata	501	Numer Methods for Partial Diff Equations
344	Design & Analysis of Algorithms	520	Theory of Parsing, Transiation, & Compiling
380	Psychology & Computers (2)	525	Operating Systems Theory
391	Directed Study (CR & Topics Arranged)	526	Computer Graphics (2)
410	Numer Methods for Scientists & Engineers I	527	Seminar in Real Time Programming (2)
411	Numer Methods for Scientists & Engineers II	528	Design & Analysis of Software Systems
423	Compiler Writing (4)	531	Computer Architecture
428	Software Workshop (2)	541	Adv Switching Theory
431	Intro Computer Architecture	542	Adv Automata Theory
440	Intro Operations Research	543	Reasoning about Programs
485	Computer Science Seminar (1)	544	Analysis of Algortihms
486	Computer Science Seminar (1)	581	Directed Study
491	Directed Study (CR & Topics Arranged)	585	Graduate Seminar (1)

Practical Courses

NEW MEXICO STATE UNIVERSITY
Las Cruces, NM 88003
(505) 646-3121

New Mexico State is a public university with a 6,250-acre campus, which is among the largest in the world. The campus supports a population of 12,500 students with a faculty student ratio of 1 to 21, and a library containing 700,000 volumes.

The Department of Computer Science offers BS, MS, and PhD programs with current enrollments of 292, 56 and 6 respectively. Undergraduates should apply through the Office of Admissions. Graduates apply through the Dean of Graduate School; deadlines: July 1 for the Fall, Nov 1 for the Spring, and April 1 for the Summer.

Computing facilities at New Mexico State include: an AMDAHL 470/V5, an IBM 4341 with OS MVT and VM CMS operating systems respectively; PDP 11/34 (UNIX), HP Shared Resourse Manager, three HP 9816s, IBM PCs, three Terak 8510 graphics system, one Ramtek 9351 color graphic system, five LSI 11/03s, and a Cambridge Ring for local network. CSNET (phonenet) is to be acquired in the near future.

The Department consists of 11 full-time members. One position may be open at the assistant professor rank. Faculty and their interests: M B Wells (prgrmng languages, algrthms); J M Adams (prgrmng languages, thry of computation); D W Dearholt (AI); J R Denk (info systems, computer systems mangmnt); V P Holmes (operating systems, ntwrks, performance modeling); K M Hussain (info systems); J B Johnston (computational system structure); A I Karshmer (graphics, minicomputer systems); T J Long (thry of computatn, complexity thry); R J Lorentz (thry of computatn, concrete complexity thry); D Partridge (AI, computatnl linguistics); T H Puckett (operating systems, systems prgrmng); R H Stark (graphics, prgrmng languages).

Course Offerings:

110	Computer Appreciation	482	Database Management Systems
171	Algorithmic Computations	484	Distributed Systems
207	FORTRAN Programming (2)	485	Computational Linguistics
222	Algorithms and Data Structures I	486	Computer Graphics in Parts Manufacture
227	Ada Programming	487	APL Programming (1)
237	APL Programming (2)	489	Independent Study
263	Machine Programming and Organization		Graduate Offerings
278	Information System Design	510	Theory of Computation
320	Operational Semantics	550	Mathematical Linguistics
322	Programming Concepts-Honors	563	Architectural Concepts II
363	Computer System Architecture	567	Simulation Concepts and Languages II
363	Computer System Architecture Lab (1)	571	Programming Language Structure II
371	Programming Principles	574	Operating Systems II
377	Introduction to Numerical Methods	575	Artificial Intelligence II
378	Information System Implementation	576	Computer Graphics II
409	Independent Study	577	Information Storage and Retrieval
450	Automata, Languages, Computability	578	Management Informatgion Systems II
457	FORTRAN Programming (1)	579	Special Topics (1-6)
460	Introduction to Semantics	581	Compiler Construction
461	Pascal Programming (1)	589	Special Research Problems (1-6)
462	Programming Concepts (2)	599	Master's Thesis
463	Architectural Concepts I	600	Predissertation Research
467	Simulation Concepts & Languages I	620	Topics in Theoretical Computer Science
469	Social Implications of Computing (1)	621	Topics in Programming Languages
471	Programming Language Structure I	622	Topics in Algorithms and Data Structures
472	Algorithms and Data Structures II	623	Topics in Computer Architecture
474	Operating Systems I	624	Topics in Operating Systems
475	Artificial Intelligence I	625	Topics in Artificial Intelligence
476	Computer Graphics I	626	Topics in Computer Graphics
477	Design and Implementation of Simulation	628	Topics in Information Systems
478	Management Information Systems I	629	Selected Topics in Computer Science
479	Special Topics	700	Doctoral Dissertation

UNIVERSITY OF NEW MEXICO
Albuquerque, NM 87131
(505) 277-0111

The University of New Mexico is a public university with a 600-acre campus, a population of 23,000 students, a faculty student ratio of 1 to 12, and a library containing 1.1 million volumes.

The Department of Computer Science offers BS, MS and PhD programs, in which 212, 74 and 8 students are enrolled respectively. In addition, the Electrical & Computer Engineering Department offers a BS in Computer Engineering for students with strong interests in hardware and systems. A dual program MBA/MS in CS is also available.

Apply through the Department of Computer Science, College of Engineering. Deadlines for graduate admissions: June 30 for the Fall; Nov 15 for the Spring; April 15 for the Summer.

Computing facilities at the University include four VAX 11/70, IBM 3032, PDP 11/44, Apples, TI 9900s. Faculty position is open at assistant professor rank. Higher ranks may be possible. Faculty and their interests:

E S Angel (image processing, image coding); W Brainerd (language development, formal languages); S Bell (microprocessor software, programming methodology, operations research); E J Gilbert (problem solving, programming methodology, computer music); C B Moler (matrix computations, vector software); D R Morrison (data structures, management of computing installations); C P Crowley (operating systems, user systems interfaces, architecture).

G F Luger (AI, knowledge engineering, cognition science); H D Shapiro (algorithmic heuristics, high level computer architecture); P Helman (combinatorial optimization, database design); M J Manthey (concurrency and quantum mechanics); A Maccabe (language design distributed computing); B M E Moret (algorithmic heuristics, system reliability, testing, image & pattern rcognition); R Veroff (automated theorem proving, design verification).

Course Offerings:

150	Computing for Business Students	475	Numerical Analysis I
154	Foundations of Cumputing Science	476	Numerical Analysis II
155	Intro to Computer Programming (4)	487	Studies in Operating Systems
237	Intro to Data Processing	491	Special Topics - Undergraduate (1-6)
253	Intermediate Programming (4)	499	Individual Study - Undergraduate (1-3)
255	Intro to Computing Systems	502	Analysis of Algorithms
263	Fundamentals of Data Structures (4)	503	Computability & Complexity
300	Block-Structured Programming (5)	506	Stochastic Optimization in Computer Science
303	Fundamentals of Algorithms	550	Programming Languages & Systems
337	Survey of Computer Systems Org & Software	552	Advanced Topics in Compiler Construction
355	Syntax & Semantics of Prgmmng Languages	553	Computer Evaluation of Math Functions
357	Operating Systems Principles	557	Selected Topics in Numerical Analysis
375	Intro to Numerical Computing	563	Design & Use of Data Base Systems
390	Introductory Topics in Prgmmng (1-3)	566	Pattern Recognition
401	Modern Computer Architecture	587	Advanced Operating Systems
403	Algorithm Heuristics	592	Colloquium (1)
405	Linear & Integer Programming	650	Reading & Research
406	Intro to Stochastic Methods in Cmptr Scnce	691	Seminar in Computer Science (1-6 hrs)
431	Cryptology in Computing	699	Dissertation (3-12 hrs.)
433	Computer Graphics	Graduate Offerings:	
438	Information Processing Models of Cognition	420	Immigration I (5)
451	Math Theory of Formal Languages	421	Immigration II (5)
452	Simulation	422	Immigration III (5)
453	Topics in Program Correctness	490	Computing for Graduate Students
454	Compiler Construction	551	Individual Study - Graduates (1-3)
457	Principles of A I Machines	559	Master's Computing Poject (3 or 6)
460	Advanced Software Methodology	591	Special Topics - Graduates (1-6)
463	Storage & Retrieval of Information		

NEW YORK

COLUMBIA UNIVERSITY
West 116 ST., NY 10027
(212) 280-2521

Columbia university is a private institution which occupies two major campuses in Manhattan, the 32-acre Morningside campus that houses haumanities, engineering & pure sciences, business, law, and the Health Sciences campus at 168th St and Broadway. Together, they serve a population of 17,000 students with a faculty student of 1 to 6, and a library with over 5 million volumes.

The Computer Science Department of the School of Engineering & Applied Science offers BS, MS, PhD, Doctor of Engineering Science, and a professional degree beyond the MS that requires no thesis, the degree of Computer System Engineer. Applications should be requested from the Office of Engineering Admissions, 530 Seeley W Mudd, Columbia University, NY 10027, (212) 280-2931. For admission as a Freshman, Part One application must be filed by Jan 1. Upon receipt of Part One, Part Two application package is sent out to the student, which is to be received by Jan 20. For admission with advanced standing, the deadline is March 15 for the Fall. Deadline for graduate admission with financial aid is Feb 1; for reuglar admission, March 15.

The University's computing center contains three IBM 4341, four DEC 2060, an IBM 3031, an IBM 3851 mass storage system, and a Xerox 9700 printer. The department has its own labs for instruction and research in: computer communications and VLSI design, microprocessors, AI, and software systems. A new $5.8 million building devoted to computer science research has been completed to house a network of four DEC VAX 11/750s, including special purpose peripherals for VLSI design, image understanding, network analysis, and document production. A hardware lab is maintained to facilitate the development of experimental multi-processors.

Faculty research interests at Columbia include: algorithmic analysis, computational complexity, software tool design, computer modeling, performance evaluation, computer networks, computer architecture, VLSI design, expert systems, natural languae understanding, computer vision, multicomputer design, VLSI applications, artificial intelligence, combinatorial modeling, and microprocessor applications. Faculty:

University Professor: S Eilenbery
Professors: T R Bashkow, J T Gross, M Schwartz, T E Stern, J F Traub, S H Unger, O Wing.
Assistant professors: R Farrow, J Kender, G Leitner, M Lebowitz, K McKeown, D E Shaw, S Stolfo, Y Yemini.
Adjuncts and Lectures: B Gilchrist, C Micchelli, H D Eskin, R Hon; D Bantz, F Cohen, J Gielchinsky, E W Klein.

Course Offerings: (3 semester units unless noted)

1001	Intro to Computer Programming A	4841	Intro to VLSI
1003	Intro to Computer Programming B	4991	Topics in Computer Science & EE
1005	Intro to Computer Programming C	4995	Special Topics in Computer Science
3011	Intermediate Computer Programming	4996	Same as above
3123	Assembly Language & Computer Logic	6101	Data Base Systems
3131	Data Structure	6119	Modeling & Analysis of Operating Systems
3203	Intro to Discrete Mathematics	6180	Modeling & Performance Evaluation
3204	Finite Mathematics	6204	Topics in Graph Theory
3232	Fundamental Algorithms	6206	Topics in Combinatorial Theory
3240	Elementary Numerical Analysis	6214	Program Verification
3261	Computablity & Formal Languages	6232	Analysis Verification
3824	Elements of Computer Organization	6262	Parallel Computation Systems
3998	Undergraduate Projects in Computer Science	6291	Theoretical Topics in Computer Science
4001	Computer Programming Engineering Applns	6741	Topics in Artificial Intelligence
4114	Assembly Language & Systems Programming	6827	Digital Computer System Design I
4115	Programming Languages & Translators	6828	Digital Computer System Design II
4117	Programming Languages & Translators II	6831	Sequential Logic Circuits
4118	Intro to Operating Systems	6832	Topics in Logic Design Theory
4125	Software Laboratory	6851	Distributed Processing
4203	Graph Theory	6865	Parallel Architectures & VLSI Systems
4205	Combinatorial Theory	6900	Tutorial in Computer Science
4231	Analysis of Algorithms	6901	Projects in Computer Science
4241	Numerical Algorithms & their Complexity	6998	Topics in Computer Science
4242	Numerical Algorithms & their Complexity II	8992	Readings in Computer Science
4261	Cmptatn Mthds in Engnrng Anlysis & Dsgn	9902	Seminar in Computer Science
4400	Computer & Society	9910	Research
4701	Artificial intelligence	9911	Doctoral Research
4705	Natural Language Processing	9951	Doctoral Research Instruction
4801	Mathematical Logic I	9999	Doctoral Dissertation
4802	Mathematical Logic II		

CORNELL UNIVERSITY
Ithaca, NY 48103
(607) 256-1000

Cornell is a private university whose 734-acre main campus is in Ithaca. Operating on a semester system with summer sessions, the university serves a population of 16,500 students with a faculty student ratio of 1 to 6 and a library with 4.5 million titles. It is a prominent research university.

The Department of Computer Science, established in 1965 and one of the oldest CS departments in the country, has produced graduates serving almost every major universities and industrial research labs. Oriented toward graduate study and primarily toward doctoral study, the Department offers BS, MS and PhD programs with current enrollments of 150, 4 and 85 students respectively. Undergraduates should apply through the Admissions Office; deadline Jan 1; graduates through the Graduate Field Representative, Computer Science Department; deadline Feb 15.

Computing facilities include two VAX 11/780, two PDP 11/60, Sun and Motorola 68000 workstations. The uiversity computer center runs an IBM 370/168, two IBM 4341s, a DECSYSTEM 2060. Lisp Symbolic 3600, 11/750, and IBM PC-XTs are to be acquired in the future.

Major research engaged here include: Programming Languages and Systems; Computing Theory; Information Organization and Retrieval; Numerical Analysis; and Robotics. There are 21.5 full-time members in the department. Faculty openings exist. Applicants showing strong research potential in programming languages, operating systems and software engineering are especially sought. Faculty and their interests:

O Babaoglu (distrbtd systems, performance evaluation); K Birman (distributed systems, signal prcssng); J Bramble (numerical analysis); T Coleman (numerical analysis); R L Constable (computational complexity, formal semantics, proof of thry of prgmng logics); R W Conway (prgmng systems); A J Demers (prgmng languages, semantics, compiler construction); J R Gilbert (analysis of algrthms, combinatorial algrthms for numerical prblms).

D P Greenberg (graphics, computer-aided design, image prcssng); D Gries (prgmng mthdlgy, prgmng languages, comiler construction); J Hartmanis (thry of computation); J E Hopcroft (algrthms, robotics); K Karplus (VLSI, computer music, computer-aided design); F Luk (numerical analysis); A Nerode (logic, applied math); P Pritchard (prgmng mthdlgy, algrthms).

G Salton (info orgnztn & retrieval); F B Schneider (concurrent prgmng, fault tolerance, distrbtd systems); D Skeen (distrbtd computing, fault-tolerant systems, databases); R Teitlebaum (prgmng languages and systems); S Toueg (networks & protocols, distributed computing); C V Loan (numerical analysis).

Course Offerings: (generally 4 units)

100	Intro to Computer Prgrmng	635	Information Organization & Retrieval
101	The Computer Age	640	Design & Analysis of Computer Network
211	Computers & Programming	652	Sparse Matrix Thry
280	Discrete Structures	681	Analysis of Algorithms
305	Social Issues in Computing	682	Theory of Computing
314	Intro to Computer Systems & Organztn	709	Computer Science Graduate Seminar
321	Numerical Methods	711	Topics in Prgrmng Langauges & Systems
410	Data Structures	712	Topics in Prgrmng Languages & Systems
411	Prgrmng Languages & Logics	713	Seminar in Operating Systems
414	Systems Prgrmng & Operating Systems	715	Seminar in Prgrmng Refinement Logics
415	Practicum in Operating Systems	719	Seminar in Programming
417	Interactive Computer Graphics	721	Topics in Numerical Analysis
432	Intro to Database Systems	722	Topics in Numerical Analysis
481	Intro to Theory of Computing	729	Seminar in Numerical Analysis
482	Intro to Analysis of Algorithms	733	Topics in Information Processing
484	Intro to Symbolic Computation	734	Seminar in File Processing
490	Indep Reading & Research	739	Seminar in Info Orgnztn & Retrieval
600	Computer Science & Programming	747	Semianr in Semantics
611	Adv Programming Languages	749	Seminar in Systems Modeling & Analysis
612	Translator Writing	781	Topics: Anlysis Algrthms & Thry Computing
613	Concurrent Prgrmng & Operating Systems	782	Topics: Anlysis Algrthms & Thry Computing
614	Advanced Operating Systems	789	Seminar: Thry of Algorithms & Computing
615	Machine Organization	790	Special Investigation in Computer Science
621	Numerical Analysis I	890	Special Investigation in Computer Science
622	Numerical Analysis II	990	Special Investigation in Computer Science
632	Database Systems		

New York University is a private university which has several campuses that include the main one in Washington Square, the Institute of Fine Arts on 78th St., Medical Center on First Ave., the Graduate Business Center in Trinity Place. The university serves a population of 45,000 students, with a faculty student ratio of 1 to 13 and a library system that contains over three million volumes. Among the university's diverse divisions of international note is the Courant Institute of Mathematical Sciences, which is operated as a research institute by senior faculty members of the Department of Mathematics and Computer Science. The Institute maintains its own library with more than 35,000 volumes and 15,000 volumes of periodicals.

Established in 1969 as a part of the Courant Institute, the Department of Computer Science has experienced rapid growth in its faculty, student population, research staff and funding. Currently, there are 640, 447 and 99 students in its bachelor's, masters and PhD programs respectively. Prospective students should apply through the Admissions Offices of University College, orGraduate School of Arts & Science; deadline for regular admission, June 1; for undergraduate financial aid, Feb 15, and for graduate financial aid, about Jan 15. For more information about the CS programs, contact Courant Institute at 251 Mercer Street, New York 10012, (212) 460-7100.

Computing facilities for research and instructional use include a Cyber 170/720, an IBM 4341, four VAX 11/780, a VAX 11/750, a Data General MV 8000/9600, a DEC 20/50, the IBM PCs, as well as computer graphics systems. Access to the ARPAnet is provided through a local IMP. In addition, the department maintains an engineering lab in which several advanced microprogrammed computers have been designed and built. A major new facility for experimental computer research and robotics is located at a different site on 715 Broadway.

Areas of current research here include: parallel computing, robotics, high level programming languages, software prototyping and testing, the ADA language software testing, natural language processing, artificial intelligence, theory of computation, compilers, operating systems, algorithmic analysis, computer vision, the design of computer systems, VLSI systems, mathematical programming and numerical analysis.

There are 18 full-time faculty members plus 5 research professors in the department. Openings exist at all ranks. Faculty and their interests:

H Berstein (scientific computation, data communctns, ntwrks, robotics); M Bastuscheck (develpmnt and implmntn of robotics devices with particular interest in vision systems); R Cole (computnl complexity, algrthm design, data strctr, complexity thry); M Condict (prgmng languages, verification, semantics logic); E Davis (AI); M Davis (math logic, thry of computation); R Dewar (prgrmng languages, compilers, operating systems, prgrmng by transformation); R Hummel (computer vision, variational inequalities); M Kalos (scientific prgrmng & simulation, Monte Carlo methods, statistical physics); M Goldstein (scientific computation, nonnumerical computatnl commnctn, minis, computer center adminstrtn); A Gottlieb (parallel prcssrs, parallel algrthms, analysis of algrthms); R Grishman (natural language prcssng, AI, computer design).

M Harrison (AI, thrm proving, design of languages & compilers, operating system design microprocessors); G Lowney (high level prgrmng languages, system prgrmng); C O'Dunlaing (thry of computation); M Overton (numerical analysis, optmztn, linear & nonlinear prgrmng, numerical sftwr); E Schonberg (prgrmng languages, compiler design, analysis of algrthms, program transformations); J Schartz (computnl complexity, computer design language design, compiler optmztn, nonnumerical computation, opeating system design); R Spirakis (distrbtd systems, performance evaluation, analysis of algrthms); R Varadhan (probability thry, stochastic prcss, PDE); U Vishkin (analysis of algrthms, parallel prcssrs, parallel algrthms); E Weyuker (program schemas, analysis of algrthms, program testing); O Widlund (numerical analysis, numerical sftwr, PDE, math analysis); C Yap (databases, VLSI design complexity thry & algrthms) Course Offerings:

0001	Computers & Society	2362	Information Theory
0002	Intro to Computers & BASIC	2420	Numerical Methods I
0007	Computer Programming	2421	Numerical Methods II
0041	Topics in Programming Languages	2432	Information Retrieval
0101	Intro to Computer Science I	2433	Database Systems I
0102	Intro to Computer Science II	2434	Database Systems II
0201	Computer Systems Organization	2463	Compiler Optimization Techniques
0310	Basic Algorithms	2520	Algrthmic Analysis & Combintrl Algrthms I
0321	Numerical Methods for Digital Computers	2521	Algrthmic Analysis & Combintrl Algrthms II
0430	System Programming	2542	Symbolic Mathematical Computation
0432	Operating Systems Design	2562	Heuristic Prgrmng & Machine Intelligence
0480	Special Topics	2563	Adv Topics in Artificial Intelligence
0997	Independent Study	2570	Robotics Devices Lab
0998	Independent Study	2632	Parallel Algorithms & VLSI Systems
1122	Intensive Intro to Computing	2643	Compiler Optimization Techniques
1133	C-PAC (Intensive Intro Computer Science)	2672	Logic of Programming
1170	Fundamental Algorithms I	2730	Linear Programming
1171	Fundamental Algorithms II	2750	Nonlinear Optimization
2110	Programming Languages I	2812	Correctness of Algorithms
2111	Programming Languages II	2862	Recursion Theory
2112	Scientific Computing	2940	Adv Num Anlysis: Computatnl Fluid Dynamics
2120	Advanced Topics in Programming Languages	2941	Adv Num Anlysis: Finite Element Methods
2130	Compilers & Computer Languages I	2950	Special Topics in Numerical Analysis I
2131	Compilers & Computer Languages II	2951	Special Topics in Numerical Analysis II
2135	Algorithm Specification	2960	Monte Carlo Methods & Simulation
2233	Computer Systems Design	3023	Topics of industrial Interest
2235	Advanced Computer Design	3032	Special Topics in Computer Science
2250	Design of Operating Systems I	3033	Special Topics in Computer Science
2251	Design of Operating Systems II	3812	Advanced Laboratory
2262	Data Communications	3813	Advanced Laboratory
2270	Computer Graphics	3820	Thesis Seminar
2273	Image Processing	3840	Master's Thesis Research
2350	Theory of Computation I	3860	Research
2351	Theory of Computation II		

POLYTECHNIC INSTITUTE OF NEW YORK
Brooklyn, NY 11201
(212) 643-5000

Polytechnic Institute of New York is a private institute resulted from the merging of New York University's School of Engineering & Science, and the former Polytech of Brooklyn in 1973. Operating on a semester basis, the institute has 5,000 students with a faculty student ratio f 1 to 14, and a technical library with 270,000 volumes.

The computer science program is administered by the Division of Computer Science of the Department of Electrical Engineering and Computer Science. Two undergraduate programs are offered: BS in CS, and computer engineering option leading to BS in Electrical Engineering. Graduate programs include: MS and PhD in computer science, and an MS in information systems. In addition, Combined Computer Science and Life Science Programs are available. Currently, there are 100 enrolled in the BS CS option,

350 in the BS Computer Engineering option, 400 in the MS, and 50 and the PhD program. Interested students should write to the department or call (212) 643-3645.

Computing facilities at PINY include: IBM 4341, IBM 370/158, DEC 11/70, DEC 11/60, Apollo, and various micros including the North Stars, TIs, Motorolas, Intels. Appolo network, and Lockheed graphics systems are available. Future plan includes a second IBM 4341 and a VAX 780.

The EE/CS department has 50 full-time members of which, 16 belong to the CS Division. Faculty positions exist at all ranks. Specialty in any area of computer science will be considered. Faculty and their interests:

E J Smith (computer organztn, automata); B L Hicks (eductnl applns of computers, graphics); M Klerer (prgmng systems, languages, AI); A E Laemmel (computer archtctr, coding); S Preiser (numerical analysis, appl math, algrthms, system performance evaluation); M L Shooman (sftwr engnrng, system reliability & safety).

R J Juels (computer archtctr, microprocessors systems); A Kershenbaum (computer comunications, algrthms); H Ruston (sftwr engnrng, prgrmng, circuit thry).

A D Klappholz (parallel prcssng, archtctr); J H Mirza (archtctr, pipeline prcssng); N Rubin (AI, prgrmng languages, compilers)

Adjuncts: M Adamowicz; B V Gordon; F Grossman; N N Gupta; J P O'Donohue; T W Parsons; R L Schoenfeld; J B Snyder; M W Wilson; J H Chang; D R Doucette; R Flynn; E J Lancevich; D Protopapas.

Course Offerings:

100	Intro to Computer Programming (2)	610	Information & Analysis & System Design II
101	Intro to Digital Computing	613	Computer Architecture I
111	Computer Programming I	614	Computer Architecture II
203	Computer Programming II	616	Microprocessors
204	Intro to Data Structures	623	Operating Systems I
205	Assembly & Machine Language Programming	624	Operating Systems II
206	Compilers	633	Info Retrieval & Natural Lang Prcssng
211	COBOL Programming	635	Principles of Data Communication Networks
217	Information Organization & Retrieval	637	Programming Languages
236	Switching Circuits & Digital Systems	641	Compiler Design & Construction I
237	Intro to Computer Architecture	642	Compiler Design & Construction II
238	Computer Systems	651	Computer Graphics & Image Processing
240	Electronic Music Composition	653	Interactive Computer Graphics
297	Computer Laboratory I (1)	661	Artificial Intelligence I
299	Computer Laboratory II (1)	662	Artificial Intelligence II
397	Senior Sem & Proj in Computer Science (2)	663	A I & Pattern Recognition
398	Senior Project in Computer Science (1)	671	Switching & Automata I
Graduate		672	Switching & Automata II
530	Intro to Computer Science	673	Formal Languages & Automata Theory
531	Intro to Digital Computing	675	Theory of Computation
540	Elements of Data Structures	907	Selected Topics in C S
550	Assembly Language Programming	935	C S Proj Related to Public Adm
603	Information Structures & Algorithms	941	Readings in Computer Science I
606	Software Engineering	942	Readings in Computer Science II
608	Data-Base Management Systems	996	Arojects in Computer Science
609	Information & Analysis & System Design I		

SUNY Buffalo's 1200-acre campus at Amherst serves a population of 27,000 students with a faculty student ratio of 1 to 17, and a library of over 2 million volumes.

The Department of Computer Science offers BS, MS, and PhD programs with current enrollments 120, 65 and 40 students respectively. Students should apply through the department; deadline is Feb 28.

University computing facilities include a Cyber 730 and a Cyber 815. The department has a VAX 780, two VAX 750s (Berkeley UNIX), the DEC 100, IBM PC, and LSI 11/23 micros, work stations, graphics and image processing equipments, plus a lab manager and a full-time systems programmer. CSNet and USENET are are accessible.

There are 8 tenured or tenure-track, 3 visting lectureres, and 5 associated faculty in the department. Positions exist at all ranks. Background in programming languages, architecture, hardware, artificial intelligence are most desirable.

Course Offerings:

Course Offerings: "/" denotes two semester course

113	Intro to Computer Science I	594	Graph and Combinatorial Algorithms
114	Intro to Computer Science II	596	Intro to the Theory of Computation
191/	Intro to Discrete Mathematics	622	Operating Systems
241	Machine Organization and Programming I	637/	Advanced Numerical Analysis
250	Data Structures	642	Techniques of Artificial Intelligence
Graduate		644	Language Processors
505	Fundamentals of Programming Systems	645/	Advanced Systems Programming
506	Fundamentals of Computer Systems	661/	Image Reconstruction
521	Intro to Operating Systems	665	Computer Graphics
531	Analysis of Algorithms	673	Computational Vision
537/	Intro to Numerical Analysis	674	Selected Topics in A I
541	Machine Organization and Programming II	675	Natural Language Understanding
543	Intro to Language Processors	681/	Formal Languages
562	Database Concepts	695/	Theory of Computation
565	Intro to Pattern Recognition	697/	Recursive Function Theory
566	Intro to Image Analysis	699	Supervised Teaching
572	Intro to Artificial Intelligence	700	Independent Study
580	Computer Graphics	701	Computer Science Seminars
591	Fundamentals of Computer Mathematics	799	Supervised Research
		800	Theses Guidance

Stony Brook's 1,100-acre campus supports a population of 16,000 students, with a faculty student ratio of 1 to 15, and a library with 1.3 million volumes.

The Department of Computer Science offers BS, MS, and PhD programs with current enrollments of 450, 50 and 30 respectively. BS students should apply through the Admissions Office, priority deadline Jan 5. Graduates should apply through Graduate Program Director, Department of Computer Science, SUNY Stony Brook; phone: (516) 246-7647. Application deadline for the Fall is March 1.

The University Computing Center operates a dual-processor Univac 1100/82. The CS Lab contains a VAX 11/780, seven VAX 11/750, a PDP 11/60, all under Berkeley UNIX;

two Sun Workstations, four Hurikon Workstations. The VAX systems are linked with an Ethernet and the PDP 11/60 has a connection to an experimental multiprocessor network consisting of LSI 11 micros. The lab has direct access to the CSNET and the ARPANET. Future plan calls for twenty more workstations.

There are 19 full-time faculty members in the department. Positions exist at all ranks. Background in programming environments, software engineering, networks, VLSI, programming languages and database systems are most desirable. Faculty and their interests:

A J Bernstein (design & correctness of operating systems, concurrent prgrmng, computer ntwrk); H Gelernter (AI, scientific applns); J Heller (info orgnztn & retrieval, humanities data prcssng, DBMS); D R Smith (archtctr digital systems design, computer systems).

P B Henderson (software engnrng, prgmng environments); Z M Kedem (database systems, graphics); L D Wittie (operating systems, networks & interconnection topologies).

H G Badr (operating systems design, prformance evaluation); M A Jones (database systems, AI); J Hsiang (prgmng language semantics, program correctness, thry of computation); E Sciore (database design, functional & applicative languages); S C Smolka (operating systems, networks, distributed systems); M K Srivas (specification of software, prgmng language semantics); D Warren (natural language understanding, program verification); A Zorat (distributed computing, architecture).

Course Offerings:

105 Intro to Computer Science and Data Processing
111 Computer Science for Engineers
112 Intro to Computer Science
113 Intro to Computer Science I
114 Intro to Computer Science II (2)
120 Computer Organization and Programming (4)
201 Advanced Programming
301 Intro to Business Data Processing
303 Intro to the Theory of Computatation
304 Compiler Design
305 Database Design
306 Operating Systems
345 Computer Architecture
346 Computer Communications
352 Heur Pgmmng & Simulation of Intlgnt Behavior
370 Digital Simulation and Modeling
371 Computer Graphics
380 Microprocessors & Programmed Logic (4)
475 Undergraduate Teaching Practicum
487 Research in Computer Science (1-6)
Graduate
502 Computer Architecture (4)
503 VLSI Design (4)
504 16 Bit Microprocessor Applications (4)
520 Techniques of Software Design (4)
521 Data Structures (4)
522 Compiler Design (4)
523/524 Laboratory in Computer Science (2-3)
525 Operating Systems (4)
526 Concepts in Modern Programming Languages

530 Simulation and Modeling
532 Database Systems (4)
535 Advanced Topics in Operating Systems
537 Artificial Intelligence
540 Foundations of Computer Science
541 Theoritical Foundations of Computing I
542 Theoritical Foundations of Computing II
543 Automata Theory I
544 Automata Theory II
546 Analysis & synthesis of Computer Comm Ntwrk
548 Analysis of Algorithims
599 Research (variable and repetitve credit)
620 Analysis of Computer Systems
621 Seminar in Programming Languages
622 Seminar in Operating Systems
630 Seminar in Artificial Intelligence
631 Seminar in Database Systems
641 Mathematical Theory of Computation
642 Seminar in Analysis of Algorithims
645 Seminar in Theory of Computation
681 Special Topics in Programming Languages
682 Special Topics in Computer Systems Design
683 Special Topics in Computer Applications
684 Special Topics in Computer Architecture
685 Special Topics in Computer Architecture
686 Special Topics in Artificial Intelligence
687 Special Topics in Computer Graphics
698 Practicum in Teaching
699 Dissertation Research

SYRACUSE UNIVERSITY
Syracuse, NY 13210
(315) 423-3611

Syracuse University is a private university whose 200-acre campus operates on a semester system with summer sessions. It has a faculty student ratio of 1 to 14, and a library with over 2 million titles.

The School of Computer and Information Science offers a BS in Systems & Information Science, BS in Computer Science, MS in Computer Science, and PhD in Computer & Information Science. Current enrollments: 300 in the BS program, 28 full time and 74 part-time students in the MS, and 5 full time and 10 part-time students in the PhD program. Undergraduate application deadline suggested: Feb 1. There is no deadline for graduate admission. Applications are handled in the order they are received. However, the number of openings is limited. It is advisable to apply as early as possible.

The University's Computer Center is equipped with: two IBM 4341s, a DEC KL10, a GT43 graphics system, MV-8000. The School operates its own computing lab consisting of two PDP 11/44s, an online DEC writer III, and many microcomputers. Local Net1 and CSNet with access to ARPANET are also available. Operating systems in use include: MVS, CMS, TOPS 10, A OS/VS. Future acquisition includes an MV 10000 and many more micros for undergraduate uses.

There are 18 full-time members in the department. Faculty positions exist at the assistant professor rank. Background in programming languages, operating systems, or logic programming is particularly desirable.

Current sponsored research at the school includes: logic programming (Air Force); grammars of programming (Air Force); covering radius of cyclic codes (NSF); math semantics for higher order programming languages (Air Force); decoding theory and techniques (NSF); design of an Algol-like language and an assiciated logic for program proving (CORADCOM); design, definition and implementation of programming languages (NSF); axiomatic approach to computer security (NSF); typechecking and implementation properties of programming languages with extended type structure (NSF). Faculty , affiliates, and their interests:

P B Berra (data mangmnt systems, OR, automated process planning); T A Bickart (dynamical systems); K Bowen (AI, logic, theorem proving); M A Brown (logic, metamath, recursion thry); J D Brule (feedback control system, dynamic systems); T C Denise (logic); V W Eveleigh (control systems); G H Foster (automata, computer systems); G M Frankfurter (finalcial modeling & simulation, portfolio selection); P W Gilbert (numerical analysis); A L Goel (statistics); J E Graver (combinatorial math, graph thry).

C R P Hartmann (coding thry, combinatorial math); M K Hu (automata, adaptive mechanisms, info prcssng); L J Lardy (numerical analysis); H F Mattson Jr (applied algebra, coding thry, combinatorial math); N J McCracken (prgmng languages, math semantics); M J McGill (info storage & retrieval systems); K G Mehrotra (applied statistics, reliability); M S Miron (psycholinguistics); F L Morris (thry of computation & its appln to prgmng languages & algrthms); E J O'Connell Jr (simulation of cognitive processes, computer prcssng of natural languages).

O O'M Pardee (numerical analysis); P L Peterson (logic, epistemology, philosophy of language, semantics); J J Pia (linguistics); R Reitman (operating systems, prgmng languages, parallel processes); J C Reynolds (programming languages); J A Robinson (logic, theorem proving, AI); M Rothenberg (linguistics, speech analysis, phonetic thry); L D Rudolph (coding thry, applied combinatorics); L E Sanchis (logic computability thry); R G Sargent (digital simulation, modeling & performance evaluation); J A Scala Jr (graphics, art engnrng).

H Schwarzlander (statistical commnctn thry, info systems); W L Semon (automata thry, switching thry); E E Silbert Jr (math logic, computer design & numerical analysis); E P Stabler (switching circuits, design automation, prgmng languages); E F Storm (prgmng languages, computational linguistics); R O Swalm (engnrng economics, decision analysis); L A Swanson (model appln); R E Ward (computer aids instruction, system design & development); M E Watkins (graph thry & combinatorics); R Wolfson (formal definitional systems for orgnztn decion thry).

Course Offerings:

181	Intro Computing Concepts	575	Seminumerical Algorithms
182	Intro Computer Programming	610	Topics in Coding Theory
183	Intro Computer Programming: Fortran	620	Topics in Computer Graphics
184	Intro Computer Programming: Cobol	621	Fund of Computer Science Math I,II
187	Intro Computer Programming: Pascal	623	Fund of Computer Prgrmmng
205	Survey of Computer & Info Science	624	Fund of Computer Systems
255	Intro Computer Science	625	Computer Graphics
275	Elementary Computer Science Math	626	Thr Foundations of Computer Science
281	Computer Org & Assembly Language	630	Topics in Prgrmmng Languages
282	APL Project (1)	631	Compiler Design
283	FORTRAN Project (1)	635	Advanced Computer Prgrmmng
284	COBOL Project (1)	636	Math Semantics
285	Computer Applications	637	Formal Languages
287	PASCAL Project (1)	645	Combinatorics & Graph Theory I
305	Intro Artificial Intelligence	646	Combinatorics & Graph Theory II
331	Intro COBOL (1)	650	Topics in Computer Systems
332	Intro PL/1 (1)	651	Prgrmmng Laboratory
333	Elementary Operating System Usage(1)	655	Computer Organization
335	Intro Assembly Language Programming	656	Concepts in Concurrent Prgrmmng
355	Interm Prgrmmng in Hi-Level Language	660	Topics in Artificial Intelligence
373	Intro Automat Theory	661	Logic & Prgrmmng I & II
375	Intermediate Computer Science Math	672	Math Logic I
383	Computer Appln for Social Scientists	673	Math Logic II
415	Intro Computational Linguistics	675	Analysis of Algorithms
445	Finite Math	685	Simulation & Modeling
475	Logic & Computable Functions	700	Topics in Computer & Info Science
542	Threshold Logic	710	Topics in Appln of Computer Systems
573	Computability Theory	715	Coding Theory
575	Seminumerical Algorithms	720	Topics in Computer Science Math

Graduate

		740	Topics in Combinatorics
525	Intro Computer Graphics	741	Linear Sequential Machines
535	Assembly Language Prgrmmng	760	Topics in Computation & Cmptnl Logic
536	Computer Prgrmmng Techniques	765	Computational Logic I,II
541	Fault Detection in Digital Circuits	767	Math Theory of Computation
542	Threshold Logic	997	Masters Thesis (6)
573	Computability Theory	999	Doctoral Dissertation (1-15)

UNIVERSITY OF ROCHESTER
Rochester, NY 14627
(716) 275-3221

The University of Rochester is a private university that has a student population of about 9,000, a faculty student ratio of 1 to 11, and a library with close to 2 million volumes.

The Department of Computer Science is a PhD research-oriented department. However, it does cooperate with other departments to provide undergraduates to include

CS in their program of study: 1. The Math program offers a computer science concentration. 2. The 3-2 Degree Program allows a student to earn a bachelor's degree in an undergraduate major and an MS in Computer Science in five years instead of the usual six. 3. Computer S-science may be used as an option in the General Science program. 4. A student may plan a specialization in computer science withen the Cognitive Science program. Contact the Center for Special Degrees, Lattimore 206. 5. A student may set up an individually tailored major through Interdepartmental Degree program. Apply through the Department of Computer Science before Feb 15, phone (716) 275-5671.

The campus computing facilities include: an IBM 3032, DEC PDP KL10, VAX 11/780, PDP-20, a CYBER 175, IBM PCs and the Apples. The Department maintains several prototype ALTO personal computers, a VAX 11/780, four VAX 11/750s, a high-resolution color displays, Optronics image scanner, a Xerox laser printer and over 2 billion bytes of on-line storages. The department operates a local network with two central gateway computers, connecting all facilities and providing connections to the campus machines and to ARPANET.

A senior faculty position in artificial intelligence exists. Faculty and their interests: J F Allen (natural language prcssng, AI, representation of beliefs, goals & actions); D H Ballard (computer vision, medical image idagnosis, geometric reprsntn of objects, planning); C M Brown (AI, computer vision, graphics, production automation, geometric modeling); C S Ellis (parallel computation, methdlgy for correct concurrent software, distributed computing, data mangmnt).

J A Feldman (AI, prgmng languages, distributed computing, biologically plausible distributed info prcssng models); P Gacs (algrthmic info thry, theoretical computer science, info thry, AI, math logic); P J Hayes (AI, logic, cognitive science); G Kedem (numerical analysis, math software, VLSI design, computer-aided design, architecture); T J LeBlanc (distributed systems, prgrmng languages, compilers). J R Low (data structures, prgmng languages, distributed systems).

G L Peterson (theoretial computer science, complexity of algrthms, parallel algrthms); J I Seiferas (automata-based complexity, algrthms, combinatorics); S L Small (AI, natural language comprehension, knowledge representation). Affiliated faculty: D A Goldstein (medical applns, real-time systems); P J Schweitzer (data communication, computer performance, configuration of teleprocessing systems); E L Titlebaum (communications, radar, sonar and computers); H B Voelcker (computer-aided design, computer graphics, production automation).

Course Offerings: (generally 4 semester hours)

110	Computer Literacy	395	Research in Computer Science
171	Intro to Computer Science	400	Problem Seminar
201	Computer Systems I	410	Computer Systems Architecture
202	Computer Systems II	420	Computer Archtctr & Operating Systems
206	Non-Numerical Computing	424	Compilers & Interpreters
207	Computer Graphics	426	Operating Systems
216	Mathematical Logic I	491	Advanced Readings in Computer Science
220	Data Structures	495	Advanced Research in Computer Science
238	Combinatorial Mathematics	509	Topics in Prgrmng Systems
240	Intro to Artificial Intelligence	520	Programming Languages
246	Computer Analysis of Images	529	Topics in Prgrmng Languages
247	Natural Language Processing	540	Artificial Intelligence
248	Theory of Graphs	549	Topics in Artificial Intelligence
280	Intro to Numerical Analysis	571	Special Seminars
286	Intro to Thry of Computation	589	Topics in Thry of Computation
287	Thry of Computation	591	PhD Readings in Computer Science
288	Dsgn & Analysis of Computer Algrthms	595	PhD Research in Computer Science
309	Topics in Computer Science	597	Computer Science Colloquia
391	Independent Study		

Adelphi is a private university with a 75-acre campus supporting 12,000 students. It has a faculty student ratio of 1 to 16 and a library with 380,000 volumes.

The Department of Mathematics and Computer Science offers an undergraduate and an MS with Concentration in Computing. Interested students should apply through the Office of Admissions. Deadline for financial aid is Feb 1 for the Fall Semester.

Computing systems in use include a Prime 850, HP 1000, PE 3230, Apple IIe, Apple II+, and the IBM PC. Prime Net is available. The department is seeking individuals with specialty in artificial intelligence.

Course Offerings: (generally 3 semester units)

Undergraduate
170 Computers and Society
171 Intro to Computer Science I
172 Intro to Computer Science II
173 Intro to Computer Science II A (4)
254 Discrete Structures
271 Software I
272 Software II
343 Data Structures
344 Combinatorial Computing
371 Systems I
372 Systems II
443 Data Base Management Systems
453 Operating Systems
490 Independent Study
491 Directed Reading
493 Special Topics
494 Special Topics
Graduate
573 Assembly Language for Microprocessors
602 Computer Programming in Pascal
612 Intro to Programming
614 Computers in Secondary Education
616 Principals of Programming Languages
643 Computational Mathematics
670 Computer Systems in Education

THE CITY COLLEGE, CUNY
Convent Ave & W 138 ST., NY 10031
(212) 690-6977

City College of New York is the oldest of the four senior colleges in the City University of New York system. Known for its academic excellence in undergraduate education, CCNY now supports a population of 13,500 students that include over 2,000 graduate students, with a faculty student ratio of 1 to 15 and a library with 950,000 volumes.

The Computer Science Department offers BS, MS and PhD (in conjunction with the Graduate Center of CUNY) programs. Prospecive should apply through the Office of Admission before Jan 15.

Computing facilities available at CCNY include Amdahl 470/V6, IBM 3033, and 2 IBM 4341's, plus many other smaller computers maintained by the department.

Faculty positions exist at all ranks. Specialty in any area of computer science will be considered, with those in architecture, data base design, distributed computing, graphics, and the theory of computing especially desired.

Course Offerings: (generally 3 semester units)

5	Computer Science Orientation	5611	Database Systems I
100	Intro to Algebraic Processes	5625	File Management Techniques (COBOL)
101	Computer Prgrmng & Numerical Methods	5630	Operating Systems/Command Languages
104	Discrete Mathematical Structure	5640	Microcomputer Systems
190	Computers in Modern Society	5660	Intro to Management Science
200	Measurements, Modeling & Computing	5700	Seminar in Computer Science
204	Discrete Math Structure	5701	Seminar in Information Systems
205	Computing for Health Care & Management	5703	List & String Processing Languages
206	Computing for Social Sciences Prgrmng	5704	Operating Systems
207	Discrete Probabilistic Models	5706	Fundamental Algorithms
210	Computers & Assembly Language Prgrmng	5707	Compiler Construction
220	Information Structure	5713	Searching & Sorting
322	Software Engineering	5714	Analysis of Algorithms
332	Computers & Programming Systems	5715	Artificial Intelligence
334	Advanced Programming	5716	Natural Languages Processing
336	Information Processing	5719	Pttrn Recognition & Adaptive Systems
338	Computational Linguistics	5720	Intro to Theoretical CS
340	Logic Design & Switching Theory	5722	Intro Computability & Unsolvability
342	Computer Organization	5724	Formal Languages & Automata
350	Combinatorics & Graph Theory	5726	Computatnl Complexity & Recursion Thry
410	Microcomputers	5728	Special Topics in the Thry of Computing
420	Algorithmic Languages & Compilers	5741	Thry of Sequential Machines
422	Computability	5742	Computer Systems
428	Formal Languages & Automata	5743	Real Time Processing Systems
440	Computatnl Methods in Num Analysis	5744	Microcomputers & Microprogramming
442	Systems Simulation	5745	Adv Topics in Switching Thry
446	Math Optimization Techniques	5747	Selected Topics in Cmptr Communication
448	Artificial Intelligence	5761	Mathematical Programming I
596	Real Time Computing Systems	5762	Mathematical Programming II
599	Selected Topics in CS	5763	Decision Analysis
604	Fundamental Concepts of Prgrmng	5764	Topics in System Simulation
Graduate		5766	Probabilistic Models in Cmptr Systems
5500	Selected Topics in CS	5824	Symbolic & Algebraic Manipulation
5604	Computatnl Methods in Discrete Math	5841	Algebraic Coding Thry
5610	Intro to Software Methodolgy		

HUNTER COLLEGE
659 Park Ave., NY 10021
(212) 570-5483

Hunter College is one of the four senior colleges within the CUNY system. Its urban campus of three city blocks supports 18,000 students with a faculty student ratio of 1 to 18, and a library with almost half a million volumes.

The Department of Computer Science offers an undergraduate major program in which 200 students are enrolled. Due to limited resources, only about 80 students out of 500 interested students can be accepted into the program each year. Apply through the Admissions Office before April 1 for the Fall.

There are 11 full-time members in the department. Faculty openings exist at the assistant and associate professor ranks. Background in operating systems, graphics or database is particularly desired.

Course Offerings: (normally 3 semester units)

120	Intro Cmptrs for Humanities & Soc Sciences	310	Data Base Management
125	Intro to Computers for the Sciences	320	Artificial Intelligence
130	Intro to Computer Science	322	Advanced Programming Languages
150	FORTRAN (1)	324	Theory of Computability
155	PL/1 (1)	330	Computer Architecture
160	COBOL (1)	350	Numerical Analysis
161	Business Data Processing	352	Software Engineering
165	Miscellaneous Programming Languages (1)	355	Intro to Linear Programming
200	Intro to Assembly Language Programming	381	Indep Workshop in Computer Science (1-3)
201	Operating Systems & Systems Programming	382	Indep Workshop in Computer Science (1-3)
204	Intro to Discrete Structures	383	Indep Workshop in Computer Science (1-3)
205	Data Structures	391	Indep Study in Computer Science (1-3)
210	Systems Analysis & Simulation	392	Indep Study in Computer Science (1-3)
230	Computer Logic	393	Indep Study in Computer Science (1-3)
250	Numerical Methods	491	Seminar (1-3)
295	Topics in Computer Science	492	Seminar (1-3)
300	Intro to Formal Languages	493	Seminar (1-3)
301	Intro to Compilers		

LONG ISLAND UNIVERSITY
Greenvale, NY 11548
(516) 299-2501

Long Island University is a private university with three independent centers: C W Post Center, the Brooklyn Center, and the Southampton College. The 350-acre campus of the C W Center serves a population of 11,500 students with a faculty student of 1 to 12, and a library with 970,000 volumes.

The Computer Science Department offers Bachelor of Professional Studies (BPS) in which 350 students are currently enrolled. The master's program is pending. Apply through the Computer Science Department. No deadline is specified.

The department has access to a VAX 11/780 (UMS). Planned acquisition in the near future includes a VAX 11/750, PDP 11/44, and a PDP 11/23.

There are 11 full-time members in the department. Faculty positions exist at the assistant and associate professor ranks. Specialty in Software Engineering is most desired.

Course Offerings: (generally 3 semester units)

01	Preparatory Computer Science (0)	14	Intro to Business Data Processing
03	Intro to Computer Science & FORTRAN	15	Advanced COBOL Programming
04	Machine & Assem Language Programming	16	Logic for Computer Science
05	Intro to Computers & COBOL	20	Data Structures
09	Computation Methods in Problem Solving	23	Statistics for Computer Science I
13	Advanced FORTRAN Programming	24	Statistics for Computer Science II

31	Non-numeric Data Processing	42	Management Information Systems II
32	The Management of Data Files	51	Operating Systems
34	Mngnt Science Methods for Computer Science	52	Computer Graphics
35	Computer Simulation	56	Computers Technology & Society
36	Data Communications & Computer Networks	60	Management of Computer Programming
37	Computer Languages	61	Computer Project I
38	Compilers	62	Computer Project II
41	Management Information Systems I	63	Advanced Topics in Computer Science

ROCHESTER INSTITUTE OF TECHNOLGY
Rochester, NY 14623
(716) 475-6631

Rochester Institute is a private institute whose 1300-acre campus serves a population of 9,000 students with a faculty student ratio of 1 to 18, and a library with 200,000 volumes.

The School of Computer Science & Technology offers: BS with options in computer science and applied software science; Computer Technology (B. Tech) with options in computer systems and system software science, BS in Computer Engineering (jointly with Department of EE); MS in Computer Science; MS in Computer Systems Management; MS in Information Sciences; and a sixth-year Certificate Program in Information Sciences intended for persons with MS in library science who need training in computer automated information processing. Undergraduates are suggested to apply early in the fall. Currently, there are 1,100 and 400 in the BS and MS programs respectively. Applications for graduate assistantships should be made through the School of Computer science & Technology before March 31 for the fall quarter.

The main computing system at RIT is a network of four VAX 11/780, one of which is dedicated to engineering graphics applications. The School runs a lab equipped with: two VAX 11/780, a PDP 11/70, a PDP 11/45, all running UNIX; a PDP 11/34 connected to four LSI-11 micros. The Ethernet and USENET are also accessible.

There are 26.5 full-time faculty members in the school. Positions are open at the assistant professor rank. Background in computer science theory is particularly desirable.

Course Offerings:

ICS

P 205	Computer Techniques (3)	P 243	Programming III:Design & Implementation
P 208	Introduction to Programming	P 305	Assembly Language Programming
P 210	Program Design & Validation	P 306	Systems Programming Fundamentals
P 216	Program Design & Validation/FORTRAN	P 307	Business Applications Programming
P 220	FORTRAN Programming for Engineers	P 319	Scientific Applications Programming
P 300	Business Applications Using COBOL	P 330	PL/I Proggramming
P 303	Advanced Business Applications	P 450	Programming Language Concepts
S 200	Survey of C S	P 488	Programming Systems Workshop
S 410	Computer Concepts & Software Systems	S 202	Introdution to Computer Science
S 411	Data Communications & Computer Networks	S 315	Digital Computer Organization
S 483	Applied Database Management	S 320	Data Structure Analysis
P 241	Programming I:Algorithmic Structures	S 325	Data Organization & Management
P 242	Programming II: Data Structures	S 355	The Human Side of Computers

S 360	Fundmntls of CS for Transfer Students	S 709	Programming Language Theory
S 400	Logical Design	S 720	Computer Architecture
S 420	Data Communication Systems	S 721	Microprocessors & Microcomputers
S 430	Numerical Methods	S 730	Modeling & Simulation ,I
S 435	Systems Spec, Design & Implementation	S 731	Modeling & Simulation,II
S 440	Operating Systems	S 735	On-Line Information Systems Design
S 470	Finite State Machines & Automata	S 736	Data Base System Implementation
S 480	Formal Languages	S 744	Data Communications & Networks,I
S 485	Data Base Concepts	S 745	Data Communications & Networks,II
S 515	Analysis of Algorithms	S 770	Fundamentals of Computer Graphics
S 520	Computer Architecture I	S 771	Advanced Topics in Computer Graphics
S 521	Introduction to Microprocessor Systems	S 809	Operating Systems ,I
S 525	Assemblers,Interpreters,& Compilers	S 810	Operating Systems,II
S 530	Fundamentals of Discrete Simulation	S 811	Topics in Operating Systems
S 540	Operating Systems Laboratory	S 836	Data Base Systems
S 541	Introduction to Computer Networks	S 846	Information Storage & Retrieval
S 545	Computer Architecture II	S 850	Computability
S 560	Compiler Construction Laboratory	S 851	Computational Complexity
S 565	Computer Systems Selection	S 852	Coding Theory
S 570	Intrduction to Computer Graphics	S 856	MS Thesis
S 580	Language Processors	S 860	Compiler Construction
S 585	Systems Programming Laboratory	S 890	Seminar(2-4)
S 590	Seminar in Computer Science (2-4)	S 895	MS Thesis
S 599	Independent Study (2-4)	S 899	Independent Study(2-4)(4-8)
S 610	EDP Auditing	M 719	Data Processing & Administration
Graduate		M 725	Systems Development
S 701	Programming,I (8)	M 765	Advanced Computer Utilization
S 702	Programming,II (8)	M 790	Seminar (2-4)
S 703	Algorithms & Data Structures	M 799	Independent Study(2-4)
S 706	Foundation of Computing Theory	I 722	Library Automation & Management
S 708	Computer Organization Programming	I 733	Information Media & Design

ST JOHN'S UNIVERSITY
Jamaica, NY 11439
(212) 990-6161

St John's is a Catholic university whose 95-acre campus in Jamaica supports a population of 11,500 students with a faculty student ratio of 1 to 20, and a library collection of 1.1 million volumes.

The Division of Mathematics, Science & Computer Science offers a BS program in Computer Science. Students are suggested to apply through the Admissions Office by March 1 for the Fall. Contact the University Information Services for further information; phone (212) 990-6161 x6114.

The Computing Lab maintains a Honeywell 68 Distributed Processing System under MULTICS. Faculty openings exist at the assistant professor rank.

Course Offerings: (generally 3 semester units)

1021	Intro to Computers	1062	Survey of Languages II
1031	Intro to Computer Programming Using BASIC	1063	Operating Systems
1032	Algorithmic Processes w FORTRAN	1064	Compilers & Program Translation
1033	Structured Programming w Pascal	1065	Data Base Management Systems
1034	Computer Architecture & Assem Language	1071	Operations Research I
1041	Business Applications w COBOL	1072	Operations Research II
1042	Commercial Systems w RPG	1073	Simulation
1043	Adv Assembler Language	1074	Hybrid Computation & System Modeling
1051	The PL/1 Programming Language	1076	Data Security & Cryptography
1052	Logical Design	1078	Computers & the Law
1053	Adv Business Applications w COBOL & PL/1	1096	Individual Rsrch: Topics in Hardware (1)
1054	Data Structures	1097	Individual Rsrch: Topics in Software (1)
1061	Survey of Languages I		

SUNY AT BROCKPORT
Brockport, NY 14420
(716) 395-2751

SUNY College at Brockport's 591-acre campus serves a population of 7,500 students with a faculty student ratio of 1 to 16, and a library with 405,000 volumes.

The Department of Mathematics and Computer Science offers an undergraduate program which has a current enrollment of 500 majors. Prospective students should apply through the Office of Admissions before Feb 1. For more information, contact the department at (716) 395-2194.

Computing facilities include a Burrough 6800, a Prime 400, plus the Apple microcomputers. Graphics and microprocessor lab are also available.

There are 7 full-time members in the department. Faculty openings exist at the assistant professor rank. Individuals with specialty in any area of computer science would be most desirable.

Course Offerings: (generally 3 semester units)

101	Programming in BASIC	426	File Processing
104	Computers in the Business World	427	Software Systems Development
203	Fundamentals of Computer Science I	431	Data Base Systems
205	Fundamentals of Computer Science II	432	Simulation
213	FORTRAN	433	Computer Graphics
214	COBOL	434	Artificial Intelligence
215	PL/I	461	Math Models for Decision Making I
311	Assembly Language Programming	462	Math Models for Decision Making II
400	Advanced Programming	471	Numerical Analysis
401	Theory of Programming Languages	481	Discrete Mathematics
402	Compiler construction	483	Theory of Computation
411	Computer Architecture	485	Analysis of Algorithms
412	Operating Systems	492	Programming Internship
417	Computer Logic Design	495	Topics in Computer Science
418	Microprocessor Systems	499	Indep Study in Computer Science
422	Computer Information Systems		

SUNY, College at Fredonia's 230-acre campus serves a population of 5000 students, with a faculty student ratio of 1 to 19 and a library with 300,000 volumes.

The college offers an undergraduate degree in computer science. Equipped with a Burroughs 6800 (CANDE), NEC 8001, Heath LSI-11 and the Apple IIe's. The college plans to add a VAX 750 or equivalent in the near future. Interested students should apply through the Admissions Office, deadline May 1.

There are 16 full-time members in the department. A faculty position exists at the assistant professor rank. Specialty in statistics, with a strong background in computer science would be most desirable.

Course Offerings: (3 semester units)

105	Intro to Computing	361	Computer Organization II
125	FORTRAN Programming	380	Algorthms
205	APL with Applications	400	Directed Study of Selected Topics
260	Intermediate Computer Programming I	450	Data Structures
261	Intermediate Computer Programming II	460	Programming Languages
265	Business Programming	480	Operating System Concepts
340	Software Design and Development	490	Theory of Computation
350	Computer Organization I		

SUNY COLLEGE AT OSWEGO
Oswego, NY 13126
(315) 341-2250

SUNY, College at Oswego's 696-acre campus serves a population of 7,500 students with a faculty student ratio of 1 to 20, and a library with half a million volumes.

The Computer Science Department offers an undergraduate program with a current enrollment of 625 majors. Apply through the Office of Admissions; deadline March 15 for the Fall, and November 15 for the Spring semesters respectively.

Computing facilities include a Burroughs B6800 (CANDE), a PDP 11/34 (RSTS, RT-11), two S100 systems, an H11, and an LSI 11/23. A VAX 780 and several supermicros are to be acquired in the near future.

There are 9 full-time members in the department. Faculty positions may exist at the assistant professor rank. Background in operating system is most desired.

Course Offerings: (3 units unless noted)

101	Survey of Computers & Their Applns	341	Prgmmng Data Strctr & Sorting Tchnques
212	Intro to Programming	353	Deterministic Models of Oper Rsrch
213	Assembly Language Programming	365	Intro to File Processing
214	Intro to Programming Using FORTRAN	431	Analysis & Technology of Cmptr Systems
215	Business Oriented Programming	443	Operating Systems
216	FORTRAN as a Second Prgmng Language	444	Compiler Construction
221	Foundations of Computer Science	453	Linear Programming & Game Theory
311	Microcomputer Architecture	454	System Simulation
313	Microcomputer Software	456	Probabilistic Models of Oper Rsrch
315	Advanced Business Programming	459	Data Base Management Systems
320	Numerical Methods	490	Selected Topics (1-3)
331	Digital Computer Logic	499	Independent Study (1-6)

SUNY COLLEGE AT PLATTSBURGH
Plattsburgh, NY 12901
(518) 564-2040

SUNY, College at Plattsburgh's 150-acre campus serves a population of 6,300 students with a faculty student ratio of 1 to 20, and a library with 350,000 volumes.

The college offers BA or BS in Computer Science with study option in scientific computing; and BS in Computer Science with study option in business. The undergraduate programs total 450 CS majors. Suggest applying through SUNY Admissions, Albany NY 12246 in October.

Computing facilities include a Burroughs B6800 (MCP), a DEC PDP 11/24, and the Apple IIe's, Apple II+'s, Comodore Super-Pets. The IBM PCs will be acquired in the near future.

There are currently 8 full-time faculty members in the department. Positions are expected to exist, rank open. Background in business or scientific applications, simulation and modelling, software systems, software engineering are particularly desirable.

Course Offerings: (3 semester units unless noted)

101 Intro to Electronic Data Processing	343 Non-Numerical Information Processing
111 Computation, Reasoning and Problem Solving	345 Artificial Intelligence
113 Intro to an Elementary Language	353 Intro to Numerical Methods
171 Computers and Society	355 Simulation and Modeling
172 Computers and Society (2)	403 Software Design and Testing
201 Intro to COBOL Programming	411 Machine and Assembly Language Programming
202 Systems Analysis	413 Programming Languages
205 Intro to BASIC with Business Applications	415 Application of Minicomputer Systems
211 Intro to FORTRAN Programming	421 Discrete Structures
221 Intro to Computer Science with PASCAL (4)	433 Operating Systems
222 Intro to Computer Science with PASCAL	435 Resource Management in D P Centers
223 Survey of Computer Science with FORTRAN (4)	441 Data Base Maagement Systems
224 Survey of Computer Science	485 Seminar in Applied Computer Science
225 Business Programming (COBOL) (4)	495 Undergraduate Research (2-6)
226 Business Programming (COBOL)	497 Instructional Practicum I (1-2)
313 Intro to a High Level Language (1)	498 Internship in Computer Science (3-15)
314 Intro to High Level Languages	499 Independent Study (2-6)
321 Intro to Data Structures	

VASSAR COLLEGE
Poughkeepsie, NY 12601
(914) 452-7000

Vassar is a private college whose 1000-acre campus serves a population of 2,200 student with a faculty student ratio of 1 to 11, and a library with 550,000 volumes.

The program in Computer Science Studies has 325 students, offering a major in CS and related disciplines under the Independent Program, and an interdepartmental majors in Math-CS. Interested students should apply through the Admissions Office; deadline Feb 1.

Computing facilities include a VAX 11/780, Apples, IBM PC's, and Terak's.

Course Offerings:

101	Intro to Computers with FORTRAN
102	Intro to Computers with PL/I
103	Intro to Computers with PASCAL
104	APL in the Non-Numerical World
155	Intro to Computing for Humanists
170	Computers & People
201	Modeling & Simulation
204	APL, A Programming Language
211	Computer Architecture
225	Data Structures

235	Programming Languages
265	Intro to Artificial Intelligence
271	Natural Language Processing
275	Intro to Numerical Methods
310	Operating Systems
312	Data Structures II
331	Compilers
375	Linear Algebra with Applns
381	Special Studies

NORTH CAROLINA

UNIVERSITY OF NORTH CAROLINA,
AT CHAPEL HILL
Chapel Hill, NC 27514
(919) 966-3621

The University of North Carolina is a public university with a 625-acre campus at Chapel Hill, a population of 21,500 students, a faculty student ratio of 1 to 14, and a library with 3 million volumes. Chapel Hill, along with two towns nearby: Durham and the state capital Raleigh, form the "Research Triangle" of North Carolina. The Research Triangle Park contains a rapidly expanding cluster of high-technology industrial and government laboratories.

The Department of Computer Science offers BS, MS, and PhD programs in which 125, 50, and 40 students are currently enrolled. Prospective students should apply through the Admissions Office or the Department of Computer Science, deadline: Feb 1 for the Fall and Nov 1 for the Spring.

North Carolina is committed to play a major role in the development of microelectronics. As a participating institution in the new Microelectronics Center of North Carolina (MCNC), the Department of Computer Science of UNC-CH: 1) has gained access to the MCNC chip design and fabrication facilities to support research projects; 2) has assumed special responsibility in the development of the MCNC Design Support Facility; 3) has been filling faculty positions with computer scientists whose interests are in broad basic areas supporting microelectronic logical and geometric design, including man-machine systems, databases and algorithms; 4) has established the Microelectronics Systems Lab to support research in digital systems architectures and to build working systems from custom-designed VLSI chips.

The university maintains an IBM 4341, 165 and one IBM 3081 located at the Triangle Universities Computation Center runng the TSO and Wylbur operating systems. Departmental facilities include: two VAX 11/780 with 1 GByte total disk capacity; one VAX 11/750-based VLSI designer's workstation; two PDP 11/45; a Ikonas RDS-3000 raster graphics processing system with 6 megabit frame buffer, a 1000-line cator monitor, fast graphics and arithmetic processors; a Evans and Sutherland PS-300 vector graphics system, two Vector General graphics system; one Ramtek 9400 raster graphics; two Vectrix VX384; two Sun workstations; Apple II+s. The IBM systems run MVS, while the VAX systems run UNIX. In addition, CSnet, USEnet and the Arpanet are all accessible.

Research areas actively pursued in the department include: interactive computer graphics and image processing, VLSI design, software engineering, the architecture of classical and cellular computers, natural language processing, databases and information retrieval, theoretical studies including algorithm design and analysis. Currently, there are 15 full-time members. Faculty openings exist at all ranks. Background in VLSI design and methodology, hardware systems, especially with VLSI orientations, software engineering, or graphics would be particularly desired. Faculty and their interests:

J D Brock (parallel computation, parallel prgrmng languages & concurrent archtctrs, formal semantics of programs & systems); F P Brooks Jr (graphics, archtctr, sftwr engnrng); P Calingaert (VLSI design tools, text prcssng & document preparation, man-machine systems, program translation); H Fuchs (graphics, man-machine systems, archtctr, design of efficient algrthms, biomedical image prcssng); K S Hedlund (VLSI design, parallel computation, archtctr); B Jayaraman (languages for concurrent prgrmng & resource sharing, functnl prgrmng, prgm verification, formal semantics of concurrent systems); G A Mago (parallel computation, archtctr, prgmng languages).

S M Pizer (picture prcssng & display, observer performance, numerical computing applns to medical imaging); J B Smith (info retrieval, natural language analysis); R T Snodgrass (user interfaces for personal computers, database systems, distrbtd systems, multiprssrs); D T Stanat (algrthms design & analysis, program verification, prgrmng language semantics); S F Weiss (info storage & retrieval, automatic analysis of natural language); B I Witt (sftwr engnrng, prgrmng methdlgy). Assiciate faculty includes: E W Danziger (business data prcssng); J W Ott (prgrmng systems); L H Williams (numerical analysis, nonnumeric math computatn, computer center mangmnt).

Course Offerings: (normally 3 semester units)

14	Intro to Programming	238	Raster Graphics
112	Scientific Programming	240	Translators
114	Systematic Programming (4)	241	Compiler Design
116	Numerical Methods	242	Design of Control Programs
118	Data Processing Techniques	244	Programming Languages
119	Information Systems in Language Research	248	Semantics & Program Correctness
120	Computer Organization	254	Picture Processing & Pattern Recognition
121	Data Structures	260	Cmptr Implementation & Microprocessors
131	Computer Systems	265	Architecture of Computers
135	Business Data Processing Laboratory	268	VLSI Sytems Design
145	Software Engineering Laboratory	281	Automata & Formal Languages
151	Numerical Computing	284	Computability & Unsolvability
171	Natural Language Processing	288	Information Theory
172	Information Retrieval	289	Error-Correcting Codes
181	Models of Languages & Computation	290	Topics in Computer Science (1-3)
190	Topics in Computer Science (1-3)	291	Professional Writing in Computer Science
220	Mathematical Theory for Computer Science	321	Tchncl Comm in Computer Science (1)
222	Programming Languages & Techniques	322	Seminar in Professional Practice (1)
224	Mathematical Models in Computer Science	323	Seminar in Research (1)
226	Computer Systems	324	Computers & Society (1)
228	Algorithm Analysis	390	Seminar in Computer Science (1-3)
230	File Management Systems	391	Reading & Research
233	Discrete Event Simulation I	393	Master's Thesis (3 or more)
234	Discrete Event Simulation II	394	Doctoral Dissertation (3 or more)
236	Computer Graphics		

WESTERN CAROLINA UNIVERSITY
Cullowhee, NC 28723
(704) 227-7317

Western Carolina University is a public university with a 400-acre campus, a population of 6,400 students, a faculty student ratio of 1 to 15, and a library with 320,000 volumes.

An undergraduate major in Computer Science is offered by the Department of Mathematics. Currently, there are over 400 students enrolled in the program. Prospective students should apply through the Office of Admissions.

Computing facilities at the University include: two DEC VAX 11/780s, a VAX 11/730, plus several microcomputer systems such as the Apple, TRS-80, DEC, and LSI-11.

There are 22 full-time department members. A faculty position exists at the assistant professor rank. Background in computer hardware would be most desirable.

Course Offerings: (normally 3 semester units)

150	Computer Programming I	452	Computer Organization
151	Computer Programming II	453	Data Base Systems
152	Basic (1)	455	Computer Design
250	Intro to Computer Systems	460	Compiler Construction I
251	Intro to Computer Organization	462	Systems Programming
252	Intro to File Processing	463	Software Design and Developement
253	Discrete Structures	464	Microcomputer Developement
300	High Level Languages (1,R3)	470	Operating Systems
303	Digital Logic	480	Artificial Intelligence
310	Data Transmission	493	Topics in Computer Science (1-6,R6)
320	Computers and Society		Graduate
351	Data Structures and Algorithm Analysis	552	Computer Organization
352	Operation of Programming Languages	555	Computer Design
361	Computer Graphics	560	Compiler Construction II
389	Co-op Education in Computing (3,R15)	564	Microcomputer Developement
393	Topics in Computer Science (1-3,R6)	580	Arificial Intelligence
443	Automata and Formal Languages	593	Topics in Computer Science (1-6,R6)
451	Algorithms	610	Computing Concepts in Programming

WINSTON-SALEM STATE UNIVERSITY
Winston-Salem, NC 27102
(919) 761-2070

Winston-Salem State University supports a population of 2,300 students with a faculty student ratio of 1 to 15 and a library with 155,000 volumes.

The Department of Mathematics/Computer Science offers a BS in computer science in which 400 students are currently enrolled. Prospective students should apply through the department. No deadline is specified.

The department has access to the Triangle Universities Computation Center's large AMDAHL and IBM systems. In addition, the following facilities are available: IBM Series/1, 32 Apples, 3 IBM 5100s, TUCC network, local OMNINET for the Apples. Twelve IBM PCs with local networking are to be acquired in the near future.

There are four full-time members in the department. Faculty positions exist at the associate and full professor ranks. Background in software & design, multiple operating systems would be most desirable.

Course Offerings: (normally 3 semester units)

1306 Intro to Computer Science	3340 Applied Algebraic Structures
1310 Computer Programming I	3341 Intro Numerical Analysis
1320 Computer Programming II	3342 Computer Graphics
2181 Programming Lab - Interactive (1)	3345 Assembler Language Programming
2183 Programming Lab - JCL (1)	3350 Software Design & Developement
2187 Fortran Programming I (1)	3355 Principles of Data Base Management
2189 Principles of Programming - APL (1)	3388 Intro to COBOL Programming
2310 Intro to Computer Systems	3389 Intermediate COBOL Programming
2320 Intro to Computer Organization	3392 Database Management System Design
2330 Intro to Computers & Their Use	4340 Organization of Programming Languages
3310 Intro to File Processing	4385 System Simulation & Modeling
3320 Operating Systems & Cmptr Architecture	4386 Intro Computability Language & Automata
3330 Data Structures & Algorithm Analysis	4387 Seminar in Computer Science
3335 Mini/Microcomputer	4388 Systems Analysis & Design

NORTH DAKOTA

NORTH DAKOTA STATE UNIVERSITY
Fargo, ND 58105
(701) 237-8643

North Dakota State is a public university whose 2,300-acre campus in Fargo supports a population of 9,000 students with a faculty student ratio of 1 to 22, and a library with 360,000 volumes.

The Department of Mathematical Sciences, which consists of 12 full-time faculty members, offers a bachelor's and master's programs in computer science. 400 and 75 students are currently enrolled in them. Prospective students should apply through the department at least one month before the start of classes. The campus operates on a trimester system with two 5-week summer sessions.

Computing facilities at the university include two IBM 4341 processors, a PDP 11/45, a VAX 11/750, a LSI 11/23, thirty two TRS-80s, and twelve IBM PCs. Operating systems in use are UNIX, VSPC, MVS, SAS. Networks ND HECN and AGNET are available. A VAX 11/780 may be acquired in the near future.

Course Offerings:

145	Intro to Computing	455	Numerical Analysis
150	Basic: Applns for Personal Computing (4)	456	Numerical Analysis
160	Scientific Programming in FORTRAN (4)	457	Numerical Analysis
161	Business Programming in COBOL & RPG (4)	465w	Data Structures & Algorithm Analysis II
170	Intro to Computer Science I (4)	474w	Operating System Concepts
171	Intro to Computer Science II (4)	475s	Operating System Design
230	Principles of Digital Systems	480f	Computer Facility Operations (2)
260	Intro to Computer Organization	481w	Computer Facilities Management
271	Assembly Language Programming (4)	482	Computer Project Implementation
310	Intro to Small Computer Systems	Graduate	
311	Intro to Computer Architecture	506w	Machine Language, Structures & Files (5)
340	Adv Programming for Personal Computers	507s	Operating Systems (5)
364	Intro to File Processing (4)	508f	Survey of Mathematical Foundations of C.S.
365	Data Structures & Algorithm Analysis I	509w	Formal Lang, Automata & Cmptr Parsng Tchnq
380s	Adv Scientific Programming in FORTRAN	523s	Compiler Construction
381s	Adv Programming in COBOL	524w	Survey of Artificial Intelligence Mthdlgy
402f	Decision Models I	525s	Computer Comprehension
403w	Decision Models II	526s	Automated Theorem Proving & Game Playing
418s	Simulation Models	527s	Computer Scene Analysis & Robotics
425f	Computer Programming Methods (5)	528f	Computer Graphics
450f	Theory of Linear Programming	529w	Computer Communication Networks
451	Mathematical Decision Models	537f	System Simulation
452	Mathematical Decision Models		

538w	Simulation Programming Languages	Variable Credit Course	
539s	Adv System Simulation	495	Field Experience (up to 15)
548s	Operating Systems Software Design	196	Special Topics (up to 5)
550	Adv Decision Models	496	Special Topics (up to 5)
551	Adv Decision Models	596	Special Topics (up to 5)
552	Adv Decision Models	497	Individual Study (up to 5)
565f	Data Based Management Systems I	597	Individual Study (up to 5)
566w	Data Based Management Systems II	498	Seminar (up to 3)
570s	Adv Data Structures & I/O Management	598	Seminar (up to 3)
		599	Graduate Thesis & Research (up to 15)

OHIO

CASE WESTERN RESERVE UNIVERSITY
University Circle, Cleveland, OH 44106
(216) 368-4450

Case Western Reserve University is the result of the merge of Case Institute of Technology and Western Reserve University in 1967. This private university serves a population of 8,500 students with a faculty student ratio of 1 to 9, and alibrary with 1.62 million volumes.

The Department of Computer Engineering and Science offers BS, MS, PhD in Computer Engineering, MS, PhD in Computing and Information Sciences. Currently, there are 255 in the BS, 60 in the MS, and 35 in the PhD programs respectively. While Computer Engineering is based mainly on physical sciences, computing and informatin Sciences are more strongly based on mathematical sciences. However, both programs emphasize a strong background in computer hardware, software, theory, as well as a substantial amount of hands-on experience. Apply through Undergraduate Admissions, or School of Graduate Studies. Feb 15 is the application deadline for financial aid. For further information, call the department at (216) 368-2800.

The research areas actively pursued at the university: applications of microprocessors, artificial intelligence, computer aided design, database systems, distributed computing, computer graphics, operating systems, program verification, system architecture, and theory of computation. These studies are being facilitated by three laboratories dedicated exclusively to research and instruction in computer engineering and science:

The UNIX Interactive Computing Lab, built around a VAX 11/780 and a PDP 11/45 running Berkeley 4.1 UNIX and UNIX V6.5 respectively, is used for computer-aided design, architecture, program verification, and database research. The Case Shaded Graphics Lab consists of a custom-built real time shaded graphics system, that operates in conjunction with a PDP 11/40 and several specialized peripherals (such as the Evans & Sutherland graphics pipeline that include LDS 2 Channel Controller, 4*4 matrix multiplier, Y-sort processor and memory, visible surface processor, Beta Scope and 35 MM Camera Station...etc) in addition to and AED 512 color graphics terminal, a Hewlett-Packard eight color plotter, and a real-time grame buffer system, all connected to the UNIX systems. The lab is used for shaded graphics, fluid dynamics, biomechanics, structure dynamics, and computer aided design of VLSI circuits. The Digital Synthesizer Lab consists of a pair of general purpose digital system synthesizers, designed and built by department staff and driven by a UNIX-based PDP 11/34. The facilities in this lab allow the creation of testing and evaluation of hardware software systems, ranging in complexity from special purpose interfaces to microprogrammed minicomputers, multiprocessor architecture, distributed systems, and microprocessor applications research.

In addition, the department maintains two PDP 11/20, a TI 960A, a voice synthesis unit, five LSI-11 systems, an AED S12 frame, an IMLC graphic system, and a number of microprocessors. University computing resources include three DEC 2060s, two VAX 11/780, VAX 11/782, three Apollo DN 300, and 50 DEC PRO 350 in the Undergraduate Computing Lab.

There are 11 full-time members in the department. Faculty positions exist at the assistant and associate professor ranks. Background in VLSI systems and design automation, distributed systems architecture, programming methodology, graphics, applied artificial intelligence, analysis of algorithms, would be most desirable. Faculty and their interests:

C W Rose (computer-aided design, systems archtctr, microprcssr appln, ntwrks); P Drongowski (VLSI systems, archtctr, graphics sftwr engnrng); G W Ernst (AI, program verification, operating systems); J Franco (analysis of algrthms, complexity of algrthms); K Gopinath (computer graphics, system simulation, computer design, archtctr); R J Hookway (sftwr reliability, program verification, operating systems); F E Hunt (functional prgrmng, graphics); P Mateti (sftwr engnrng, operating systems, prgrmng languages, correctness proofs); M Ozsoyoglu (DBMS, algrthms); F Way III (numerical methods, computer systems, sftwr, info storage & retrieval).

Other affiliated faculty includes: M R Buchner (simulation, distrbtd computer control, signal prcssng); Y H Pao (applied AI, pattern recgntn, knowledge based systems); H W Mergler (digital systems, systems engnrng, logical dsgn, digital servo-mechanisms, computer control, metrology).

Course Offerings: (generally 3 semester units)

		Graduate	
CMPS131	Elementary Computer Programming (2)	MATH410	Math Thr: Automata & Formal Language
CMPS231	Introductory Computer Programming	ECMP420	Computer Systems Architecture
ECMP315	Computer Design I (4)	ECMP423	Introduction to Operating Systems
ECMP316	Computer Design II (4)	ECMP424	Advanced Computer Systems Architecture
ECMP335	Programming Structures I (4)	CMPS425	Computer Communication Networks
ECMP336	Programming Structures II	ECMP431	Software Engineering
CMPS380	PASCAL Programming (1)	ECMP432	Compiler Construction
CMPS381	APL Programming (1)	CMPS433	File Processing & Data Mangmnt Systems
EEAP381	Digital Systems II	CMPS441	Program Verification
CMPS382	FORTRAN Programming (1)	CMPS443	Intro to Logic & Computability
EEAP382	Introduction to Microprocessors	CMPS454	Analysis of Algorithms
CMPS383	COBOL Programming (1)	ECMP461	Artificial Intelligence
CMPS384	LISP Programming (1)	CMPS466	Computer Graphics
CMPS385	SNOBOL Programming (1)	CMPS470	Seminar in Computer Science
CMPS386	C Programming (1)	ECMP470	Seminar in Computer Engineering
CMPS387	ALGOL Programming (1)	ECMP522	Analytic Models in Operating Systems
ECMP396	Special Topics in Computer Engineering	ECMP531	Adv Topics in Compiler Construction
ESYS401	Digital Signal Processing	CMPS541	Mathematical Linguistics
ESYS403	Cmptr Based Data Acq & Control Systems	CMPS571	Seminar in Database Systems
ESYS416	Introduction to Optimization	CMPS574	Adv Sem in Computer Systems Design
ECMP420	Computer System Architecture	CMPS601	Indep Study in Computer Science
OPRE433	Information Systems	ECMP601	Indep Study in Computer Engineering
EEAP480	Digital System Synthesis		

Ohio State is a major public university with a 3250-acre campus, a population of 58,000 students, a faculty student ratio of 1 to 16, and a library with 3.7 million volumes.

The Department of Computer and Information Science in the College of Engineering offers BS, MS, and PhD programs. Apply through Graduate or Undergraduate Admissions. For further information, contact: Department of Computer & Informatin Science, The Ohio State University, 2036 Neil Ave Mall, Columbus, OH 43210; Phone: (614) 422-1408. In addition, admission applicatin forms and the College of Engineering Bulletins can be obtained from the Admissions Office, The Ohio State University, Third Floor Lincoln Tower, 1800 Cannon Drive, Columbus, OH 43210.

The Department has about 28 full-time equivalent faculty members, all active in sponsored research on a broad front. Their research interests include: analysis of algorithms, artificial intelligence, biomedical information processing, computer graphics, computer networks, data security and database computers, parallel and distributed processing, real-time computer systems, software engineering, and theoretical computer science.

Computing facilities in the Department include: a DEC 2020 time-sharing system dedicated to faculty and graduate student research; a seven-node network for research in distributed systems, configured with six DEC 11/13 micros and a DEC 2020; a data base computer laboratory with a VAX 780 and two DEC 11/44 for experimental database research. In addition, the Computer Graphics Research Group has a VAX 11/780, two 11/23's, and special graphics processors and display peripherals for advanced research in computer graphics.

Course Offerings:

100	Computers in Society	675	Intro to Computer Architecture
201	Elementary Digital Cmptr Prgmng	676	Minicomputer & Microcomputer Systems
211	Cmptr Prgmng for Problem Solving	677	Computer Networks
212	Computer Data Processing	680	Data STructures
221	Programming & Algorithms I	693	Individual Studies
222	Programming & Algorithms II	694	Group Studies
294	Group Studies	707	Math Fundtns of Cmptr & Info Science II
313	Intro to File Design	712	Man-Machine Interface
321	Intro to File Processing	720	Intro to Linguistic Analysis
380	File Design & Analysis	726	Intro to Automata & Language Theory
411	Design of On-Line Systems	727	Intro to Theory of Algorithms
489	Professional Practice in Industry	728	Topics in Thry of Computing
493	Individual Studies	730	Basic Concepts Artificial Intelligence
505	Fundmntl Concepts of Cmptr & Info Science	735	Statiscal Mthds in Pattern Recognition
511	Cmptr Systems & Prgmng Adminstrv Sciences	741	Comparative Operating Systems
541	Survey of Numerical Methods	745	Num Soln of Ord Diff Equations
542	Intro to Computing in the Humanities	746	Adv Numerical Analysis
543	Intermediate Digital Cmptr Programming	750	Modern Mthds of Info Storage & Retrieval
548	Intermediate Digital Cmptr Prgmng	751	Fundmntls Document-Handling Info Systems
551	Elements of Database Systems	752	Tchnqs for Simulation of Info Systems
555	Survey of Programming Languages	753	Theory of Indexing
557	Minicomputer Programming Systems	755	Programming Languages
560	Elmnts of Cmptr Systems Programming	756	Compiler Design & Implementation
594	Group Studies	757	Software Engineering
607	Math Foundation of Cmptr & Info Science	760	Operating Systems
610	Prncpls of Man-Machine Interaction	761	Intro to Operating Systems Lab
640	Numerical Analysis	765	Management Info Systems
642	Numerical Linear Algebra	770	Data Base Systems
643	Linear Optimztn Tchnqs in Info Prcssng	775	Computer Architecture
660	Intro to Operating Systems	780	Analysis of Algorithms

781 Aspects of Cmptr Graphics Systems
788 Intermediate Studies Cmptr & Info System
805 Info Theory in Physical Science
820 Computational Linguistics
835 Special Topics in Pattern Recognition
850 Thry of Information Retrieval I
852 Dsgn & Analysis of Info Systems Simulation

855 Adv Topics in Programming Languages
875 Adv Computer Architecture
885 Research Topics in Cmptr & Info Science
888 Advanced Studies in Cmptr & Info Science
889 Advanced Seminar in Cmptr & Info Science
899 Interdepartmental Seminar

BOWLING GREEN STATE UNIVERSITY
Bowling Green, OH 43403
(419) 372-2086

Bowling Green State University is a public institution whose 1,250-acre campus serves a population of 17,000 students with a faculty student ratio of 1 to 17, and a library with 700,000 volumes.

The Department of Computer Science offers BS and MS programs in which 763, and 45 students are currently enrolled. Undergraduate students should apply through the Office of Admissions by May; graduates, through the Graduate College by March 15. Deadline for financial aid is Feb 1.

Computing facilities at the university include an IBM 4341(MVS), a DEC System 20 (TOPS-20), a VAX 780 (UNIX), and a microcomputer lab that contains numerous Apples and IBM PCs. The Department of Computer Science has its own microcomputer lab with 12 Apples and two 10-megabyte CORVUS drives with a CONSTELLATION system, plus several graphic terminals.

There are 16 full-time members in the department. Faculty openings exist at all ranks. Background in software systems or programming languages is most desirable.

Course Offerings: (generally 3 semester units)

100 Computer Basics
101 Intro to Programming
180 Intro to Programming 1-3
201 Assembler Language Programming
202 Systems Programming
205 Advanced Programming Techniques
260 Business Programming Principles
305 Data Structures
306 Programming Languages
307 Computer Organizatioin
313 Elementary Mathematical Logic
360 COBOL Programming
390 Practicum in Computer Science 1-6
Graduates and Undergraduates
407 Advanced Computer Organization
408 Operating Systems
409 Language Design and Implementation
410 Formal Language Theory
420 A I and Heuristic Programming
425 Computer Graphics
428 Microcomputer Systems
440 Optimization Techniques

442 Techniques of Simulation
451 Numerical Analysis I
452 Numerical Analysis II
462 Database Management Systems
464 Software Development
480 Seminar in Computer Applications 1-3
Graduate
500 Computing for Graduate Students
501 Intro Graduate Study in Computer Science 2
502 Computer Systems Organization 2
503 Statistical Packages 2
507 Architecture of Computers
508 Advanced Operating Systems
509 Advanced Compiler Design
511 Automata and Computability Theory
512 Analysis of Algorithms
529 Communication Networks
540 Mathematical Programming Systems
562 Techniques of Database Organization
564 Computer Center Management
570 Readings in Computer Science 1-4

155

MIAMI UNIVERSITY
Oxford, OH 45056
(513) 529-2531

Miami University is a public university whose 1,100-acre campus serves a population of 15,000 students, with a faculty student ratio of 1 to 23, and a library with 1.1 million volumes.

The Systems Analysis Department offers an undergraduate program in which 950 students are currently enrolled. Apply through the Admissions Office. Deadline for financial aid is Feb 1 for the Fall Semester.

Computing facilities include an IBM 4341 and an IBM 370/148 with VM/CMS, PDP 11/34, plus many IBM PCs, and Cromemco S-100 micros. There are 20 full-time faculty members in the department. Openings exist at all ranks.

Course Offerings: (generally 3 semester units)

141 Fundamentals of Computing 2	281 Systems Software
152 Intro to SAS Programming 1	282 PL/I Programming 4
153 Fundamentals of Computing 2	285 Programming 2
154 Intro to Microcomputers	351 Systems Techniques
155 RPG Programming 2	372 Analysis of Stochaic Systems
156 BASIC Programming 1	381 Computer Systems Archtr & Teleprcssng
157 Intro to COBOL Programming	382 Analysis of Continuous Systems
158 Intro to PL/I	383 Numerical Methods with FORTRAN
171 Intro to Systems Analysis 2	384 Microcomputer Systems
172 Assembler Language Programming 4	385 Applied Data Management
173 Intro to Programming	471 Simulation 4
253 Computational Methods with FORTRAN	Graduate
271 COBOL Programming 4	671 Informatiion Storage and Retrieval
272 Systems Analysis and Design	672 Advanced Simulation

OHIO UNIVERSITY
Athens, OH 45701
(614) 594-5174

Ohio University is a public university whose 600-acre campus serves a population of 15,000 students with a faculty student ratio of 1 to 14, and a library with 1.15 million volumes.

The Computer Science Department offers an undergraduate major in computer science. The department does not offer an advanced degree. However, graduate students may choose MS in Math with Computer Science Option, which requires 75% course work offered by the CS Department. Currently, 374 are enrolled in the bachelor's program, and 47 in the MS program. Interested students should apply through the Office of Admissions; deadline June 15 for the Fall Quarter.

Computing facilities include an IBM 4341, IBM 370/158, HP 3000, PDP 11/10, PDP 11/20, PDP 11/34, many micros such as LSI 11/2, OSI model C3, and the Apple II+s. PDP 11/23, and a VAX 11/780 with UNIX will be acquired in the near future.

There are 7 full-time faculty members in the department. Openings exist at the assistant and associate professor ranks. Background in networking, artificial intelligence, or data base design is particularly attractive.

Course Offerings: (generally 5 quarter units)

120	Computer Science Survey	
220	Intro to Computing	
230	Computer Programming I	
231	Computer Programming II	
238	Intro to Computer Systems	
300	Intro to Discrete Structures	
320	Organization of Programming Languages	
321	Computing for Engineers and Scientists	
322	Computing with Statistical Packages	
340	Intro to Computer Organization	
361	Data Structures	
404	Design and Analysis of Algorithms	
406	Computation Theory	
410	Formal Languages and Syntactic Analysis	
442	Operating Systems and Computer Architecture	
444	Data Communications	
451	Modeling and Analysis of Computer Systems I	
452	Modeling and Analysis of Computer Systems II	
456	Software Design and Development	
458	Operating Systems and Computer Architecture	
462	Files and Data Bases	
464	Information and Organizational Retrieval	
468	Data Base Design	
480	Artificial Intelligence	
481	Info Organization and Retrieval Projects-15	

Graduate Offerings

500	Intro to Discrete Structures
504	Design and Analysis of Algorithms
506	Computation Theory
510	Formal Languages and Syntactic Analysis
520	Organization of Programming Languages
521	Computing for Engineers and Scientists
522	Computing with Statistical Packages
540	Computer Organization
542	Operating Systems and Computer Architecture
544	Data Communications
551	Modeling and Analysis of Computer Systems I
552	Modeling and Analysis of Computer Systems II
556	Software Design and Development
558	Operating Systems & Computer Architecture II
561	Data Structures
562	Files and Data Bases
564	Information Organization and Retrieval
568	Data Base Design
580	Artificial Intelligence
581	Information Organization & Retrieval Projects

OREGON

UNIVERSITY OF OREGON
Eugene, OR 97403
(503) 686-3201

The University of Oregon is a public university whose 190-acre campus serves a population of 17,500 students with a faculty student ratio of 1 to 19, and a library with over 2.1 million volumes.

The Computer & Information Science offers BS, MS, MA, and PhD programs. The department also coordinates interdisciplinary master's degree in other fields such as Computers in Education for teachers. In addition, doctorates in numerical analysis and combinatorics are offered by the Department of Mathematics, a doctorate in computer science education by the College of Education, and a doctorate involving considerable work in computers in business by the College of Business Administration. Prospective students should apply through the department or other colleges for admission. Application deadline for financial aid is March 1.

University computing facilities include an IBM 4341, a DEC 1091, over 100 smaller computers and 400 terminals. The CIS department has Symbolics 3600 Lisp Machines and DEC VAX 11/750s.

Faculty and their interests: G P Ashby (systems prgrmng); A M Farley (AI); D G Moursund (computers in education, numerical analysis); A Proskurowski (combinatorial algrthms, complexity of computation); G B Shaw (computer vision, picture languages); G W Struble.

Course Offerings: (generally 4 quarter units)

121	Concepts of Computing		Upper Division with Graduate Credit
131	Intro to Business Information Processing	342	Business Information Processing
133	Intro to Numerical Computation	407	Seminar
150	Special Topics in Computer Science	409	Supervised Consulting
199	Special Studies in Computer Science	410	Experimental Course
201	Intro to Computer Science I	413	Information Structures
203	Intro to Computer Science II	414	Intro to Programming Systems
234	Adv Numerical Computation	415	Operating Systems
241	Intro to Information Systems	422	Software Methodology I
242	Business Data Processing	423	Software Methodology II
245	Intro to Time-Shared Computing	424	Assembly Language Programming
311	Computer Organization	435	Business Information Systems
313	Intro to Information Structures	441	Computer Graphics
315	Analysis of Programs	445	Modelling & Simulation
405	Reading & Conference	451	Database Processing
		472	Computers in Education I
		473	Computers in Education II

Graduate

503	Thesis	526	Compiler Construction
505	Reading & Conference	529	Computer Architecture
507	Seminar	530	Adv Operating Systems
510	Experimental Course	531	Parallel Processing
513	Advanced Information Structures	532	Computer & Information Networks
520	Formal Languages & Machines	551	Data Base Systems
521	Thry of Computation: Complexity	571	Artificial Intelligence
522	Thry of Computation: Computability	573	Pattern Recognition
524	Structure of Programming Languages	574	Computer Vision
525	Strctr of Prgrmng Languages: Compiling	575	Natural Language Processing

PENNSYLVANIA

PENNSYLVANIA STATE UNIVERSITY
University Park, PA 16802
(814) 865-4700

Penn State is a public university whose campus at University Park has 35,000 students and the campus at Commonwealth, about 27,000 students. The university maintains a 4-term system, a faculty student ratio of 1 to 22, and a library with 2.4 million volumes.

The Department of Computer Science in the College of Science offers BS, MS, and PhD programs in which 1146, 97, and 18 students are currently enrolled. Apply through the Undergraduate Admissions at 201 Shields, or the Graduate School. Graduate deadlines are: June 30 for the Fall Semester and Dec 1 for the Spring Semester. Undergraduates are suggested to apply by Nov 30.

The university's Computation Center operates: an IBM 3081 with 16 megabyte memory and 3 billion bytes of disk storage running OS/VS2 MVS; an IBM 4341 running VM/CMS; an Evans & Sutherland Multipicture System for high performance graphics attached to a PDP 11/34. The department runs its own Computer Systems Lab that consists of: a VAX 11/780;two PDP 11/34s; a Microdata 1600/30; a Burroughs Loop System that contains 6 nodes (DEC Q-bus backplanes); a PDP 11/23 that runs UNIX and provides a testbed for distributed computing software, plus 5 PDP 11/03, each of which can run a standalone processor memory peripheral system; a Burroughs B80, and several 8080-based micros. CSNet and BITNet are used. Additionally, electronic mail may be forwarded to nodes associated with ARPANet by routing information through a USENet site attched to it.

There are 15 full-time faculty members in the department. Openings exist at all ranks. Applicants in all areas of computer science will be considered. Background in artificial intelligence, databases, numerical analysis, operating systems, and programming languages would be of particular interest. Faculty research areas include: analysis of algorithms, automata and formal language theory, operating systems, databases, information retrieval, numerical analysis, theory of computation, and computer arithmetics. Members and their interests:

J M Lambert (numerical analysis, apprxmtn thry, operations research); G N Frederickson (analysis of algrthms, computnl complexity, data strctrs); J Goldstine (automata & formal languages); J J Ja (arithmetic complexity, combinatorial & graph algrthms, parallel computnl complexity); D B Johnson (algrthms, computatnl complexity, scheduling thry, graph & ntwrk thry); G G Johnson Jr (pttrn recgntn, image prcssng, lab automatn); D T Laird (computer system); J Simon (computnl complexity).

H Alt (formal languages, complexity thry, analysis of algrthms); J Barlow (numerical & scientific computing and computer arithmetic); P Berman (automata); J G Deshpande (ntwrks, operating systems); C Forney (computer systems); S Gupta (analysis, operations research); M Hafen (automata & language thry, data bases); D E Heller (analysis of algrthms, numerical algebra, parallel computatn); M J Irwin (archtctr, computer arithmetic, ntwrks & distrbtd prcssng); S J Laskowski (computnl complexity, analysis of algrthms); B Mahr (complexity thry); R M Owens (archtctr, computer arithmetic, large data bases, distribtd prcssng); W J Sakoda (geometric complexity, automata ntwrks, inductive inference); L E Snyder (numerical analysis); C M Smith Jr (computer languages & systems); D W Wall (Prgrmng languages & compilers, concurrent prgrmng, algrthms & data strctrs, CS education).

Course Offering:

101 Intro to Computing	512 Operating Systems II
120 Intermediate Programming	515 Architecture of Arithmetic Processors
211 Intro to Systems Programming	521 Compiler Construction (4)
Upper Division and Graduates	522 Parsing, Translation & Compiling
412 Systems Programming	534 Algorithm Design & Analysis (4)
415 (EE 415) Computer Systems Architecture	535 Theory of Graphs & Networks
430 Combinatorics & Graph Theory	539 Complexity of Combinatorial Problems
434 Fundamentals of Computer Science I	541 Database Management Systems (4)
435 Fundamentals of Computer Science II	542 Information Processing Systems
442 Advanced Programming & Job Control Language	550 (Math 550) Numerical Algebra
444 Systems & Program Design in EDP	551 (Math 551) Num Soln of Ordinary Diff Eq
453 (Math 453) Numerical Computations	552 (Math 552) Num Soln of Partial Diff Eq
454 (Math 454) Matrix Computations	553 (Math 553) Intro to Approximation Theory
468 Mathematical Machine Theory	561 Machine-Based Computional Complexity Theory
Graduate Offerings	568 Theory of Formal Lang & Automata
511 Operating Systems I (4)	581 Machine Intelligence & Heuristic Programming

TEMPLE UNIVERSITY
Philadelphia, PA 19122
(215) 787-7000

Temple University is a public university with a 235-acre campus, supporting a population of 31,000 students with a faculty student ratio of 1 to 8, and a library with 1.8 million volumes.

The Department of Computer & Information Science (CIS) offers two undergraduate and four graduate programs: BBA in the School of Business Administration, BA in the College of Liberal Arts, MA, MBA with CIS as Major Field, MS/Phd in Business Administration with CIS as Major Field, and PhD in CIS. Currently, there are 1200 in the bachelor's, 200 in the master's, and 30 in the PhD programs. Undergraduates should apply through the Office of Undergraduate Admissions in September. Graduates should apply through the Department of Computer & Information Sciences.

University Computing facilities include a CDC dual Cyber 172/174, and a DEC VAX 780. The CIS Department has an 8,000-sq-ft lab that contains a fully-equipped logic lab, a vision graphic robotics lab, 10 PDP 11/34-type mini computer systems, and many micros. Advanced work stations are to be acquired in the near future.

There are 25 full-time faculty members in the department. Several openings exist at each of the ranks. Background in any of the computer science areas will be considered. Faculty and their areas of interests:

P Bagley (system & prgm dsgn, data strctrs, prgmng languages, on-line busnss applns, computer based printing & publishing); A Beller (pattern regntn, AI, databases); G Berry-Rogghe (knowledge reprsntatn, natural languae based info systems, extensional query systems); B Farley (neutral ntwrk models, numerical analysis); R Epstein (algebraic data types, AI); F L Friedman (sftwr portability, sftwr dsgn, sftwr quality measuremnt, prgrmng language dsgn & language translatn, CS education); L J Garrett (DP, business simulation, mini systems, database dsgn, word prcssng); M Halpern (AI, non-numerical computatin, symbolic math, system simulation).

G Ingargiola (sftwr engnrng, language dsgn, operating systems); C A Kapps (hardwr sftwr relationship, microprcssrs, real-time prcsses, logic dsgn); E B Koffman (AI, computer aided instruction); J F Korsh (algorithms, combinatorics, computatnl complexity, operations rsrch); E M Kwatny (applns of computers, lab automation, &signal prcssng); P Lafollette (biomedical computatn, robotics, pattern recgntn, mini & micro computer systems, image & signal prcssng); M Negin (image & signal prcssng, pattern recgntn, robotics biomedical computatn, mini & micro systems); A Pelin (CS computatn, prgrmmng languages, automatic prgm geneation).

A T Poe (automata thry, combinatorics, thry of computatn, CS education); A Ramer (computatnl complexity, AI heuristics, database techniques); N Relles (human factors, user assistance, natural language access to database, data base mangmnt); C S Sankar (mangmnt info systems, data base mangmnt systems, decision support systems, office automation); D M Sherr (info systems develpmnt methdlgy, sftwr engnrng, human services info systems, health planning & evaluation systems); R L Stafford (picture prcssng, graphics, realtime systems, small computer systems); J A Stebulis (info systems, prgrmng languages & language translation); A Waksman (info storage & retrieval, data base mangmnt systems, systems develpmnt); E J Weiner (computatnl linguistics, computer aided instruction, AI).

Course Offerings: (generally 3 semster hours)

001	Intro to Computer Programming	324	Compiler Design
005	Computers and Society	330	Data Management Systems
061	Computers and Computer Programming	335	Management of Computer Activities
062	Data Structures	337	Applications of Modern Operating Systems
066	Mathematical Concepts in Computing	338	Software Design
072	Assembly Language Programming	340	Logical Design Laboratory
082	COBOL and Sequential Data Structures	345	Seminar on Prblms & New Developments in D P
091	The Arts and Science of Computing	350	Seminar in Topics in Computer Science
120	Hardware/Software Systems	397	Independent Study
153	COBOL & Info Retrieval & File Management	401	Intro to Computer Programming & Applns
200	Intro to Computerized Mngmnt Info Systems	500	Survey of Information Systems
201	Information Systems Analysis & Design	502	Computer Simulation
203	Intro to Artificial Intelligence	505	Advanced Programming Techniques
205	Programming Lang	535	Information Systems
207	Intro Systems Prgmmng & Operating Systems	545	On-Line Systems & File Management
209	Introduction to Numerical Computation	551	Programming Techniques
211	Automata, Computability and Languages	561	Operating Systems
214	Intro to Computer Simulation	563	Logical Design
215	Computer Simulation in Business	573	Automata & Formal Languages
218	Logical Design Laboratory	581	Computer Graphics & Image Processing
220	Computer Graphics & Image Processing	587	Artificial Intelligence
223	Data Structures & Algorithms	594	Intro to Robotic Systems
242	Discrete Structures	598	Independent Study (Courses 598-599)
272	Lang for Non-Numeric & Linguistic Prcssng	601	Project in Info Systems of Simulation
301	Information Systems Implementation	604	Seminar in Problems in Info Science
305	Real Time Computer Systems		

651	Compiler Construction	675	Theorem Proving & Program Verification
661	Data Management	681	Mathematical Structures of Heuristics
662	Computer Networking & Communication	682	Expert Systems & Natural Language Prcssng
663	Machine Architecture	683	Principles of Algorithm Analysis
664	Advanced Logic Design	684	Intro to Combinatorics
665	Topics in High Order Lang & Translation	686	Advanced Topics in Numerical Computation
667	Systems Performance Measurement & Analysis	690	Software Engineering
668	Operating Systems Theory	691	Information Systems Analysis & Design
673	Design & Analysis of Algorithms	692	Practicum in Information Systems

UNIVERSITY OF PENNSYLVANIA
Philadelphia, PA 19104
(215) 243-7507

The University of Pennsylvania is a private university with 260-acre campus on the west bank of the Schuylkill River that winds through William Penn's "greene countrie towne" between Center City and the university. The water is part of some the university's oldest traditions. Over the years, it has provided riverside parks for picnickers and a perfect course for Penn scullers. The campus supports a population of 16,000 students with a faculty student ratio of 1 to 7, and a library with over 3 million volumes.

The Computer and Information Science of the School of Engineering & Applied Science, offers a Bachelor of Applied Science in Computer Science, an master's program (MSE) and a PhD program in which 220, 70, and 50 students are enrolled respectively. In addition, a dual degree program MBA/MSE is jointly sponsored by the School and the Wharton School of Business and Management. Undergraduates should apply through the Admissions office; deadline January 1. Graduates should apply through the Department of Computer & Information Science by Feb 1.

Computing and research facilities include: an UNIVAC 1100/61 with one megaword memory, and 3 billion bytes disk storage; a Graphics Lab consisting of a Ramtek GX 100B, a Vector General 3404 high performance interactive display, Tektronix 4010 storage tube; a VAX 11/780 for natural language processing and database systems research; a VAX 11/750 for atutomatic program generation and testing research; a PDP 11/05 and PDP 11/60 for computer vision research; HP 9836 work stations and a file server for distributed database research; a Computer Structures Lab that includes such microcomputers as the IBM PC's, Z-80 based micros, DEC micros...etc; a Computer Assisted Lab for electronic experiment setup, control and evaluation. Other facilities with limited access include: a PDP 10KL at Wharton, which supports an ARPAnet link; PDP 10KA at the School of Medicine; an IBM 4341 in the Physics department; and an IBM 370/168 at the UNICOLL Corporation. Future plans call for more VAX 11/780s, VAX 11/750, and LISP machines.

There are 18 full-time faculty members in the department. Openings exist at all ranks. Background in computer architecture, artificial intelligence, and theory of computation would be of particular interest. Faculty members are actively engaged in the research of the following areas.

I. Artificial Intelligence and Man-Machine Communication: computer graphics and computer vision; natural language proessing; integrated systems, vision and language; mathematical learning theories; sound and speech synthesis; applications to data base and biomedical systems.

II. Automation of Software and Data Base Design: automatic generation of computer programs; data base systems; simulation in economics and business.

III. Computer Systems: computer architecture; microprocessor networks; design automation and automatic testing.

IV. Theory of Computation: analysis of algorithms; mathematical linguistics; program verification.

Members of the department: A K Joshi (Chair); J Bordogna; J W Carr III; Z Domotor; J C Emery; D Garfinkel; J L Garner; C D Graham Jr; H J Gray; G T Herman; H Hiz; J F Lubin; H L Morgan; N S Prywes; M Rubinoff; H S Wilf.

N I Badler; R Bajcsy; O P Buneman; E K Clemons; F D Ketterer; D Ness; E Prince; W D Seider; B L Webber. S Davidson; T W Finin; J H Gallier; R Gerritsen; S M Goldwasser; I Lee; E Ma; D Miller; F Nourani.

Adjuncts: J Emery; B W Lampson; E Lieblein; A Patel; E W Reigel; R K Gupta; D B MacQueen; N F Maxemchuk; C Moss; L P Rubinfield.

Course Offerings:

514 Intro to Computer Commnctn Network	627A Number Systems & Arithmetic
523 Intro to Cmptrs: Prgrmng & Logic	627B Computer-Aided Digital System Dsgn
540 Theory of Computation	634 Applns Cmptrs to Busnss Indstrl Systems
543 Intro to Cmptrs; Systems & Devices	640 Seminar on Thry of Computation
560 Combinatorics & Graphs	671 Adv Topics in Operating Systems
570 Intro to Operating Systems	672 Microprogramming
574 Intro to Mechanical Languages	673 Data Mangmnt Systems Anlys & Dsgn
576 Design of Numerical Prcdrs & Cmputatns	674 Topics in Mechanical Languages
578 Algebraic Foundatns for Cmputr Science	675A Programming Langauges & Compilers
580A Intro to Computer Graphics	675B Seminar in Adv Prgrmng Languages
580B Microprocessors	677 Numerical & Graphcl Comptatn of ODE
580D Intro to VLSI Systems Design	679 Seminar: Natural Language Processing
581 Basic Logic for Computer Science	680E Seminar: Artificial Intelligence
590 Analysis of Algorithms	680E Seminar: Biomedical Computing
591 Intro to Artificial Intelligence	680H Adv Topics in Computer Architecture
594 Image Reconstruction from Projections	899 Indep Study
595 Microprocessor System Orgnztn & Dsgn	999 Dissertation Research

UNIVERSITY OF PITTSBURGH
Pittsburgh, PA 15260
(412) 624-4141

University of Pittsburgh is a private university with a 125-acre campus, a student population of 30,000 and a library with 3.8 million volumes.

The Department of Computer Science offers BS, MS, and PhD programs in which there are 1200, 75 and 25 students are enrolled currently. In addition, a joint major in computer science and mathematics is available for BS students in the College of Arts and Sciences or the College of General Studies. Contact the Department of Computer Science for appropriate application forms; Phone (412) 624-6458.

The University Computer Center operates a dual DEC-SYSTEM 1099s. The department has several PDP 11 minicomputers, including a VAX 11/780, two graphics systems, and numerous microcomputers. LAN and CSNet are both available. A DEC

11/750 and more graphics system will be acquired in the near future. In addition, the Computer Science Library contains about 5,000 volumes and subscribes to more than a 100 journals.

There are 15 full-time faculty in the department. Positions are open at all ranks. Faculty are actively engaged in research here. The departmental colloquium and lecture series are regularly held to promote professional contact with individuals whose interests and specialties cover the entire spectrum of computer science. Speakers include department faculty, members from other universities, or computer scientists from government and industry.

General areas of faculty research include: adaptive system design and analysis; AI research and machine learning; operating system design and analysis; theoretical studies in computer science, computational complexity and mechanized induction; development of new theories and strategies for using computing environments to enhance human learning; microcomputer systems and applications; fault-tolerant and fail-safe digital systems; consistency, concurrency, crash recovery, and query processing in distributed database management systems; database design; the simulation and analysis of database control algorithms; intelligent query systems; design and analysis of software systems; compiler design; test generation for detecting program errors; software reliability; standardization of data structures and the automatic selection of storage structures; design and analysis of algorithms; user-oriented design of interactive graphics systems; user-computer interaction languages; modeling of systems and program behavior for performance evaluation and enhancement; text processing; linguistics; teaching methods in computer science; development of tools for investigating language implementation; modeling and analytical characterization of control structures in programming languages.

Members of the department and their interests: A T Berztiss (prgrmng language & data strctrs, graph & ntwrks, parallel proceses, curriculum dsgn); B Bhargava (distrbtd database mangmnt; medical info systems, sftwr reliablty, crash recovery); C Borkowski (txt prcssng, info retrieval, linguistics); H Y Chuang (swtchng thry, logical dsgn, fault-tolerant computing, archtctr, sftwr engnrng, micros); R P Daley (comptatnl complexity, theoretical CS, mechanized induction); K A De Jong (adaptive systems, AI, Operating systems, sftwr dsgn).

T A Dwyer (num analysis, computer-augmented learning, micros, cmptr ntwrks, personal computing). J P Kearns (operating systems, prgrm behavior, performance evaluation); C C Li (pttrn recgntn, image prcssng, biomedical applns); E L LLoyd (dsgn & analysis of algrthms, computatnl complexity, VLSI); J Placek; H Shapiro; M L Soffa (prgrmng language & systems, sftwr tools); O E Taulbee (pttrn recgntn, info systems, computing resources mangmnt, instructnl computing, networking); S Treu (user-computer interaction, networking, interactive graphics, distrbtd procssng, simulation).

Course Offering: (generally 3 units)

Non-Major Courses		Major Courses	
2	Intro to Programming FORTRAN	105	Data Structures & Files
3	Intro to Programming COBOL	110	Discrete Mathematical Structures
4	Intro to Programming BASIC	111	Intro to Thry of Computation
7	Intro to Computer Science	112	Boolean Algebra & Computer Logic
11	Computational Mthds & Accuracy	121	Structure of Prgrmng Languages
21	Data Entry, Statistical Analysis & Output	123	List Processing Programming
31	Interactive Text Generation & Analysis	124	Programming Languages
41	Intermediate Programming	125	Software Systems Design
42	Intro to Information Structures	132	Numerical Math: Analysis
43	Computers & Programming	133	Numerical Math: Linear Algebra
62	Computer-based Simulation	134	Industrial Numerical Analysis
65	Files & Database Systems	142	Intro to Simulation
80	Exploration into Computing & CS	150	Systems Programming
91	Computer-based Data Systems	151	Computer Operating Systems

155 Database Management Systems	251B Models of Computer Systems
156 Intro to Computer Graphics	252 Computer Networks
157 Computer Organization	254A Computer Architecture
158 Microcomputer Systems	254B Adv Computer Architecture
160 Directed Study	255 Principles of Database Systems
161 Topics in Computing Systems Management	256 Interactive Computer Graphics
181 Computer-based Systems Analysis & Design	267 Economics of Computing
191 Scientific Prgrmng for Graduate Students	271 Pattern Recognition
192 Computer Prgrmng for Graduate Students	277 Artificial Intelligence
200 Master's Thesis	281 Inforamation Processing Systems
202 Topics in Computer Science	283 Automatic Text Processing
209 Master's Directed Project	296 Computer Augmented Learning
211A Theory of Computation I	298 Microcomputer-based Learning Envrnmnts
211B Theory of Computation II	299 Independent Study
215 Modern Algorithms	300 Research & PhD Dissertation
217 Switching & Coding Theory	309 Directed Study
221A A Language Design	311 Seminar: Theory of Computation
221B Compiler Construction	321 Seminar: Programming Languages
231A Numerical Methods I	331 Seminar: Math of Computation
231B Numerical methods II	351 Seminar: Computer Systems
235 Intro to Statistical Computing	362 Seminar: Computing Resources Management
236 Modelling & Simulation	363 Seminar: Social Implctns of Computers
251A Advanced Computer Operating Systems	371 Seminar: Artificial Intelligence

EDINBORO UNIVERSITY OF PENNSYLVANIA
Edinboro, PA 16444
(814) 732-2000

Edinboro University is a state university whose 590-acre campus serves a population of 6,000 students with a faculty student ratio of 1 to 17, and a library with 340,000 volumes.

The Department of Mathematics/Computer Science offers an undergraduate program in which 600 students are currently enrolled. Apply through the Admissions Office before August 15 for Fall Semester. Application for financial aid is March 15.

There are 22 full-time members in the department. Faculty positions exist at the associate professor rank. Computing facilities here include a UNIVAC 90/60 running VS9 and an Apple microcomputer lab.

Course Offerings: (generally 3 semester units)

CS100 Computers & Society 1	217 Advanced BASIC Programming
101 Intro to Word Processing on Micros 1	221 Assembly Language Programming
102 Intro to Spreadsheets on Micros 1	300 Numerical Calculus
103 Intro to File Management on Micros 1	321 Adv Assembly Language Prgrmng
115 PASCAL Programming	530 Numeric Linear Algebra
116 RPG Programming	532 Linear Programming
118 FORTRAN Programming	CT101 Intro to Information Processing
119 PL/I Programming	110 Computer Operations
120 COBOL Programming	208 Systems Analysis
211 Advanced COBOL	212 Computer Systems

213 Data Base Management Systems	412 Advanced Computer Systems
215 Computer Technology Practicum	413 Adv Data Base Mangmnt Systems
313 Data Structures	490 Independent Study
314 Information Processing Management	700 Computer Literacy
408 Advanced Computer Systems	701 Computer Applications

INDIANA UNIVERSITY OF PENNSYLVANIA
Indiana, PA 15705
(412) 357-2230

Indiana University of Pennsylvania is a public university, whose 95-acre campus serves a population of 13,000 students with a faculty student ratio of 1 to 19, and a library with 520,000 volumes.

A BS in computer science, with a current enrollment of 600 students, is offered here. Prospective students should apply through the Admissions Office before March 1.

There are 10 full-time faculty members in the department. Computing facilities include a Honeywell Level 66, a Microdata 1600, and the Ithaca microcomputers. Contact the Computer Science Department for more information; Phone (412) 357-2524.

Course Offerings: (generally 3 semester units)

110 Intro to Computer Science	Adv Courses in Programming Applns & Theory:
200 Intro to Computers	420 Modern Programming Languages
210 Programming the Computer (2)	450 Applied Numerical Methods
220 Applied Computer Programming	460 Theory of Computation
250 Intro to Numerical Methods	481 Sp Topics: Computer Graphics
300 Assembly Language Programming	
310 Data Structures	Adv Courses in Machines & Systems Programming:
315 Large File Organization & Access	410 Processor Architecture & Microprogramming
	430 Intro to Systems Programming
Intermediate & Adv Courses in Data Processing:	481 Sp Topics: Micro & Minicomputer Applns
320 Software Engineering	481 Sp Topics: Digital Systems Logic
345 Data Communications	481 Sp Topics: Compilers & Interpreters
370 Computer Resource Management	481 Sp Topics: Operating Systems
399 Internship in Computer Science (4-12)	
441 Data Base Management	
480 Seminar: Current Topics in CS (2)	

LA SALLE COLLEGE
Olney Ave., Philadelphia, PA 19141
(215) 951-1500

La Salle is a private college operated by the Brothers of the Christian Schools. Its 60-acre campus supports a population of 6,200 students with a faculty student ratio of 1 to 17, and a library with 350,000 volumes.

The Department of Mathematical Science offers an undergraduate program in which 450 students are currently enrolled. Apply through the Admissions Office. Deadline for financial aid is Feb 1.

The College has a DEC System-20 running TOPS 20, and about twenty Intertec Superbrains micros (CPM). A time-shared microsystems running UNIX will be acquired in the near future.

There are 17 full-time faculty members in the department. Openings exist at the assistant and associate professor ranks.

Course Offerings: (generally 3 semester units)

150	Intro to Computer Sci in Sci & Math	355	Discrete Structures
151	Intro to Computer Sci in Bus Adm	356	Programming Languages
153	Algorithms and Data Structures	357	Assemblers, Loaders and Compilers
154	COBOL in Bus Data Processing	358	Computer Architecture
254	File and Data Management Systems	454	Adv D P & Data Base Management
257	Computer Struct & Assembly Language	455	Formal Lang & Automata Theory
Upper Division		457	Operating Systems
354	Data Structures		

MANSFIELD STATE COLLEGE
Mansfield, PA 16933
(717) 662-4243

Mansfield University of Pennsylvania is a public university with a 175-acre campus, a population of 2,500 students, a faculty student ratio of 1 to 14, and a library with over 200,000 volumes.

The Department of Business, Economics, and Computer Science offers BS with an emphasis in compter and information sciences. There are 150 students currently enrolled in the program. Prospective students should apply through the Admissions Office before June 30 for the Fall Semester.

The university has an UNIVAC 9060 running VS/9 and the IBM PCs. Faculty positions exist at both the assistant and associate professor ranks.

Course Offerings: (generally 3 semester units)

101	Computers in Society	325	Operating and Programming Systems
104	Introduction to Computer Science	335	Assembly Language Programming
105	Programming and Information Processing	401	Management Information Systems
205	Introduction to File Processing	420	Special Prblms in Computer Applns (1-3)
225	Automated Accounting Systems	430	Organization of Programming Languages
230	Language and Structure of Computers	480	Operations Research
301	Data Structure	497	Independent Study (1-3)
310	Introduction to Systems Analysis		

Slippery Rock University of Pennsylvania is a public university with a 600-acre campus, a population of 5,800 students, a faculty student ratio of 1 to 17, and a library with half million volumes.

An undergraduate program in computer science with a current enrollment of 250 students is offered. Interested students should apply through the Director of Admissions. Dec 31 is the suggested application deadline.

Current computing facilities include an IBM 370/148 (DOS), NOVA-3, and the SAGE microcomputers. A VM Operating System, and an IBM 3000, will be acquired in the near future.

There are six full-time members in the department. Faculty positions exist at the assistant and associate professor ranks. Background in programming languages, database systems, microprocessors, software engineering, or analysis of algorithms, would be most attractive.

Course Offerings:

151 Computer Concepts	265 Data Base Systems
160 Intro Programming and Information Systems	274 Assembly Language and Machine Organization
161 FORTRAN	275 Simulation
162 COBOL	283 Computers in Education
170 Small Computer Languages	366 Small Computer Systems
171 Modern Imperative and Procedural Programming	350 Concurrent Programming & Operating Systems
172 Functional Programming	374 Compiler Design and Implementation
200 Applied Advanced Programming	375 Computer Architecture
260 Fundamental Structures of Computer Science 1	393 Analysis of Algorithms
261 Programming Languages	460 Senior Seminar in Computer Science
262 Fundamental Structures of Computer Science 2	490 Independent Study

SPRING GARDEN COLLEGE
Chestnut Hill, PA 19118
(215) 242-3700

Spring Garden College is a private college whose 7-acre campus serves a population of 1,500 students, with a faculty student ratio of 1 to 15. The college is a member of the two million Tri-State College Library Cooperative system.

An undergraduate program in Computer Systems Technology is offered with an current enrollment of 300 students. Apply through the Admissions Office. The college has an IBM 4331/K2 running VM/CMS, and a HP 3000/33 running MPE VI. There are six full-time faculty in the department. A position is open at the assistant professor rank. Background in assembly language is desirable.

Course Offerings:

3502 Introduction to Data Processing	3512 PL/I Programming
3504 RPG II-Programming	3515 COBOL Programming I
3507 Assembly Language Programming	3516 COBOL Programming II
3508 Advanced Assembly Language	3518 Computer-Based Business Systems & Applns
3510 FORTRAN Programming	3519 Systems Techniques
3511 Advanced FORTRAN Programming	3520 Systems Analysis and Design

3535	Management Information Systems	3546	Microcomputer Programming
3536	Data Base Processing	3547	Telecommunications
3540	COBOL Programming III	3550	Job Control Language
3545	Applied BASIC Programming		

VILLANOVA UNIVERSITY
Villanova, PA 19085
(215) 645-4000

Villanova is a private Catholic university with a 240-acre campus, a population of 7,700 students with a faculty student ratio of 1 to 15, and a library with 460,000 volumes.

The College of Arts & Sciences offers a BS in Computer Science, and the Graduate School offers an MS in Computer Science. The current enrollments are 120 and 400 students for the two programs respectively. Prospective students apply through the Admissions Office or the Graduate School. The undergraduate deadline is Jan 20, while the graduate, June 15.

Computing facilities include an IBM 4341-2 (IBM) and a VAX 11/780 (UNIX), a VAX 11/730, Apple II+s, and the IBM PC's. Acquisition plans in the future call for the development of a microcomputer network.

There are 10 full-time faculty members in the department. Openings exist at the assistant and associate professor ranks. Background in operating systems or artificial intelligence would be of great interest to the department.

Course Offerings: (generally 3 semester units)

CPS 1051	Algorithms & Data Structures I (4)	EE 8400	Computer Organization
CPS 1052	Algorithms & Data Structures II (4)	Com 8410	Systems Programming
CPS 1061	Computer Programming (4)	Graduate	(Elective)
CPS 1071	PL/1 Computer Programming (4)	EE 8425	Microprocessors & Microcomputers
CPS 1081	Computer Business programming-COBOL (4)	EE 8428	Switching & Automata Theory
CPS 1111	Compiler Construction (4)	EE 8442	Computers Structures & Performance
CPS 1200	Computer Organization	EE 8445	Advanced Computer Organization
CPS 1300	Discrete Structures	Com 8460	Minicomputers & Microprocessors
CPS 1401	Assembler Languages Programming (4)	Com 8470	Computer Graphics
CPS 1500	Principles of Data Base Systems	Com 8480	Principles of Operating Systems
CPS 1600	Operating Systems	Com 8490	Data Base System & File Management
CPS 1700	Analysis of Algorithms	Com 8500	Formal Grammars & Prgmnng Lang Theory
CPS 1800	Organization of Programming Languages	Com 8505	Compiler Construction
CPS 1900	Logic of Computation	Com 8510	Theory of Computability
CPS 5900	Seminar in Computer Science	Com 8520	Artificial Intelligence
Graduate	(Required)	Com 8530	Distributed Processing Systems
Com 8301	Data Structures & Algorithms	Com 8540	Software Engineering
Com 8310	Programming Languages & Techniques	EE 8730	Information Theory & Coding

RHODE ISLAND

UNIVERSITY OF RHODE ISLAND
Kingston, RI 02881
(401) 792-2164

The University of Rhode Island is a public university whose 1200-acre campus serves a population of 10,000 students with a faculty student ratio of 1 to 14, and with a library that contains 1.3 million volumes.

The Department of Computer Science and Experimental Statistics offers BS, MS in Computer Science, and a PhD in Applied Mathematical Sciences with a specialization in CS. Currently, there are 200, 40 and 5 students enrolled in the three programs respectively. Demand for computer science has far exceeded available resources. Only 35 undergraduates are admitted each January. Selection is is based primarily on GPA.

Department's computing facilities include: a VAX 11/750, a PDP 11/34, and a Microcomputer Applications Lab that contains several Appolo Work Stations. The university's Academic computer Center has a National Advanced System AS/7000N (equivalent to an IBM 370/3033), and a PRIME 750 minicomputer. The College of Engineering has two VAX 11/780, two PDP-9 with a graphics display console, and a Data General Eclipse linked to the computer center.

There are 10 full-time faculty members in the department. Openings exist at all ranks.

Course Offerings: (generally 3 semester units)

201	Intro to Computing I	382	Intro to JCL
202	Intro to Computing II	406	Microcomputer Applns Lab
220	Computers in Society	411	Computer Orgnztn & Prgrmng
240	Intro to Non-Numerical Computation	412	Programming Systems
283	Intro to PL/I Coding	413	Data Structures
301	Comparative Programming Languages	416	Microcomputer Systems Architecture
302	Prgrmng Languages & Compiler Dsgn	491	Directed Study in Computer Science
311	Machine & Assembly Language Prgrmng	492	Special Topics in Computer Science
350	Intro to Numerical Computation		

BRYANT COLLEGE
Smithfield, RI 02917
(401) 231-1200

Bryant College is a private college whose 295-acre campus serves a population of 6,300 students with a library that contains over 100,000 volumes.

A bachelor's degree in Computer & Information Systems (CIS) is offered here with a current enrollment of 500 students. A new MBA in CIS program starts in the Fall of 1983. Prospective students should apply through the Admissions Office or the Graduate Office. No application deadline is specified.

Computing facilities include: a Data General MV 8000 Eagle, TRS 80s, Apples, Super Pets, and 20 IBM PCs. More IBM PCs will be acquired in the near future.

There are 10 full-time faculty members in the department. Openings exist at all ranks. Background in system analysis, business microcomputer systems, COBOL programming, or decision support systems would be most welcome.

Course Offerings: (generally 3 semester hours)

Undergraduate

102	Intro To Computer Data Processing	331	Systems Analysis and Design
211	Cobol Structured Programming	361	Data Communication Systems
251	Fortran Programming	391	Systems Management Internship
261	Problem Solving and Decision Making	401	Management Info Systems
311	Applied Data Structures	402	Seminar in Computer Info Systems
321	Management Science	461	Data Base Management
		471	Microcomputers & Cmptr Architecture

SOUTH CAROLINA

UNIVERSITY OF SOUTH CAROLINA
Columbia, SC 29208
(803) 777-7700

University of South Carolina is a public university with a 262-acre campus serving a population of 26,000 students, a faculty student ratio of 1 to 17, and a library with 3.7 million volumes.

The Computer Science Department offers BS and MS programs in which 600 and 50 students are currently enrolled. A new PhD program begins in the Fall Semester of 1983. Write to the department for applications and information regarding deadline and financial aids.

Computing facilities include an IBM 3033, Amdahl S/470-VS, VAX 11/780, PDP 11/44, and the Cosmos, Cromenco, and Motorola microcomputers. The CSNet is accessible. Operating systems in use include VMS, MV, CMS for the mainframes, UNIX for the minis.

There are 10 full-time members in the department. Openings exist both at the assistant and associate professor ranks.

Course Offerings: (generally 3 semester units)

101	Intro to Computer Concepts	501	Systems Simulation
140	Intro to Algorithmic Design I	508	Computer Methods for Humanistic Problems
205	Business Applications Programming	508L	Lab for Comp Meth Humanistic Probs 1
206	Scientific Applications Programming	510	Systems Programming
210	Cmptr System & Assembly Lang Programming	511	Operating Systems I
240	Intro to Algorithmic Design II	520	Database System Design
310	Intro to Computer Architecture	530	Programming Language Structures
320	Information Structures	540	Advanced Program Design
360	Numerical Calculus	541	Software Design and Development
399	Independent Study-9	550	Discrete Math for Computer Science
420	File Management	551	Intro to Automata Theory
498	Undergrad Research Project in Comp Sci I	560	Numerical Analysis I 4
499	Undergrad Research Project in Comp Sci II	561	Numerical Analysis II 4
500	Fundamentals of Computer Science	580	Artificial Intelligence

CLEMSON UNIVERSITY
Clemson, SC 29631
(803) 656-2287

Clemson University is a public university with a 600-acre campus located in a small town where recreational opportunities abound in the nearby mountains, lakes and the Atlantic Ocean. The university supports a population of 12,000 students, a faculty student ratio of 1 to 12, and a library of 805,000 volumes.

The Department of Computer offers a bachelor's and master's programs in which 550 and 60 students are enrolled respectively. In addition, the Department of Electrical & Computer Engineering offers many hardware courses. Prospective students should apply through the Office of Admissions or the Graduate School; deadlines are Dec 1 and July 1 for the undergraduate and graduate students respectively.

Computing facilities here include an IBM 3081, a VAX 11/780, a PDP 11/35, and various microcomputer systems. The CSNet is available. Future acquisition plans call for several microcomputer systems.

There are 18 full-time faculty members in the department. Their research interests cover almost all software areas including: operating systems, database systems, algorithms, programming languages ...etc. Openings exist at all ranks. Background in database systems, operating systems, programming languages, software engineering, or artificial intelligence would be most attractive.

Course Offerings:

110	Elementary Computer Programming	429	Translation of Prgrmng languages
120	Intro to Info Processing Systems	430	Computer Performance Evaluation
130	Data Processing with COBOL	435	Microprogramming
150	Intro FORTRAN Programming	450	Thry of Computation
151	Intro PL/I Programming	462	Teleprcssng & Database Mangmnt Systems
152	Intro PASCAL Programming	463	Online Systems
154	Intro Snobol Programming	471	Systems Analysis
155	Intro RPG Programming	472	Software Development Methodology
156	Intro BASIC Programming	480	Fundamentals of Computer Science
210	Programming Methodology	481	Special Topics in Computer Science
230	Assembly Language Programming	823	Operating Systems Design
250	Advanced FORTRAN Programming	825	Sftwr Systems for Data Communications
251	Adv PL/I Programming	828	Thry of Programing Languages
253	APL Programming	840	Design & Analysis of Algorithms
330	Computer Systems Organization	862	Database Management System Design
340	Intro to Data Structures	864	Computer Architecture
360	Peripherals & File Design	881	Special Topics
422	Systems Programming	891	Master's Research
423	Intro to Operating Systems		(Note: courses 422 to 481 are same as 622 to 681)
428	Dsgn & Implmntatn of Prgrmng Languages		

FURNAM UNIVERSITY
Greenville, SC 29613
(803) 294-2034

Furman is a Baptist university with 3,000 students, a 750-acre campus, a faculty student ratio of 1 to 14, and a library with 450,000 volumes.

The Department of Computer Science offers two undergraduate programs: a Computer Science-Mathematics Major, and a Computing-Business Major. Currently, there are 600 students taking CS courses.

About 35 will recieve Computer Science degrees in 1984. Prospective students should apply through the Admissions Office. Deadline for financial aid is Feb 1 for the Fall Quarter.

Furman is a Baptist university with 3,000 students, a 750-acre campus, a faculty student ratio of 1 to 14, and a library with 450,000 volumes.

The Department of Computer Science offers two undergraduate programs: a Computer Science-Mathematics Major, and a Computing-Business Major. Currently, there are 600 students taking CS courses. About 35 will recieve Computer Science degrees in 1984. Prospective students should apply through the Admissions Office. Deadline for financial aid is Feb 1 for the Fall Quarter.

Computing facilities at Furnam include: an HP 3000 Series 64; an HP 1000; two networks composing of twelve HP 9836s, and eight HP 9836s. There are 5 full-time members in the department. An opening exists at the assistant professor rank.

Course Offering: (generally 4 quarter units)

20	COBOL	33	Artificial Intelligence
21	Introduction to Computing	35	Software Design
24	Programming Languages Structures	40	Data Base Management Systems
25	Computer Organization	41	Systems Analysis
30	Information Structures	44	Computational Theory
31	Microprocessors	49	Introduction to Numerical Analysis
32	Computer Architecture		

LANDER COLLEGE
Greenwood, SC 29646
(803) 229-8307

Lander is a public college with a 75-acre campus supporting 2,000 students, a faculty student ratio of 1 to 22, and a library with 150,000 volumes.

A bachelor's program in computer science is offered with a current enrollment of 132 students. Interested students should apply through the Admissions Office before August for the Fall Semester.

The faculty and student have access to an IBM 3081. Microcomputers in use include the Apples and the Commodores. More micros will be acquired in the near future. In addition, software at Clemson University is made availabl to the faculty and students here.

There are 4 full-time faculty in the department. Openings exist at the assistant professor rank.

Course Offering: (generally 3 semster units)

LANDER COLLEGE

105	Intro to Computer Science	350	Data Structures
201	Fortran	360	Database Design
220	COBOL	370	Prgmmng Packages w Statistial Computation
240	PL/I	380	Systems Analysis
260	Principles of Programming	390	Special Topics 1-3
290	Computer Science Practicum 1	410	Computer Architecture
300	Numerical Analysis	420	Organization of Programming Languages
310	Assembly Language Programming	430	Microprocessors
320	Computer Organization I	460	Intro to Operating Systems
330	Computer Organization II	499	Computer Science Project
335	Intro to File Processing	554	Computers in Education

SOUTH DAKOTA

SOUTH DAKOTA
SCHOOL OF MINES & TECHNOLOGY
Rapid City, SD 57701
(605) 394-2411

South Dakota School of Mines & Technology is a public institution with 2800 students, a faculty student ratio of 1 to 19, and a library with 190,000 volumes.

The Department of Mathematical Sciences offers BS and MS degrees in Mathematics and Computer Science. Currently, there are 300 and 10 students in the two programs respectively. Apply through the department for admission before April 1.

Computing facilities include: a CDC Cyber 170/720, a PDP 11, and several microcomputer systems. A second CPU for the Cyber 170 is to be acquired in the near future.

There are 13 full-time faculty members in the department. Openings exist at the assistant and the associate professor ranks. Individuals who can teach general computer science courses will be considered.

Course Offerings:

101	Computer Literacy	471	Theory of Compilers
111	Elmntry Num Analysis for Engnrs & Scientists	472	Operating Systems
172	Computing in BASIC	478	Topics in Computer Science
173	Intro to COBOL	491	Special Prblms in Computer Science
197	Programming Techniques in BASIC	611	Software Design
271	Intro to Computer Science	615	Discrete Structures
298	Programming Techniques	651	Data Base Design
299	Intro to Computer Science Lab	671	Theory of Computation
341	Computer Organization & Design	673	Network, parallel & Distrbtd Prcssng
370	Comparative Languages	685	Statistical Tchnques in Digtl Simulation
371	Data Structures	700	Thesis
399	Advanced COBOL		

TENNESSEE

VANDERBILT UNIVERSITY
Nashville, TN 37212
(615) 322-2561

Vanderbilt is a private university with a 320-acre campus, a population of 9,000 students, a faculty student ratio of 1 to 9, and a library with 1.5 million volumes.

The Computer Science Department offers BS, MS, Master of Engineering, and PhD programs. Currently, there are 240 in the BS, 20 in the master's, and 12 in the doctorate programs. Apply through the Undergraduate Admissions Office at 401 24th Ave S., Nashville, TN 37212; or through the Graduate School at 336 Kirkland Hall, Nashville, TN 37240, before Feb 1 for the Fall Semester.

The university's Computer Center maintains a DEC 1099, DEC 2070, 2 VAX 11/780s and several PDP 11s. The CS Department has a Perkin Elmer 3220, two IBM PCs, and a HP-200. The Engineering School owns seven Commodore Super Pets. Both CSNet and EDUNet are available. More DEC VAX computer systems will be acquired in the near future.

There are 9 full-time members in the department. A faculty position is open at the assistant professor rank. Members of the faculty:

C F Fischer, P C Fischer, R L Hemminger, M D Plummer, W H Rowan Jr, H E Williams, R I Winner, L W Dowdy, J L Grefenstette, B D McKay. Adjuncts and lecturers: C L Bradshaw, W A Brown, M Chrestenson-Becker, W S Donelson II.

Course Offerings: (generally 3 semester units)

152 Intro to Scientific & Engineering Computing	282 Operating Systems Principles II
200 Intro to Computing (4)	286 Intro to Database Management Systems
203 Intro to Computer Organization	288 Artificial Intelligence & Heuristic Prgmmng
208 Intermediate Programming	305 Topics in Artificial Intelligence
212 Intro to Discrete Structures	315 Advanced Systems Programming I
214 Business Information Systems	316 Advanced Systems Programming II
240 Undergraduate Research (1-3)	320 Algorithms for Parallel Computing
241 Computer Science Project Labratory	325 Numerical Computing
242 Special Topics in Computer Science (1-3)	330 Large Scale Data Management Systems
253 Data Structures	340 Topics in Theory of Computation
254 Computer Systems Architecture	350 Theory of Compiler Design
261 Intro to Organization	371 Digital Computer Architecture
263 System Simulation	380 Design & Analysis of Algorithms
268 Intro Automata, Formal Lang & Computation	390 Individual Studies (1-3)
271 Computer Logic	391 Seminar (1-3)
272 Sequential Machines	395 Special Topics
275 Programming Languages	396 Special Topics
276 Compiler Construction	399 PhD Dissertation Research
281 Operating Systems Principles I	

MEMPHIS STATE UNIVERSITY
Memphis, TN 38152
(901) 454-2000

Memphis State is a public university with a 200-acre campus, a population of 20,000 students, a faculty student ratio of 1 to 17, and a library with 860,000 volumes.

The Department of Mathematical Sciences offers BS and MS majors in computer science. Currently, there are 574 and 406 in the programs respectively. Prospective students should apply through the Office of Admissions, Administrative Bldg Suite 215; deadlines are Aug 1 for the Fall Semester, Dec 1 for the Spring.

Computing facilities include a Univac 1100/60, a Tektronics Graphics system, and 28 IBM PC's. The Corvus OMNI Net is available. Two Pixel 100 A/P will be acquired in the near future.

There are 7 full-time faculty members in the department. Faculty positions are open, one each, at the assistant and the full professor ranks. Background in operating systems, databases, analysis of algorithms, or cryptography would be highly desirable.

Course Offerings: (generally 3 semester units)

1000	Computer Programming I	6001	Thru 6901 Same as 4001 Thru 4901
2010	Computer Programming II	7041	Compiler Design
3230	Assembly Language Programming	7111	Microcomputer Programming I
3420	Computer Organization	7112	Microcomputer Programming II
4001	Computer Programming	7115	Database Systems
4002	Accelerated Computer Programming	7177	Minicomputer Software
4003	Computer Orgnztn & Assmbly Language	7271	Operating Systems
4040	Programming Languages	7601	Automata theory
4041	Intro to Compilers	7713	Design & Analysis of Algorithms I
4081	Software Development	7714	Design & Analysis of Algorithms II
4150	Information Structures	7715	Computational Complexity
4160	File Processing	7815	Pictorial Information Systems
4242	Intro to Computer Graphics	7825	Fault Tolerant Computing
4270	Intro to Operating Systems	7912	Computer Center Operations
4601	Intro to Automata	7991	Problems in Computer Science
4715	Artificial Intelligence	7993	Seminar in Computer Science
4901	Topics in Computer Science		

UNIVERITY OF TENNESSEE
Knoxville, TN 37996
(615) 974-2591

The University of Tennessee, Knoxville, is a public university with 30,000 students, a faculty student ratio of 1 to 18, and a library with 1.6 million volumes.

The Department of Computer Science offers both BA and MS programs. About 325 and 100 students are enrolled in the two programs. Admission to the BA program is administered through the Admissions Office, 320 Student Services Building. Graduates apply through the Office of Graduate School Office, 218 Student Services Building. Deadline for nonservice fellowships offered by the Graduate School is Feb 1. Apply through the Department of Computer Science for graduate assistantship by March 1. Some additional assistantships are available through the Image processing Lab in Electrical Engineering. Contact the Department at 8 Ayres Hall; Phone (615) 974-5067, for further information.

The University's Computing Center contains two IBM 370/3031s, an IBM 4341/2, a DEC system-10 with dual KL10 processors, a PDP 11/55, a Calcomp 1051 plotter. The

IBM 370/3031s run under MVS with JES2, and SVS with HASP IV; the DEC system-10 under TOPS-10. Time-sharing features include VM/CMS on the 4341, Coursewriter III on the 370/3031s and extensive graphics software support.

The Department's Minicomputer Lab includes: VAX 11/780, PDP 11/34, NCR TOWER 1632, HP 64000 Logic Analyzer, 2 DEC Professional 350s each with color graphics capability, 3 DEC LSI 11s running RT-11, 4 Z80 micros running CPM, 2 Apples with color graphics. The VAX system has 4 MB memory, Floating Point Accelerator, User Writable Control store, a VS11 color raster graphics terminal, and runs VMS and UNIX.

The VAX and NCR TOWER system are connected to the DCA network that links all major computers on the campus with the massive facilities at the Oak Ridge National Lab. DECNet is supported by the VAX and PDP 11/34, which supports a virtual terminal facility and provides access to the EE Department's VAX 11/780 and the VAX 11/780 at the UT Space Institute. In addition, the nationwide computer science network, CSNet, is available on the VAX.

There are 13 faculty members in the Department. Openings exist at the assistant and associate professor ranks.

Course Offerings: (generally 3 semester units)

1410	Intro to Business Oriented Programming	4980	Special Topics in CS (1-4)
1510	Intro to Programming-FORTRAN	5000	Thesis (3-15)
1610	Intro to Structured Programming	5002	Nonthesis Graduation Completion
1620	Intermediate Structured Programming	5010	Computer Assisted Instruciton
2215	Discrete Structures I	5050	Modeling & Simulation of Physical Systems
2610	Programming Techniques	5100	Immigration to CS (5)
2710	Machine Organization	5109	Immigration to CS Practicum (2)
3010	Computers & Society	5175	Intro to Logic Design
3150	Intro to Num Algorithms & Programming	5210	Artificial Intelligence
3155	Intro to Num Algorithms	5230	Intoduction to Program Verification
3180	Logic Design of Digital Systems	5250	Medical Computing
3215	Discrete Stuctures II	5310	Computer Networks
3410	Computer Programming-COBOL	5430	Adv Compiler Design
3520	Assembly Language Programming	5455	Finite Differnece Mthds of Partial Diff Eq
3910	Commercial Computer Concepts & Control	5465	Finite Element Methods
4050	Number Systems for Digital Computers	5475	Adv Topics in Num Partial Diff Eq
4210	Intro to Artificial Intelligence	5570	Adv Database Mgmt Systems
4225	Num Solution to Equations & Num Approx	5655	Num Mathematics
4235	Num Methods for Ordinary Diff Eq	5665	Num Mathematics
4245	Num Llinear Algebra	5675	Num Mathematics
4310	Statistical Data Processing	5670	Adv Operating Systems
4330	Indep Study in CS (1-3)	5680	Adv Operating Systems
4340	Interactive Statistical Data Processing	5680	Adv Operating Systems
4470	Programming Languages (4)	5710	Finite Automata Theory
4510	Data Structures & Nonnumeric Programming	5730	Computability & Computational Complexity
4550	Systems Programming	5750	Theory of Formal Languages
4570	Intro to Database Mgmt Systems	5775	Combinatorial Algorithms
4590	Adv Systems Programming	5790	Computer Architecture
4610	Operating Systems--Concepts & Facilities	5810	Information Organization & Retrieval
4620	Operating Systems--Case Studies	5840	Pattern Recognition
4660	Principles of Compiler Design	5850	Pattern Recognition
4710	Formal Language & Automata	5880	Data Security
4730	Analysis of Non-numeric Algorithms	5910	Special Topics in Computer Science (1-6)
4750	Interactive Computer Graphics	5920	Special Topics in Computer Science (1-6)
4820	Intro to Pattern Recognition	5930	Special Topics in Computer Science (1-6)
4830	Digital Image Processing	5940	Adv Small Computer Systems
4850	Small Computer Systems	5950	Adv Small Computer Systems
4910	Analysis & Mgmt of Computer Installations	5970	Indep Study in Computer Science (1-3)

TEXAS

NORTH TEXAS STATE UNIVERSITY
P O Box 13797, Denton, TX 76203
(817) 788-2681

North Texas State is a public university with a 380-acre campus, a population of 18,000 students, a faculty student ratio of 1 to 16, and a library with 1.4 million volumes.

The Department of Computer Sciences offers bachelor's, master's and PhD programs in which 100, 200 and 20 students are currently enrolled. Prospective students should apply through the Department of Computer Science.

Computer systems in use include: NAS, VAX 11/780, TI 990, Apples, TI 99/YA, TI PC, IBM PC. Corvus, LAN. UNIX, ADA are available.

There are 17 full-time members in the department. Faculty openings exist at all ranks.

Course Offerings: (generally 3 semester units)

101	Computers in Society	
110	Intro to Computer Science	
111	Program Development	
201	Assembly Language Programming	
232	Programming Laboratory (1-4)	
310	Computer Systems Analysis	
340	Data Structures	
370	Advanced Assembly Language Programming	
378	Data Communications	
387	Logic Laboratory	
395	Internship in Computer Science	
401	Software Development Analysis	
402	Software Testing Methodologies	
408	Cultural Impact of the Computer	
410	Computer Science for the Teacher	
420	Intro to Systems Programming	
425	Survey of Computer Languages	
430	File Organization and Processing	
435	Intro to Data Base Design	
440	Intro to Digital Logic	
442	Intro to Computer Graphics	
445	Algorithm Analysis and Complexity Theory	
451	Machine Structures	
454	Intro to Operating Systems	
488	Special Computer Application Problem (1-4)	
489	Directed Study Computer Sciences (1-4)	

Graduate
501	Intro to Computer Applications
502	Computer Methods
503	Problem Solving in High-Level Languages (4)
504	Systems Analysis & Assmb Lang Prgrmng (4)
505	Data Structures and Systems Programming (4)
510	Computers in Education
511	Computer-Assisted Instruction
514	Seminar in Current Activities in C S (1)
515	Research Methods (1)
521	Text Processing
525	Programming Languages
527	Human Factors in Computer Science
530	Information Structures
533	Topics in Computer Applications
535	Database Systems Design
541	Artificial Intelligence
543	Methods of Numerical Computations
544	Topics in Computations and Modeling
547	Computer-Aided Modeling
552	Advanced Software Development
554	Operating System Design
555	Compiler Design
557	Systems Programming
558	Topics in Programming

561	Digital Logic Design	595	Thesis (6)
568	Topics in Digital Engineering	596	Computer Sciences Institute (1-6 each)
570	Computer Structures	610	Topics in Cmptr Assisted Intruction Systems
572	Topics in Microcomputers	628	Computability
578	Communication System Design	633	Topics in Computer Science Research
587	Digital Logic Laboratory	642	Topics in Computer Graphics
588	Special Computer Appln Problem (1-4)	651	Software Verification and Reliability
589	Directed Study (1-4)	654	Topics in Advanced Operating Systems
590	Special Problems (1-3)	670	Systems Performance Measrmnt & Evaluation
592	Research Problems in Lieu of Thesis	678	Distributed Computing & Data Communictns

TEXAS A & M UNIVERSITY
College Station, TX 77843
(713) 845-1031

Texas A & M is a public university with a 5,200-acre campus, a population of 35,000 students, a faculty student ratio of 1 to 25, and with the Sterling Evans Library whose capacity has been recently expanded to 2 million volumes.

The Department of Industrial Engineering offers Bachelor's, Master's (Master of Computing Science, and MS in compting science), and PhD programs with current enrollments of 1,200, 80, 20 students. Prospective students should apply through the Office of Admissions and Records. Application deadlines: April 1 for financial aid, May 1 for regular admission.

Mission-oriented graduate research has been conducted in: artificial intelligence and automation, computer graphics, software engineering, systems engineering, operations research and optimization. Research is supported by facilities that include: Amdahl 470 V/6 II, Amdahl 470 V/8 running MVS/JES3, MV/8000, Eclipse 130, Apples, and the TI Profesional microcomputers.

Several faculty openings exist at all levels. Background in software engineering is particularly desired. Members of the Computer Science Division within the Department: S B Childs; D Colunga; D D Drew; D K Friesen; J E Kalan; W M Lively; U W Pooch; S V Sheppard; D B Simmons; G N Williams.

Course Offerings: (generally 3 semester units)

201	Computer Programming for Engineers	407	Scientific Programming
202	Intro to Computer Programming	458	Programming of Digital Computers
203	Intro to Computing	481	Seminar
204	Computers & Programming	485	Problems
205	Intro to Data Processing	489	Special Topics
301	Computer Organization	603	Assembly Language (4)
302	Intro to Discrete Structures	611	Survey of Programming Languages
303	Data Structures	612	Progamming Methodology
401	Programming Languages	613	Computer Software Systems
402	Compiler Design	614	Computer Architecture
403	Systems Programming	615	Database Systems
404	Information Processing	621	Computer Methods in Applied Sciences
405	Data Processing Systems Orgnztn	622	Computer Communications and Networks
406	Mechanical Languages	623	Software Engineering

624 Simulation	681 Seminar (1)
625 Artificial Intelligence	684 Professional Internship (1)
627 Formal Languages and Automata Theory	685 Problems (1-4)
628 Compiler Construction	689 Special Topics (1-4)
629 Analysis of Computer Algorithms	691 Research (1)
630 Information Storage and Retrieval	

UNIVERSITY OF TEXAS AT ARLINGTON
Arlington, TX 76019
(817) 273-3401

The University of Texas at Arlington is a public university with 21,000 students, a 340-acre campus, a faculty student ratio of 1 to 23, and a library with 760,000 volumes.

The Department of Computer Science & Engineering offers BS, MS, and PhD programs in computer science, and computer science & engineering. Currently, there are 780 in the BS, 200 in the master's, and 10 in the PhD programs respectively. Prospective students should apply through the CSE Department, PO Box 19015, Arlington, TX 76019-0015; Phone (817) 273-3785. Application deadline for financial aid is March 15. Deadline for regular admission is open.

Computer systems in use include: IBM 4341, DEC 2060, VAX 11/780, TE 990/12, IBM PC and the Apple II+. Operating systems include MVS, TOPS 20, VMS/EUNICE. A local area network is to be acquired in the near future.

There are 20 full-time faculty members in the department. Positions exist at the assistant and associate professor ranks. Background in computer graphics, database, microcomputers would be very attractive.

Course Offerings: (generally 3 semester units)

5300 Introduction to Programming	5323 Continuous System Modeling
5301 Advanced Information Structures	5324 Software Engineering
5302 Computer Graphics	5325 Design of Hybrid Computing Systems
5303 Design of Operating Systems	5326 List Processing & Symbol Manipulation
5304 Compiler Design I	5327 Mathematical Theory of Computation
5305 Compiler Design II	5330 The Computer & Natural Language
5306 Database Systems I	5331 Artificial Intelligence
5307 Computer Organization I	5332 Infological Data Models
5308 Computer Organization II	5333 Information Retrieval
5309 Adv Computatnl Meth for Eng & Sci I	5334 Microcomputer Organization & Programming
5310 Adv Computatnl Meth for Eng & Sci II	5335 Advanced Micro Systems Design
5312 Data Processing Management	5336 Design of File & Database Structures
5313 Algorithmic Languages	5337 Computer System Performance Evaluation
5315 Computer Networks & Communications Systems	5338 Mini-Micro Computer Controls
5316 Information Processing Systems	5345 Discrete Structures
5317 Appln of Digital Computers to Eng Prob	5346 Information Structures
5318 Computer Applns in the Social Sciences	5391 Individual Study in Computer Science
5319 Assembly Language	6301 Algorithm Analysis
5320 Computer Simulation Techniques	6304 Formal Language Theory
5322 Computer Simulation Techniques	6311 A Operating Systems

6321	Computerized Image Manipulation	6341	Design of VLSI Systems
6324	Advanced Software Engineering	6343	Fault Tolerant Computing
6328	Signal Processing	6392	Special Topics in Adv Computer Science
6329	Database System II	6997	Research in Computer Science
6339	Advances in Computer Architecture	6999	Dissertation

THE UNIVERSITY OF TEXAS
Austin, TX 78712
(512) 471-1711

The University of Texas at Austin, the largest member of the University of Texas system, has 48,000 students, 110 buildings on a campus with more than three hundred acres, a faculty student ratio of 1 to 22, and the eighth largest academic library in the nation with 4.6 million volumes.

The Department of Computer Sciences offers bachelor's, master's and PhD programs in which 1400, 124, and 81 students are currently enrolled. Prospective students should apply through the Director of Admissions. Application deadline for admission with financial aid is March 1, for regular admission, June 1.

Computing facilities at UT Austin include: two CDC Cyber 170/750 operated under a dual operating system UT-2D developed by the Computation Center's staff; a DECsystem-10 and a DECsystem-20, an IBM 370/158 under VM/SP. The Center's Advanced Graphics Lab uses a VAX 11/780, a Vector General subsystem, a Grinnell system for image processing, a Matrix 4007 camera. A PDP 11/70 under UNIX, used as an External Network Gateway Processor, connects the campus to the ARPANet national network. In addition, the Center operates a DECsystem-20 for research projects in the computing sciences. This system provides communication ports and an interface to the APARNet. Departmental research facilities include a VAX 11/780 and workstations interconnected by a local network, a LISP machine subnetwork, several mini and microcomputer systems. Planned acquistion includes the CRAY computer and more VAX's.

Faculty and their interests: J Bitner (computing thry, analysis of algrthms); W Bledsoe (AI, automatic thrm proving); R Boyer (automatic thrm, prgm verification); F Brown (AI, automatic thrm proving); J C Browne (systems, archtctr, performance measurement); J Brumfield (systems; performance measurement).

K M Chandy (systems, distrbtd prgrmng); A A Cline (numerical analysis, math softwr); A G Dale (database management); N B Dale (instructional systems); A E Emerson (computing thry); D Fussell (database mngmnt, graphics, VLSI dsgn); M Gouda (system modelling, communication protocols); D Kincaid (numerical analysis); V Kumar (distributed systems).

S S Lam (computer networks); C Lengauer (programming languages); N Martin (computer archtctr); J Misra (distrbtd systems, prgrmng languages); A Mok (distrbtd systems, prgrmng environments); M Molloy (performance measurement, modelling); J S Moore (automatic thrm proving, prgrm verification); G Novak (AI).

J Peterson (operating systems, office ntwrks, word processing); E Rich (AI, user interfaces); L Rosier (computing thry); D Scott (numerical methods, numerical sftwr); A Silberschatz (operating systems, data mangmnt, prgrmng languages); R Simmons (computational linguistics); D M Young (numerical analysis); H Korth (database); D Batory (database).

Course Offerings:

372 Intro to Operating Systems	115L A Brief Intro to PASCAL
375 Algorithmic Languages and Compilers	206 Accelerated FORTRAN Programming
378 Undergraduate Topics in Computer Sciences	301 Computers in the Modern World
379H Computer Sciences Honors Course	304F FORTRAN Programming
Graduate	304P PASCAL Programming
380K Statistical Applns of Electronic Computers	315 Computer Science Concepts
380L Advanced Operating Systems	318 A Survey of Numerical Techniques
380M Operating Systems Theory	410 Computer Organization & Programming
380N Systems Modeling II	325 Discrete Mathematics
381K Artificial Intelligence	327 Programming Applications & Practice
382 Switching Theory	328 Data Structures
382L Theory of Computational Complexity	333 Intro Formal Languages & Automata Theory
382M Functional Logical Design	135 Computer Programming
383C Num Analysis: Linear & Nonlinear Algebra	336 Analysis of Programs
383D Num Analysis: Approx, Quadrature & Diff Eq	343 Artificial Intelligence
385 Intro to Theory of Computation	345 Programming Languages
386 Data Base Management	347 Data Management
386K Num Treatment of Differential Equations	352 Computer Systems Architecture
386L Advanced Programming Languages	353 Elements of the Theory of Computation
386M Data Communications & Networks	354 Computer Graphics
388 Computational Linguistics	368K Numerical Mathematics for Applications
390 Advanced Systems Laboratory	369 Systems Modeling I
393D Topics in Num Analysis	370 Undergraduate Reading and Research

BAYLOR UNIVERSITY
Waco, TX76706
(817) 755-1011

Baylor is a private Baptist university with 11,000 students, a 350-acre campus, a faculty student ratio of 1 to 20, and a library with 970,000 volumes.

The Computer & Engineering Sciences Department, located in CSB 403, Baylor University, Waco, TX76798, offers a BS in computer science with a current enrollment of 350 students. Prospective students should apply through the Admissions Office. Deadline for scholarship is March 1.

Computer systems in use include: VAX 11/780 (VMS), PDP 11/34, PDP 11/44 running RSX and UNIX, Apple II+, and the IBM PC. In addition, the DECNet is available.

There are 10 ful-time faculty in the department. Openings exist at the assistant professor level. No particular area in computer science is specified.

Course Offerings: (generally 3 semester hours)

1301 Personal Computing	3324 Numerical Methods
1325 FORTRAN Programming	3331 Survey of Programming Languages
1330 Intro to Computer Science I	3333 Simulation Models
1340 Intro to Computer Science II	3338 Computer Organization
2332 Intro to File Processing	3437 Digital Logic and Electronics
2334 Assembly Language Programming	3439 Digital Computer Fundamentals

4103 Intro to Computer Programming	4334 Data Structures
4104 Intro to Command Language	4335 Database Design
4105 Intro to Computer Packages	4336 Intro to Computation Theory
4301 Cultural Impact of the Computer	4337 Intro to Operating Systems
4322 Numerical Analysis	4420 Instructional Applications of Computers
4331 Prgmng Language Design & Implementation	4438 Mini/Microcomputer Systems
4333 Systems Programming	

SOUTHWEST TEXAS STATE UNIVERSITY
San Marcos, TX 78666
(512) 245-2364

Southwest Texas State is a public university with a population of 15,000 students, a 180-acre campus, a faculty student ratio of 1 to 25, and a library with 720,000 volumes.

The Department of Mathematics and Computer Science offers BS and MS programs in computer science in which 300 and 60 students are currently enrolled. Apply through the Admissions Office. Deadline for scholarship is March 15 for the Fall Semester.

The university has a DEC-1091, several PDP 11's, LSI 11's, Apples, and the Commodore microcomputers. Local network is available.

There are 11 full-time members in the department. Faculty positions exist at the assistant and associate professor levels. Individuals with a PhD in computer science or computer science education are welcome to apply.

Course Offerings: (generally 3 semester units)

1308	Computers and Society	4328	Systems Programming II
1318	Fundmntls of Computer Math & Flowcharting	4338	Mathematical Modeling
2308	FORTRAN Programming	4348	Programming for Teachers
2318	Assembly Language	4358	Computers in Education
2328	Non-Mathematical Statistics	4368	Survey of Computer Languages
3305	Intro Probability and Statistics	4378	Adv Applns in Computer Science
3318	Computer Applns to Statistical Methods	Graduate	
3348	Operations Research	5305	Adv Probability and Statistics
3358	Data Structures	5308	Adv Systems Programming
3368	Small Scale Computer Systems (3-2)	5318	Adv Programming Techniques
3378	Theory of Sequential Machines	5328	Data Structures
3408	Intro Computer Architecture (3-2)	5338	Formal Languages
3428	Intro Num Analysis w Computer Applns	5348	Computer Organization and Design
4305	Probability and Statistics	5368	Topics in Computer Science
4318	Systems Programming I		

STEPHEN F. AUSTIN STATE UNIVERSITY
Nacogdoches, TX 75962
(713) 569-2504

Stephen F Austin is a pubic university with a 400-acre campus, a faculty student of 1 to 23, and a library with 350,000 volumes.

Bachelor's and a master's programs in computer science are offered which consist of 2000 and 20 students respectively. Prospective students should apply through the Office of Admissions. Application deadline for financial aid is April 1.

Computer systems in use include: a Honeywell Dual B3 DPS System running CP-6, TI 990/12, Apple II+, IBM PC, IMSAI 8080 microcomputer systems. More micros will be acquired in the near future.

There are 12 full-time members in the department. Faculty openings exist at the assistant professor rank. Background in data processing systems, or data base systems would be highly desirable.

Course Offerings:

Undergraduate
101 Intro to Computing
201 Intro to Computer Programming
202 Computer Programming Principles
211 Programming w Business-Oriented Languages
214 Assembly Languages
221 Intro to Information Processing Systems
301 A Contemporary Programming Language
321 Programming Methods for DP Applications
326 Data Base File Oriented Systems
331 Programming Methods for Scientific Applns
341 Data Structures
343 Computer Architecture Basics
344 Microprocessing
401 Contemporary Topics in Computer Science
412 Computer Science Practicum
421 Applied Operations Research
426 Systems Analysis & Design
431 System Simulation & Model Building
432 Applied Numerical Methods
435 Teleprocessing & Data Communications

441 Principles of Systems Programming
442 Organization of Programming Languages
485 Internship in Computer Science
Graduate
421 Applied Operations Research
431 Systems Simulation & Model Building
435 Teleprocessing & Data Communications
441 Principles of Systems Programming
501 Intro to Computers & Info Processing
502 Fundamentals of Computer Science
511 Programming Languages
513 Elements of Programming Style
525 Contemporary Systems Design
531 Applied Simulation
532 Advanced Numerical Processess
541 Language Translators & Interpretars
542 Operating Systems
561 Microcomputer Technology
565 Computer Architecture
575 Advanced Graduate Studies
578 Seminar

UNIVERSITY OF TEXAS AT EL PASO
El Paso, TX 79968
(915) 747-5550

University of Texas at El Paso operates on a semester system with a faculty student ratio of 1 to 21 and a library with 625,000 volumes.

The Department of Computer Science offers bachelor's and master's degrees in which 900 and 40 are enrolled respectively. Prospective students should apply through the Admissions Office; deadline for financial aid is March 1.

Computing systems include: IBM 4341-M2 running VM/SP, MVS-JES3, IBM 4331-K2, PDP 11/45. Operating systems and noteworthy software in use: MUSIC, UCSD P-System for micros, UNIX. In addition, the department owns 57 personal computers.

There are 6 full-time members in the department. An opening exists for individuals with background preferably in data base or architecture; rank negotiable.

U T EL PASO

Course Offerings:

1471	Computer Science Problems Seminar	3513	Computer Architecture
3100	Computers Individual & Society	3516	Data Acquisition & Processing
3110	Intro to Computer Programming	3473	Mini Computers
3310	Research Techniques with FORTRAN	3474	Design of Operating Systems
3325	COBOL Programming	4360	Computer Organization & Design
3330	Programming Language Organization	MATH	
3335	Systems Programming	3429	Numerical Methods
3340	Data Structures	3528	Numerical Linear Algebra
3345	Systems Analysis & Design	3529	Numerical Analysis
3350	Automata Theory & Formal Languages	Graduate	
3425	The Appln Programming Environment	3335	Systems Programming
3430	Design & Implmnt of Prgrmng Languages	3350	Automata Theory & Formal Languages
3442	Data Base Management	3425	The Appln Programming Environment
3445	Advanced Systems Design	3430	Design & Implmntn of Prgrmng Languages
3450	Systems Simulation	3442	Data Base Management
3452	Compiler Construction	3445	Advanced Systems Design
3475	Theory of Operating Systems	3450	Systems Simulation
3495	Special Topics in Computer Science	3452	Compiler Construction
4120	Intro to Digital Computation	3475	Theory of Operating Systems
4225	Intro to Structured COBOL Programming	3495	Special Topics in Computer Science
4130	Intro to Digital Computation	3510	Computer Graphics
4332	Assembler Language Programming	3511	Survey of Programming Languages
CIS		3515	Theory of Computation
3482	Management Info Systems	3522	Adv Info Storage & Retrieval Systems
3490	Data Processing Management	3530	Data Communications
EE			

WEST TEXAS STATE UNIVERSITY
Canyon, TX 79016
(806) 656-3331

West Texas State is a public university with 6,800 students, a 124-acre campus, a faculty student ratio of 1 to 18, and a library with over 700,000 volumes.

The Department of Business Analysis offers an undergraduate and a master's programs in computer information systems, in which 400 and 20 students are enrolled respectively. Prospective students should apply through the Department. No application deadline is specified.

Computing facilities include a DEC System 10, several PDP 11's, Apples, IBM PC's, and the PET microcomputers. There are 5 full-time faculty members in the department.

Course Offerings: (generally 3 semester units)

Undergraduate
201 Using the CIS Lab
205 Principles of Computer & Info Systems
260 Advanced Programming Techniques
305 Computer Applications in Research
315 Assembler Language Programming
314 Contemporary Programming Methods
360 Structured Systems Analysis & Design
380 Data Structures
399 Special Topics
450 Database Concepts & Design
462 Computer Center Management
476 Supervised Reading & Info Systems
485 Logic & Algorithms
490 Computer Systems Developement & Design
497 Internship & Conference

498 Applied Problems in Computer & Info Systems
499 Honors
Graduate
5450 Database Concepts & Design
5462 Computer Hardware & Software Developement
5482 Logic & Algorithms
5485 Computer Systems Developement & Design
5500 Computer Systems & Their Use
5510 Seminar in Computer & Info Systems
5520 Analysis & Design of Info Systems
5530 Data Base Management Info Systems
5540 Decision Support Systems
5576 Reading & Conference
5586 Computerwise Management Info Systems
5599 Special Topics

UTAH

UNIVERSITY OF UTAH
Salt Lake City, UT 84112
(801) 581-7200

The University of Utah is a public university whose 1,500-acre campus is situated at the base of the spectacular Wasatch Mountain Range, allowing its 22,000 students access to some of the world's finest skiing, backpacking, camping, boating ...etc. The university has a faculty student ratio of 1 to 19, and a library system with 1.9 million volumes.

The Department of Computer Science offers bachelor's, MS, Master of Engineering (a professional degree), M Phil, and PhD programs. Current enrollment for these five programs, respectively: 400, 36, 30, 1, and 30. Interested students should apply through the Department at 3160 MEB, University of Utah. Application deadlines: Feb 1 for the Autumn Quarter, Oct 1 for the Winter, and Jan 1 for the Spring. For information about financial aid, contact the Administrative Officer of the Computer Science Department.

Research and computing facilities consist of five laboratories: the Software Research Lab, the Computer Aided Design & Graphics Lab, the Small Computer Lab, the Computer Aided Instruction Lab, and the Digital Signal Processing Lab.

1) Software Research Lab. It is the primary support facility for research in software system and computer architecture. It contains a DEC System 2060 with 5 megabyte memory, a PDP 11/40 front-end communications concentrator, a PDP 11/34 front-end network communications processor for connection to the TELENET network using x.25 interface to the 10 megabit/second Ethernet, a PDP 11/34 front-end driving a Photocomposer, a HP 7221 four and eight color plotters, and AN20 ARPAnet interface for connection to C/30 IMP. In addition, the lab contains a VAX 11/750 with 6 megabyte memory, floating point accelerator, 670 megabyte disk storage, tape drive, interface to the Ethernet and the ARPAnet's C/30 IMP.

2) Computer Aided Design and Graphics Lab. It houses a VAX 11/750 with 6 megabyte memory as the host computer for many specialized pieces of computer graphic hardware such as: Evans & Sutherland Multi Picture System PS300, Grinnell and Jupiter raster color 512*512 frame buffers, Lexidata Solidview 3D real-time solid viewing system, Megatek 7290 color raste graphics system, Matrix Instruments 9000 graphics recorder, interface to the Ethernet ...etc. In addition, there is the Computervision Design CAD system with a raster interactive design station, 134MB disk storage, CGP-100 Central Processor ...etc.

3) Small Computer Lab. It houses 18 Apollo Workstations, 2 Apollo Domain DN400, 1 Apollo Domain DN600, 15 Domain DN300, Apollo disk server/Ethernet gateway, 4 HP 9836 68000-based systems, a Three Rivers PERQ bit mapped workstation, and a Wicat 150 68000-based system.

4) Computer Aided Instruction Lab. It houses various microprocessor systems which are connected to various host systems for use in developing tools for computer aided instruction.

5) Digital Signal Processing Lab. It contains a VAX 11/750 for research work in

real-time applications of image and sound processing. The VAX has 3 megabyte memory, floating point accelerator, 400MB disk storage, tape drive, and interface to the Ethernet.

Other important Department facilities include a darkroom and scientific photo laboratory. The College of Engineering operates a research-scale integrated circuit fabrication facility which is used heavily by the Department. Additionally, the Department operates an integrated circuit testing facility which is used to test and debug both internally and externally fabricated circuits, and which contains state-of-the-art Hewlett Packard and Tektronix automated IC testing equipment.

The department consists of 14 full-time highly active faculty members. Recruiting continues at all levels. Computer scientists in all areas of CS will be considered, especially those with background in computer graphics, CAD/CAM, VLSI, Robotics, and artificial intelligence.

A partial listing of funded research include: "A 3D Tomogram Viewer for Cancer Detection and Therapy", NIH to B Baxter; "A Multi-Sensor Kernel System" NSF to T C Henderson; "Applicative Multi-Processor Simulation" IBM Federal Systems to R M Keller; "Asynchronous Control for VLSI Circuits: Methods for Automated Design and Testing Using a Direct Mapping Technique" NSR to L Hollaar; "Computer-Aided Design" NSF to R Riesenfeld and L Hollaar; "Computer-Aided Geometric Design" ONR to R Riesenfeld and E Cohen; "Continued Analysis and Development of Specialized Backend Processors for Very Large Text Database" NSF to L Hollaar.

"Coordinated Experimental Computer-Aided Design" NSF to R Riesenfeld and L Hollaar"; "Discrete B-Splines as an Approach to Computer Aided Geometric Design" Army Research Office to E Cohen and R Riesenfeld; "High Level Control Description in Programming Languages" NSF to G Lindstrom; "Modelling and Architecture for High Speed VLSI" General Instrument Corporation to K Smith; "Subdivision Algorithms for Curved Surface Representation and Display" NSF to R Riesenfeld; "Transformation of ADA Programs into Silicon" Defense Advanced Research Projects Agency to E Organick; "Very General Purpose Multiprocessing" NSF to R Keller.

Faculty, research adjuncts and their interests: R E Barnhill (computer aided geometric dsgn, apprxmatn & reprsntatn of surfaces, numerical analysis); B S Baxter (visual perception & digtl signl prcssng); R C Brandt (computer aided instruction); E Cohen (computer aided geometric dsgn); E Ferretti (computer music); R M Fujimoto (archtctr, parallel computatn, communication ntwrks, VLSI, multi microprocessor systems); D H Hanscom (communicatns prcssr hardware dsgn); T C Henderson (AI, computer vision & robotics); L A Hollaar (archtctr, logic dsgn, info retrieval, systems prgrmng, data communctn).

R M Keller (thry of asynchronous comptatn & its applns to hardwr dsgn & operating systems); L C Knapp (computer aided geometric dsgn); G E Lindstrom (prgrmng language dsgn & implmntatn, data strctr); E I Organick (prgrmng languages, computer system archtctr, dsgn automatn). R F Riesenfeld (computer aided geometric dsgn); K F Smith (IC dsgn & appln of IC to computer systems); P A Subrahmanyam (prgrm synthesis, VLSI synthesis, sftwr engnrng, theoretical computer science); S Thomas (computer aided geometric design and computer graphics, modelling geometric object bounded by freeform surfaces); W J Viavant (man machine communication, dsgn of small interactive systems for educational use).

Course Offering:

101	Programming with FORTRAN	534	Intro Theoretical Computer Science
103	Programming with BASIC	536	Operating Systems
104	Programing with PASCAL	539	Fundmntls of Integrated Circuit Design
105	Intro to Computer Science	540	Modelling of Integrated Circuits
301	Understanding Computers	542	Simulation of Discrete State Systems
306	Intro to Programming Linguistics	543	Adv Discrete State System Simulation
321	Intro to Logic Design	551	Intro to Computer Graphics
322	Intro Cmptr Archtctr & Machn Level Prgmng	561	Intro Waveform Processing
323	Advanced Logic Design	562	Advanced Waveform Processing
334	Discrete Structures	563	Sensory Information Processing
335	Discrete Structures	565	Computer Music Seminar
376	Interactive Numerical Methods	566	Computing With Symbolic Expressions
395	Special Studies for Undergraduates	570	Special Topics
410	Low Level Computer Programming	590	Independent Study
411	Prgrmng Linguistics & Data Structures	591	Seminar
412	same as above	601	Formal Languages
417	Programming Laboratory	612	Computational Complexity
418	Programming Laboratory	628	Organization of Computing Systems
427	Digital Systems Lab	631	Software Engineering
428	Digital Systems Lab II	632	Software Engineering
431	Intro to Coomputer Graphics	638	Data Base Systems
432	Computer Aided Geometric Modelling	641	Large Scale Integrated Circuit Design
433	Computer Graphics Applns Programming	647	Artificial Intelligence
490	Senior Project	652	Computer Graphics
495	Special Studies for Undergraduates	653	Computer Graphics
501	A Survey of Prgmng Thry & Practice	656	Symbolic Computation
502	A Survey of Modern Computer Languages	667	Computer Aided Geometric Design
511	Programming Linguistics	668	same as above
519	Programming Lab	669	same as above
520	Compiler Construction	670	Advanced Topics in Computer Science
521	Prgmng Intro to Logic Design	680	Seminar
522	Logic Design Lab	690	Independent Study
523	Program Verification	698	Research Consultation: Master's
524	Switching Circuit Theory	797	Thesis Research PhD
525	Data Commnctns Systems & Cmptr Ntwrks	798	Research Consultation PhD
529	Digital Project Lab		

UTAH STATE UNIVERSITY
Logan, UT 84322
(801) 750-1000

Utah State is a public university with 11,000students, a 130-acre campus located in a mountain valley which abounds in recreational facilities, a faculty student ratio of 1 to 20, and a library with 1 million volumes.

Bachelor's and master's programs in computer science are offered by the university with a current enrollment of 339 and 72 students respectively. Interested undergraduates should apply through the Admissions Office, while graduates through the Office of Graduate Studies. Deadline for regular admission in the Fall Quarter is September 1; for financial aid is March 15.

Computing facilities include an IBM 4341, three VAX 11/780 (VMS), three Victor 900, five TS 802. There are 11 members in the department. Faculty positions exist at all ranks. Background in any area of CS will be considered.

Course Offerings:

150	Introduction to Computer Science	521	Data Base Management Systems Lab 2
200	Computer Science	525	Computer Modeling & Simulation
210	Computer Prgrmmng Basic	50	Compiler Construction
215	Info Systems 1: Fundamental Concepts	550	On-line Comuter Systems
225	Cooperative Work Experience	551	Microcomputer Fundamentals
235	Computer Prgrmmng & Problem Solving Tchnqs	552	Software Tchnqs
236	Computer Prgrmmng & Problem Solving Tchnqs	595	Independent Study
241	FORTRAN Prgrmmng	597	Seminar
251	COBOL Prgrmmng		Graduate
00	Computer Science: An Intensive Intro (12)	610	Operating Systems
41	Advanced FORTRAN	620	Management Info Systems
51	Advanced COBOL	616	Structured Analysis
60	Systems Utilization	625	Cooperative Work Experience 1-9
56	Introduction to Computer Architecture	65	Appln Sm Cmptrs in Bus, Industry & Engnrng
70	Computer Prgrmmng with PASCAL	655	Software Development
425	Cooperative Work Experience 1-9	656	Software Applications
455	Computer Software Methodology	660	Adimini stration of Computing
441	Computer Graphics	670	Prgrmmng Languages: Anlys & Comparison
490	Special Projects 1-5	695	Reading & Reports
495	Directed Reading 1-5	690	Seminar 1-5
515	Info Systems II: Management Info Systems	697	Thesis & Research
516	Info Systems III: Analysis & Design	699	Continuing Graduate Advisement
520	Data Base Management	727	Software Engineering

WEBER STATE COLLEGE
Ogden, UT84408
(801) 626-6000

Weber State is a public college with 10,000 students, a 376-acre campus, a faculty student ratio of 1 to 18, and a library with 290,000 volumes.

A BS in Computer Information Systems is offered here with a current enrollment of 562 students. Prospective students should apply through the Admissions Office. Deadline for financial aid is Feb 1.

Computer systems in use include: DEC 2060, DEC 2020, Harris H800 and H100, Charles River, Apple, Commodore, and the IBM PC XT. There are 9 full-time faculty members in the department.

Course Offerings:

WEBER STATE COLLEGE

101	Concepts & Appln of data Processing	310	Operating Systems
120	R.P.G. Programming	311	Organization of Programming Languages
130	BASIC Programming	312	Compiler Design
140	Fortran Programming for Business	328	Computer Graphics
160	COBOL Programming	360	Adv COLBOL Programming
201	Data Management & File Design Concepts	370	Data Comunications Systems
215	Computer Architecture	380	Adv Systems Programming
240	PASCAL Programming	395	Adv Systems Concepts
250	Survey of Programming Languages	410	Microcomputer Systems
260	Technical & Scientific Computing (3)	430	Adv Fortran Programming
274	Systems Analysis & Design	440	Modeling & Simulation Methods
275	Computer Systems Applications	470	Adv Prgmnng & Prblm Solving Techniques
280	Assembler Language Programming	480	Individual Projects & Research
289	Cooperative Work Experience	499	Seminar in Computer Info Systems (1-3)
302	Data Structures		

VIRGINIA

UNIVERSITY OF VIRGINIA
UNIVERSITY Station, Charlottesville
VA 22903 ; (804) 924-7751

The University of Virginia is a public university with a 2000-acre campus, a population of 16,500 students, a faculty student ratio of 1 to 10, and a library with over 2.5 million volumes.

Bachelor's, master's and PhD programs are offered with current enrollment of 150, 75, and 20 students respectively. Apply through the Department of Applied Mathematics & Computer Science, Thornton Hall. No deadline is specified.

Computing facilities include: a CDC dual 730, three Prime 750's, a Prime 550, a VAX 11/780, plus many micros such as the North Stars, Imlacs, and the IBM PC's. The CSNet is available.

There are 12 full-time faculty members in the department. Several openings exist at the assistant professor rank, one each at the associate and the full professor ranks. Background in database management, programming environments, VLSI, software engineering, computer systems, design automation and robotics would be highly desirable. However, all areas of CS will be considered.

Course Offerings: (generally 3 semester units)

159	Intro to Computing	585	Software Engineering
250	Digital Computer Programming	545	Computer Graphics
251	Intro to Computer Programming	595	Supervised Project Research
260	Cmptr Solns of Prblms in Appl Science	751	Selected Topics in Computer Science
261	Intro to Computer Science	752	Same as Above
270	Intro to PASCAL	756	Models of Computing Systems
352	Adv Programming & Data Structure	757	Computer Networks
361	Archtctr & Assembly Language Prgrmng	773	Combinatorics & Graph Theory
384	Computer Systems Lab	771	Compiler Construction
454	Cmptr orgnztn & Operating Systems	780	Artificial Intelligence
455	Programming Languages	793	Independent Study
461	Analysis of Algorithms	854	Topics in Computer Architecture
485	Software Engineering Lab	855	Topics in Programming Langauges
551	Special Topics in Computer Science	856	Topics in Operating Systems
554	Computer Organization	860	Topics in Theoretical Computer Science
555	Programming Languages	862	Topics in Database Systems
556	Operating Systems	885	Topics in Software Engineering
560	Intro to Computation Theory	872	Digital Picture Processing
561	Design & Analysis of Algorithms	895	Supervised Project Research
562	Database Systems	898	Thesis
584	Microcomputer Systems Design	999	Dissertation

BETHANY COLLEGE
Bethany, WV 26032
(304) 829-7000

Bethany College is a private college affiliated with the Disciples of Christ Church. Its 300-acre campus serves a population of 900 students, with a faculty student ratio of 1 to 12, and a library with 145,000 volumes.

A BS in computer science is offered with a current enrollment of 60 students. Interested students should apply through the Admissions Office. Deadline for admission with financial aid is March 15 for the Fall Semester.

The college has a Prime 550 and Apple II microcomputers. Faculty openings exist at the assistant and associate professor ranks.

Course Offerings: (generally 4 semester units)

100 Computers in Society	280 Assembly Language
140 Programming in BASIC	290 Data Structures
142 Programming in FORTRAN	330 Computer Organization
143 Programming in PL/I	370 Operating Systems
144 Programming in COBOL	380 Intro to Data Base Design
145 Programming in RPG II	450 Data Base Concepts
201 Intro to Computer Science I (PASCAL)	478 Senior Seminar
202 Intro to Computer Science II	490 Senior Project
250 Intro to Data Management	

HOLLINS COLLEGE
Hollins College, VA 24020
(703) 362-6000

Hollins College is a small woman's college with a 450-acre campus, a population of 1,000 students, a faculty student ratio of 1 to 10, and a library with 210,000 volumes.

The Department of Computer Science offers an undergraduate program in computer science. For students interested in quantitative methods, a program in computational sciences is also available. Apply through the Director of Admissions. Deadline for admission with financial aid is March 1.

Computing facilities at Hollins include a VAX 11/780 (VMS), a Microcomputer Lab that consists of the IBM PC's, Apple IIe's and II+'s, TRS-80s, Sinclairs plus others. More microcomputers will be acquired in the near future.

Faculty positions exist at the assistant professor rank. Background in graphics would be highly desirable.

Course Offerings: (generally 4 units)

100 Computers & the Problems of Society	253 Intro to CS, Assembly Language
130 Intro to Computer Programming	350 Special Studies in Computer Science
150 Special Studies in Computer Science	352 Computer Architecture & Organization
152 Advanced Computer Programming	393 Adv Topics in Computer Graphics
160 Adv Computer Programming	

JAMES MADISON UNIVERSITY
Harrisonburg, VA 22807
(703) 433-6147

James Madison is a public university with a 365-acre campus located in the beautiful Shenandoah Valley of Virginia. It has a population of 9,000 students, a faculty student ratio of 1 to 17, and a library with 380,000 volumes.

The Department of Mathematics and Computer Science offers an undergraduate major in computer science. Students may also choose a major in mathematics and select computer science as a concentration within that major. A new MS in CS is being developed. Currently, there are 500 students in the department. Apply through the Office of Admissions before Feb 1. Early action is available for highly qualified students.

The university has a VAX 11/780, plus numerous micros including the Apple III, Intertec Superbrain, HP, Corvus, in addition to remote access to an IBM 3032 at Virginia Tech.

The department consists of 26 full-time members. Of these, 9 teach in the CS discipline. One or more openings exist at the assistant / associate professor ranks.

Course Offerings: (generally 3 semester units)

100	Intro to BASIC	452	Discrete Methods
101	Intro to FORTRAN	455	Prgrmng Languages
238	Digital Computer Programming	456	Implmntatn of Prgrmng Languages
240	Assembly Language	465	File Processing
248	Cmptr Mthds in Engnrng & Science	474	Database Design & Applns
345	Adv Prgrmng & Data Structures	480	Selected Topics in Computer Science
350	Cmptr Systems & Architecture I	497	Independent Study
351	Cmptr Systems & Architecture II	499	Honors
352	Design & Analysis of Algorithms	548	Numer Math & Computer Applns
448	Numer Math & Computer Applns I	585	Selected Topics
449	Numer Math & Computer Applns II	590	Operation Research

VIRGINIA WESLEYAN COLLEGE
Virginia Beach, VA 23502
(804) 461-3232

Virginia Wesleyan College is a private college affiliated with the Methodist Church. Its 80-acre campus serves a population of 1,700 students with a faculty student ratio of 1 to 14, and a library with 160,000 volumes.

An undergraduate major in Computer Science/Mathematics is offered with a current enrollment of 160 students. Interested students should apply through the Admissions Office before May 1.

Computing facilities here include a prime 750, Apple IIe's, and Alpha Micro's. PRIMOS, MUSE, INFO, EMACS are available. More microcomputer systems will be acquired in the near future.

Faculty openings exist at the assistant professor rank. Specialty in any CS areas will be considered.

Course Offerings: (generally 3 semester units)

100	Intro to Computers	310	Intro to Computer Systems
110	Intro Programming in BASIC	311	Data Structure
211	Computer Programming I, PASCAL	330	Operations Research
212	Computer Programming II	430	Database Mangmnt Systems Design
213	Structured COBOL	440	Operating Systems

WISCONSIN

UNIVERSITY OF WISCONSIN, MADISON
Madison, WI 54408
(608) 262-3961

University of Wisconsin, Madison, is a public university with 42,000 students, a 900-acre campus, a faculty student ratio of 1 to 16, and a library containing over 3.6 volumes.

The Department of Computer Science offers BS, MS, and PhD programs, in which about 200 undergraduates and 250 graduate students are currently enrolled. For information on admission and financial aid, write to Chair, Admissions and Awards Committee, Computer Science Department, The University of Wisconsin, 1210 W Dayton Street, Madison, WI 53706. Application for financial aid must be completed by Jan 15 preceding the Fall Semester. Applications for admission without financial aid can be made for August, January or June, any time up to two months before the term begins. Because of the demand, department requirements for admission are more stringent than those of most other departments.

The university's Computing Center has a Sperry 1100/82, four PDP 11/70's, two Data General C-330 Eclipses providing MUMPS interactive services, and a VAX 11/780, a Harris 800, a collection of color-graphics, plotter, and phototypesetter equipments. The CS Department Lab contains: a PDP 11/40, two PDP 11/40's, two PDP 11/70's, a VAX 11/750, two VAX 11/780's, an HP 3000, and an assortment of microcomputers for instructional use. Research equipment includes: three VAX 11/780's, eight VAX 11/750's, one VAX 11/730, an IBM 4341, a Britton-Lee Ingres database machine, an Intel development system, 5 DEC GIGI systems, 5 HP Chipmunk 9836 systems, a Chromatics 68000-based color-graphics terminal, an HP 2648 graphics terminal, a Tektronix 4112 graphics terminal, a Tektronix eight-pen plotter, an HP 7580A plotter. All research equipment and some instructional equipment are interconnected by a local network, which in turn, is linked to the ARPANet via CSNet.

The department is active in research. Regular colloquia and public lectures are often offered by the department. They cover a wide range of subjects and are given by department faculty or visiting computer scientists. In addition, for the past several years, the department, in conjunction with the Mathematics Research Center and with corporate sponsors, has presented the Distinguished Lecture Program whereby research results were presented by personnels from the academia, as well as from prominent industrial research labs. Faculty's specialization covers such diverse areas as: computer architecture, VLSI design, data base systems, operating systems, programming languages, artificial intelligence, automata and computing theory, analysis of algorithms, computer algebra, microprogramming, applications of microcomputers, optimization problems, numerical analysis and social implication of computing. Faculty and their interests:

J Barwise (logic, math linguistics, natural language semantics); G E Collins (algebraic algrthms, computer algebra); C W Cryer (numerical methods); C H Davidson (computer education, intelligent computer assisted instruction for teaching prgrmng); C W R deBoor (apprxmtn thry, numerical analysis); E J Desautels (systems prgrmng, time sharing systems, prgrmng languages, microcomputer systems & applns); J H Halton (computational methods, Monte Carlo method).

S Klein (computatnl linguistics, text grammar, cognitive symbolic anthropology); K Kunen (logic, automatic thrm proving); L H Landweber (automata thry, computatnl complexity, ntwrks, electronic mail); O L Mangasarian (math programming thry, algrthms & applns); R R Meyer (nonlinear, integer, and mixed integer prgrmng); E F Moore (graph thry, combinatorial computatns, automata thry); B Noble (integral equations, variational mthds); S V Parter (numerical mthds for PDE).

T B Pinkerton (dsgn of prgrmng languages & compilers, operating system algrthms, performance measurement, system evaluation); S M Robinson (operations research, systems analysis); A Thesen (info system dsgn, analysis & implmntatn); L E Travis (mechanization of deduction, knowledge reprsntatn, expert systems, social implications of computing); L M Uhr (pattern recgntn, learning, integrated wholistic systems, models of intelligence); D J DeWitt (microprgrmng, archtctr, database mangmnt systems).

R A Finkel (prgrmng languages, robotics, analysis of algrthms, database mngmnt systems); C N Fischer (compiler dsgn & parsing, dsgn & implmntatn of prgrmng languages); D R Fitzwater (formal models, specification, analysis, devlpmnt mthdlgy & dsgn thry of distrbtd systems, applns of dsgn automation tools, operating systems, database mngmnt systems, real time control systems); I Kaneko (oprtns rsrch, linear complemntrty, math progrmng mthds of engnrng analysis); E C Koenig (general system thry, intelligent systems). G C Oden (natrl language comprehension, pttrn recgntn, knowledge reprsntatn).

M H Solomon (prgrmng languages, thry of computatn). S W Bent (math analysis of algrthms, dsgn of graph algrthms, data strctrs, abstract complexity thry, music printing); R P Cook (prgrmng languages, operating systems); C R Dyer (AI), J R Goodman (archtctr, database mngmnt systems); R H Katz (database mngmnt systemes, engnrng databases, CAD/CAM, VLSI); A C Klug (database mngmnt systems); U Manber (parallel algrthms, comptatnl complexity, cryptology & security of ntwrks, fault tolerance); A R Pleszkun (archtctr & dsgn, sftwr development); J C Strikwerda (numerical analysis).

Course Offerings: (generally 3 semester units)

132	Intro to Computing Machines	509	Logical Foundations of Computing Theory
211	Fortran Programming for Numerical Methods	510	Intro to Computability & Unsolvability
212	Elementary Numerical Methods	513	Numerical Analysis
302	Algebraic Language Programming	525	Linear Programming
303	COBOL Programming	536	Intro to Programming Languages & Compilers
304	Machine Language Programming	537	Intro to Operating Systems
332	Intro to Computing Machines	540	Intro to Artificial Intelligence
364	Intro to Database Management Systems	545	Natural Language & Computing
371	Technology of Computer-Based Busnss Systems	550	Computers & Society
374	Intro Linear Programming & Business Applns	552	Intro to Computer Architecture
412	Intro Numerical Methods	564	Database Mngmnt Systems: Dsgn & Implmntn
433	Intro Optimization Methods	568	Monte Carlo Techniques
436	Machine Organization & BASIC Systems	635	Survey of Mathematical Programming
454	Logical Design of Digital Computers	638	Topics in Computing
460	Complex Information Processing	681	Senior Honor Thesis
465	Special Topics in Info Systems Applns	691	Senior Thesis
467	Intro to Data Structures	698	Directed Study
471	Intro to Statistical Data Processing	699	Undergraduate Reading & Research
475	Intro to Combinatorics	701	Programming Languages & Compilers

702	Compiler Construction	768	The Monte Carlo Method
703	Adv Topics in Prgmng Languages & Compilers	771	Computational Linguistics
712	Applied Numerical Methods	773	Problems in Computational Linguistics
717	Numerical Functional Analysis	774	Same as above
718	Numerical Functional Analysis II	787	The Analysis of Algorithms
719	Network Flows	812	Arithmetic Algorithms
720	Integer Programming	813	Algebraic Algorithms
723	Dynamic Programming & Assoc Topics	814	Same as above
725	Convex Programming	815	Transcendental Function Algorithms
726	Nonlinear Prgmmng Theory & Applns	820	Automata Theory
730	Nonlinear Programming Algorithms	822	Advanced Automata Theory
731	Artificial Intllgnce & Models of Thinking	830	Formal Grammars
732	Artificial Intllgnce & Models of Thinking	837	Topics in Numerical Analysis & Optmztn
736	Advanced Operating Systems	838	Topics in Computing
737	Computer System Performance Evaluation	881	Num Methods for Ord Diff Equations
752	Advanced Computer Architecture	882	Same as above
755	VLSI Systems Design	883	Num Methods for Part Diff Equations
761	Deduction & Problem Solving by Computers	884	Same as above
762	Same as above	885	Matrix Theory in Numerical Analysis
764	Topics in Database Management Systems	887	Approximation Theory
765	Pttrn Recgntion & Adaptive Systems & Learnng	990	Thesis & Research
767	Graph Theory	999	Independent Study & Research

UNIVERSITY OF WISCONSIN, EAU CLAIRE
Eau Claire, WI 54701
(715) 836-5415

The University of Wisconsin, Eau Claire, located in the northwest part of Wisconsin, supports a population of 11,000 students with a faculty student ratio of 1 to 19, and a library with 430,000 volumes.

An undergraduate program in computer science is offered here, with a current enrollment of 427 students. Prospective students should apply through the Admissions Office. Application for financial aid must be completed before March 1.

Computing facilities here include a Honeywell DPS 8/20, a DEC PDP 11/34, and microcomputers from Apple, IBM, TRS80, TERAC. EDUNET is accessible.

There are 8 full-time faculty members in the department. Positions exist at the assistant and associate professor levels. Background in all areas of computer science will be considered.

Course Offerings: (generally 3 semester units)

130	Elementary Computing Concepts	275	Data Structure 1
135	Computer Programming in BASIC	291	Special Topics (Lower Division)
151	Computer Programming in FORTRAN	310	Computers & Modern Society
155	Computer Programming in PASCAL	330	Programming Languages
165	Problem Solving in PASCAL	345	Data Structures 11
240	Mathematical Foundations of Computing	350	Non-Numeric Programming
252	Cmptr Structure & Assembler Lang Pgmmng	360	(see CS 490)
253	(see CS 240)		

370 Switching Theory
390 Operating Systems Principles
398 Cooperative Education-Juniors(2-8)
399 Independent Study-Juniors (1-3)
410 Compiler Writing Techniques
452 Systems Programming
490 Contemporary Computer Architecture
491 Special Topics (upper Division)

495 Computer Science Seminar (1-3)
498 Cooperative Education-Seniors (2-8)
499 Independent Study-Seniors (1-3)
710 Educational Computer Usage (2)
720 BASIC Language in Educational Usage (2)
730 FORTRAN Language in Educational Usage (2)
797 Independent Study (1-3)

UNIVERSITY OF WISCONSIN, MILWAUKEE
Milwaukee, WI 53201
(414) 963-4572

The University of Wisconsin, Mulwaukee, has 26,000 students on its 90-acre campus, a faculty student ratio of 1 to 15, and a library with 1.5 million volumes.

The Department of Electrical Engineering & Computer Science offers an undergraduate major, and an MS in Computer Science. Undergraduate apply through the Department of Admissions, while graduate students through the Graduate School Office. Deadline for graduate financial aid is Feb 10.

Computing facilities include: Univac 1100/81, a computer graphics lab which includes a DEC GT-46 minicomputer and Tektronix, Magnavox plasma, and Diablo terminals, Houston and Calcomp plotters.

There are 13 full-time members in the department. Faculty positions exist at all ranks. All areas in CS or Computer Engineering will be considered, but preferred areas are systems, theory, data bases, image processing and artificial intelligence.

Course Offerings: (generally 3 semester units)

132 Intro to Computing Machines
151 Into to Computer Science
251 Computer Tchnques for Engnrng & Science
315 Thry & Operation of Computing Machines
317 Discrete Information structures
351 Intro to Prgrmng Languages
352 Intermediate Programming
401 Intermed prgrmng for Non-CS Majors
403 Computer Systems
416 Logic of Computer Arithmetic
438 Software Enginering Lab
452 Applications of I/O Devices
458 Computer Architecture
535 Data Structures
536 Intro to Systems Programming
537 Intro to Operating Systems
631 The Structure of Prgrmng Languages
654 Introduction to Compilers
657 Topics in Computer Science
704 Analysis of Algorithms
753 Automata & Formal Languages

754 Compiler Construction & Theory
757 Data Base Orgnztn & File Structure
790 Advanced Topics in Computer Science
Related Courses in EE
407 Intro to Microprocessors
421 Communication Systems
431 Computer-Aided Network Analysis
457 Digital Logic Lab
511 Symbolic Logic
533 Advanced Active Networks
541 Integrated Circuits & Systems
710 Artificial Intelligence
711 Pattern Recgntn & Machine Learning
712 Image Processing
731 Linear Network Theory
732 Advanced Network Sunthesis
751 Switching & Automata Theory I
752 Switching & Automata Theory II
755 Information Theory
756 Coding Theory
819 Adaptive & Self-Optmztn Control Thry

UNIVERSITY OF WISCONSIN, PARKSIDE
Kenosha, WI 53141
(414) 553-2000

The 700-acre Parkside campus of the University of Wisconsin supports 5,500 students with a faculty student ratio of 1 to 20, and a library with 310,000 volumes.

An undergraduate major in Applied Computer Science is offered by the Division of Engineering Science with an enrollment of 362 students. Prospective students should apply through the Admissions Office, D187 Wyllie Library Learning Center, before Aug 1. Deadline for financial aid is March 15.

Computing facilities include a PDP 11/70, PDP 11/20, LSI 11/23, plus Zenith Z-100, and several 8085-based microcomputes. A DEC VAX computer system may be acquired in the near future.

The department consists of 5 ful-time members. An opening exists at the assistant professor level. Background in all areas of computer science will be considered.

Course Offering: (generally 3 semester units)

Lower Division
105 Computer Application	365 Discrete-time Systems Analysis
130 Computer Programming in BASIC (1)	368 Mathematical Modeling
131 Advanced Programming in BASIC (1)	370 Operating Systems
132 FORTRAN Programming (2)	405 Artificial Intelligence and Heuristics
145 Computers and Computing 1	420 Analog and Hybrid Computation
146 Computers and Computing 11	425 Computer Simulation of Systems
245 Assembly Language Programming	440 Programming Language Implementation
250 Digital Logic & Computer Organization (4)	450 Mini/Micro Computer Applications (4)
270 File Management Software	465 Information and Communication Theory
290 Sp Topics in Applied Computer Science	467 Computability and Automata

Upper Division
320 Computer Graphics	475 Software Applications Engineering
340 Data Structures & Programming Languages	490 Sp Topics in Applied Computer Science (1-4)
350 Microprocessors and Microcomputers (4)	491 Senior Design Project (1-3)
360 Numerical Methods	494 Cooperative Education (1-2)
361 Numerical Analysis	495 Seminar in Applied Computer Science (1)
	499 Independent Study (1-3)

UNIVERSITY OF WISCONSIN, SUPERIOR
Superior, WI 54880
(715) 394-8101

The University of Wisconsin, Superior, is a public university with a population of 2,200 students, a 230-acre compus, a faculty student ratio of 1 to 15, and a library with 220,000 volumes.

Undergraduate programs in computer science and business data processing are being offered with a combined enrollment of about 400 students. Apply through the Director of Admissions; deadline is Aug 15 for the Fall Quarter; deadline for financial aid is Mar 15.

Computing facilities include a PDP 11/70 and many Apple II and IBM PC microcomputer systems. The university plans to acquire a network of micros.

There are 4 full-time equivalent faculty in the CS/DP program. A faculty position is open at the assistant professor rank. No specialty is specified.

Course Offorings: (generally 4 quarter units)

101	Computers, Individuals, and Society (2)	402	Operating Systems 11 (3)
102	Intro to Computers (2)	450	Database Management
110	The BASIC Computer Language (2)	457	Business Simulation
201	Computer Programming 1 (PASCAL)	458	Systems Analysis and Design
202	Computer Programming 11	475	Numerical Analysis 1 (3)
203	Computer File Processing	476	Numerical Analysis 11 (3)
211	The FORTRAN Computer Language	543	Systems Programming 1 (COBOL)
310	Organization of Programming Language	544	Systems Programming 11 (COBOL) (2)
325	Assembly Language (3)	545	Systems Programming 111 (FORTRAN) (3)
326	Advanced Assembly Language (3)	606	Word Processing Techniques
343	Computer Systems Programming-COBOL 1	607	Word Processing Practicum
344	COBOL 11 (3)	650	Data Base Management
355	Data Structure	657	Data Communications
400	Computer Architecture	658	Systems Analysis and Design
401	Operating Systems 1 (3)		

WYOMING

UNIVERSITY OF WYOMING
Laramie, WY 82070
(307) 766-5160

The University of Wyoming is a growing public university. Wyoming's only 4-year institution, it has close to 10,000 students, a 795-acre campus, a faculty student ratio of 1 to 11, and a library with 900,000 volumes.

The Computer Science Department offers bachelor's and master's programs in which 300 and 20 students are currently enrolled. Interested students should apply through the Admissions Office. Deadline for financial aid is Feb 15.

Computer systems in use include: CDC Cyber 170/730 and 170/760 (NOS), Terak, DEC 11/03, DEC GIGI, and SWTP M6809-based microcomputers.

There are 10 full-time faculty members in the department. Positions exist at all ranks. Computer scientists in all specialty areas are considered. Preference is given those with research interests in management information systems, data bases, operating systems or hardware design.

Course Offerings: (generally 3 semester units)

300D Intro to Computer Programming (1)	753D Compiler Construction
301F Intro to Computer Science	755D Artificial Intelligence
301G Intro to Computer Science	770D Computer Architecture
309D Structured Programming Languages (1)	798M Graduate Topics in Computer Science
311D Computers in Society	799M Seminar in Computer Science
401D Intro to Programming Using Calculus	**Graduate**
499M Seminar in Computing (1-3, Max. 6)	602D Program & Data Structures
501D Computers & Programming	620D Prgmng Languages & Representations
521F Business Data Processing	640K Numerical Algerbra
530D Intro to Discrete Structures	641K Numerical Analysis
540D Computer Languages	645D Computer Graphics
602D Program & Data Structures	650D Systems Programming
620D Programming Lang. & Representations	661D Intro to Computation Theory
640K Numerical Algerbra	665D Formal Language Theory
641K Numerical Analysis	670D Computer Organization (5)
645D Computer Graphics	691M Topics in C S for Educators
650D Systems Programming	699M Special Topics in Computer Science
661D Intro to Computation Theory	720D Computational Linguistics
665D Formal Language Theory	735D System Simulation
670D Computer Organization (5)	750D Operating Systems
691M Topics in C S for Educators	753D Compiler Construction
699M Special Topics in C S	755D Artificial Intelligence
720D Computational Linguistics	770D Computer Architecture
735D System Simulation	798M Graduate Topics in Computer Science
750D Operating Systems	799M Seminar in Computer Science

APPENDIX

INDUSTRIAL AND PUBLIC EMPLOYERS
OF COMPUTER SCIENCE GRADUATES

Below is a sample list of major corporations of various industries with strong interest in recruiting computer science graduates. The description includes nature of primary business and recruitment interest in computer science or related areas. B – bachelor's degree, M – master's and D – doctorates; CS – Computer Science, EE – Electrical Engineering, MIS – Management Information Systems. PR – permanent residency.

The Boeing Company

College Relations
PO Box 3707 M/S 9H–13, Seattle, WA 98124
Aerospace, Electronics, Computing. B, M, D in CS or EE or Computer Engineering. US citizenship required; primarily emphasis in Scientific Application; Secondary interest in Business Application.

Chemical Abstract Services

Employment Department
PO Box 3012, Columbus, OH 43210.
International Scientific & Technical Information Service. Seeks computer scientists with B or M and a strong technical & problem solving skills. Knowledge of chemistry not required.

US citizenship or PR required.

E I Du Pont De Nemours & Company, Inc.

Bruce C Holberg, Consultant,
Business & Computer Systems Staffing,
Employee Relations, 1007 Market Street,
Wilmington, DE 19898
Professional Staffing, B, M in CS. US citizenship or PR required.

Exxon Production Research Co

Mr W B Everett, Jr.
P O Box 2189, Houston, TX 77001
Exporation/Production Research & Engineering. B, M, D in Computer Science. US citizenship or Permanent Residency Required.

General Mills, Inc.

Corporate Recruiting, ATT: Marvin Trammel
PO Box 1113, Minneapolis, MN 55440.
Diversified food company offering a variety
of consumer goods & services. B, M in CS,
MIS, Business or Mathematics. US citizenship
or Permanent Residency Required.

I B M Corporation

Manager, Corporate College Relations,
Department 86, One Barker Ave.,
White Plains, NY 10601; or
One IBM Plaza, Chicago, IL 60611;
Central Employment, 3424 Wilshire Blvd.,
Los Angeles, CA 90010.
Manufacturers of computer systems and
other information processing products. B, M,
D in CS, and Computer Engineering.

Lawrence Livermore National Laboratory

Recruiting Manager,
P O Box 808-LA1, Livermore, CA 94550.
Diversified basic and applied Research. M, D
in CS or Engineering for systems, business,
scientific programming and systems development. U S citizenship required.

Eli Lilly and Company

Manager, College Relations
307 E McCarty St., Indianapolis, IN 46285
Manufacturers of pharmaceuticals; biolog-
icals, agrichemicals, cosmetics and health
products. M in CS for business & scientific
programming.

Lincoln Laboratory - M I T

Personnel Manager,
P O Box 739, Lexington, MA 02173.
Research and development of advanced
electronics and related areas. CS personnels
for scientific programming and systems
development at all levels.

Lockheed Missiles & Space Co., Inc.

Manager, College Relations
P O Box 504, Sunnyvale, CA 94086.
Research & development in spacecraft,
satellite and other high technology systems.
CS or Computer Engineering at all levels for
business & scientific programming. U S
citizenship required.

McDonnell Douglas Automation Company

Personnel Offices in St. Louis or Cypress,
Box 516, Dept. KO50, St. Louis, MO 63166
or 5701 Katella, K34-051 Level 2W,
Cypress, CA 90630
Software development & services. B, M in
CS, MIS, Math, or Computer Programming
emphasis in Engineering majors. US Citiz-
enship required.

Merrill Lynch & Co. Inc.

Manager, College Relations.
One Liberty Plaza, 165 Broadway,
New York, NY 10080.
Financial Services. Seeks CS and business
programming personnels.

Metropolitan Life Insurance Co.

Manager, Human Resources.
One Madison Ave., NY, NY 10010.
Life, health, auto, home & other insurances.
CS personnels for business programming &
systems analysis.

N C R Corporation

Manager, Employments Office.
World Headquarters, Dayton, OH 45479.
Manufacturers of business information processing systems, and a wide range of high
technologies and products. CS, EE and
business graduates. Regional opportunites
exist throughout the nation.

Northrop Corporation

Manager, College Relations
1800 Century Park E., Century City East,
Los Angeles, CA 90067.
High technology in aircraft, defense electronics, and other technical services. CS at
all levels. US citizenship required.

Occidental Chemical Corporation

Director, Staff Planning.
P O Box 4289, Houston, TX 77210.
Manufacturer of industrial chemicals and
plastics products. CS and MBA for systems
development.

Pacific Gas & Electric Co.

Manager, College Relations.
215 Market St., SF, CA 94106.
Gas and electric company serving north and
central California. M, D in CS for business &
scientific programming systems.

Pacific Telephone & Telegraph Co.

Manager, Management Placement Office.
44 Montgomery St., Suite 1300,
San Francisco, CA 94104; or
1001 Wilshire, Room 200, LA, CA 90017.
Telephone and other communication services. Seeks M, MBA in CS, Math, or Business.

Peat, Marwick, Mitchell & Co.

Partner-in-Charge of Recruiting
345 Park Ave., NY, NY 10022.
International firm of CPA providing all
accounting services. M, MBA in computer
systems design for management consulting.

Pennzoil Co.

Manager, College Relations.
P O Box 2967, Houston, TX 77252.
Exploration and production of oil and gas,
marketing of petroleum based products. M, D
in CS for business or scientific programming
and systems.

The Perkin-Elmer Corporation

Manager, Human Resource Planning
Main Ave., M/S 16, Norwalk, CT 06856.
Manufacturers of analytical instruments,
minicomputers, semiconductor processing
equipments. M, D in CS for scientific or
business programming and systems.

Polaroid Corporation

Manager, College Relations.
750 Main St., Cambridge, MA 02139.
Research, development, and manufacturing
of film, camera, and photographic systems.
CS personnels for programming.

Procter & Gamble International

Manager, International Recruiting.
301 E Sixth St., Cincinnati, OH 45202.
Manufacturer of detergent goods and other consumer products. M, MBA and CS personnels for system development.

Rand Corporation

Personnel Director
1700 Main St., Santa Monica, CA 90406.
Non-Profit research institution performing fundamental studies in policy, planning, and national security affairs. M, D in CS for scientific programming and systems.

R C A

Director, College Relations
Cherry Hills, NJ 08358
Electronics and communications services. CS personnels for scientific programming and systems.

Shell Companies

Recruitment Manager
Box 2465, Houston, TX 77001.
Exploration and production of petroleum products. CS personnels for business & scientific programming and systems.

Sperry Corporation, Computer Systems

Employment Manager
Box 500, Blue Bell, PA 19424.
Manufacturer of hardware / software computer systems and peripheral equipments. CS and EE for systems development, application programming, and design of computer systems.

Standard Oil Co. of California

Manager, Professional Employment
P O Box 7137, SF, CA 94120.
Involved in all phases of petroleum and petrochemical industry. CS personnels for scientific and business programming.

State Farm Insurance Companies

Director, Personnel Relations.
One State Farm Plaza, Bloomington, IL 61701.
Auto, life, home, health and other insurances. CS and Math personnels.

Tektronix Inc.

Manager, College Relations.
P O Box 500, Beaverton, OR 97077.
Manufacturer of computer graphic systems, microcomputer developments, test and measurement equipments. M, D in CS or Engineering for scientific programming, hardware / software system development.

T R W Electronics & Defense

Manager, College Relations
One Space Park, Redondo Beach, CA 90278.
Spacecraft, defense, software, computer, communication and energy systems. B, M, D in CS or Computer Engineering. US citizenship required.

Union Carbide Corporation

Manager, University Relations.
One Ridgebury Rd., Danbury, CT 06817.
Manufacturer of alloys, metals, electronic components, plus other materials and products. M, D in CS or Computer Engineering for scientific programming, system analysis.

United States Steel Corporation

Manager, College Relations
600 Grant St., Pittsburgh, PA 15230.
involved in all phases of production of iron
and steel products. CS for business systems
analysis, research and technical services.

United Technologies Corporation
– Hamilton Standard Division

Manager, College Relations
Hamilton Standard Division
Bradley Field Rd., Windsor Locks, CT 06096.
Diversified high technology company. CS
personnels for businesss & scientific programming, systems analysis, engineering and
business applications.

United Technologies Corporation
– Pratt & Whitrey Aircraft Group

Manager, Professional Recruitment
400 Main St., East Hartford, CT 06186.
Development ard production for gas turbine
engines for aircraft propulsion. CS personnels for business, scientific programming,
and software design.

Wang Laboratories, Inc.,
– Research & Development Operation

Manager, College Relations 1402B
One Industrial Ave., Lowell, MA 01851.
Manufacturers of information processing
equipments, word processors, and medium to
large computer systems. CS personnels,
computer engineers, systems programmers.

Westinghouse Electric Corporation

Manager, Employment and Placements Office
Ardmore Blvd & Brinton Rd.,
Pittsburgh, PA 15221.
Electric utility, industrial and construction
production, defense and space, electronic
devices. Seeks M in CS.

Xerox Corporation

Manager, College Relations
Xerox Square 024, Rochester, NY 14644; or
2200 E McFadden Ave., Santa Ana, CA
92705; or
1341 W Mockingbird Lane, Dallas, TX 75147.
Information processing products worldwide.
CS, Computer Engineering for business,
scientific programming, systems development, and sales positions.

Arthur Young & Company

Director of Personnel Development in:
277 Park Ave., NY, NY 10172;
1025 Connecticut Ave., NW.,
Washington DC 20036; One IBM Plaza,
Chicago, IL 60611;
4300 First International Bldg,
Dallas, TX 75270;
515 S Flower St., LA, CA 90071.
International CPA firm providing all accounting services and management advisory
services. M and MBA for consultants in
computer systems.

Zenith Radio Corporation

Manager, Salaried Personnels
1900 N Milwaukee Ave., Glenview, IL 60025.
Consumer and industrial electronics products. CS or business personnels for application
programming for mainframe and microcomputers, business system design and maintenance, and engineers for microcircuit
design and development.

U S GOVERNMENT AGENCIES

Department of Agriculture

Office of Personnel CEU,
14th & Independence, Washington, DC 20250
Food grading and inspection, nutrition education, agricultural research, farm programs,
international agriculture. Seeks computer
specialists for audit & investigation.

Air Force Logistics Command

Office of Staffing & Recruitment
Robins Air Force Base, GA 31098
Logistics management. Seeks CS personnels
for scientific programming and computer
engineers.

Air Force Electronic Systems Division

Office of Recruitment, 3245 ABG/DPCSD,
Hanscom Air Force Base, MA 01731.
Development of command, control, and
communication systems, project manage-
ment, and systems engineering. Seeks MS in
CS.

Department of Commerce

Employment Officer, Office of Personnel,
14th & Constitution, Washington, DC 20230
Foreign and domestic trade, statistical and
economic analysis, measurement standards.
CS personnels for programming and systems
analysis.

N A S A

Personnel Offices at:
Ames Research Center, CA 94035;
Goddard Space Flight Center, MD 20711;
Kennedy Space Center, FL 32899;
Johnson Space Center, TX 77058.
All phases of aeronautical and space resea-
rch and development for peaceful purposes.
Seeks M, D in CS for scientific programming.

National Security Agency

College Recruitment Manager
Office of Employment, Fort George G Meade,
Maryland 20755.
Seeks CS or MIS personnels for systems
analysis & design, operating systems, scien-
tific applications programming, networking,
computer security, graphics, development of
DBMS and office automation technologies.
US citizenship required.

Naval Civilian Personnel Command

Staffing and Recruitment
801 N Randolph St., Arlington, VA 22203.
Seeks CS personnels for project engineering,
logistics management, test and evaluation,
research and development, design and maintenance.

Office of Naval Research

Director, Civilian Personnel Office
Naval Research Lab-58, 4555 Overlook Ave.,
SW.,
Washington, DC 20375.
Basic & applied research in physical sciences
and engineering sciences: microelectronics,
aerospace systems, and telecommunication
systems. Seeks M, D in CS or information
processing personnels.